DZOKCHEN

Dzokchen

A COMMENTARY ON DÜDJOM RINPOCHÉ'S
Illumination of Primordial Wisdom

B. Alan Wallace

EDITED BY
Virginia Craft and Martha J. Hanna

Wisdom

Wisdom Publications
132 Perry Street
New York, NY 10014 USA
wisdom.org

Library of Congress Cataloging-in-Publication Data
Names: Wallace, B. Alan, author. | Craft, Virginia, editor. | Hanna, Martha J., editor.
Title: Dzokchen: a commentary on Düdjom Rinpoché's Illumination of primordial
    wisdom / B. Alan Wallace; edited by Virginia Craft and Martha J. Hanna.
Description: First edition. | New York: Wisdom Publications, 2024. |
    Includes bibliographical references.
Identifiers: LCCN 2024011410 (print) | LCCN 2024011411 (ebook) |
    ISBN 9781614299165 (paperback) | ISBN 9781614299318 (ebook)
Subjects: LCSH: Spiritual life—Rnying-ma-pa (Sect) | Rnying-ma-pa (Sect)—Doctrines. |
    Rdzogs-chen. | Bdud-'joms 'Jigs-bral-ye-shes-rdo-rje, 1904–1987. Bdud 'dul dbang drag
    rdo rje gro lod kyi rdzogs rim ka dag gi khrid yig ye shes snang ba.
Classification: LCC BQ7662.6 .W35 2024 (print) | LCC BQ7662.6 (ebook) |
    DDC 294.3/444—dc23/eng/20240511
LC record available at https://lccn.loc.gov/2024011410
LC ebook record available at https://lccn.loc.gov/2024011411

ISBN 978-1-61429-916-5   ebook ISBN 978-1-61429-931-8

27 26 25 24   5 4 3 2 1

Cover design by Marc Whitaker / MTW Design and Kat Davis.
Interior design by Gopa & Ted 2. Set in DGP 11/14.9.

Cover image © "Guru Rinpoche" by Enlightenment | Dakini As Art | www.dakiniasart.org.

The biography of Gyatrul Rinpoché is reprinted with permission from Sangyé Khandro,
taken from Gyatrul Rinpoché's *Generation Stage of Buddhist Tantra* (Ithaca, NY: Snow
Lion Publications, 1996). The biography of His Holiness Düdjom Rinpoché by Tulku
Orgyen Phuntsok Rinpoché first appeared on https://www.vairotsana.org/dudjom-lineage
and is used with permission from Tulku Orgyen Phuntsok Rinpoché and the Vairotsana
Foundation.

The material from Gyatrul Rinpoché's *Meditation, Transformation, and Dream Yoga* is used
with permission of the publisher (Ithaca, NY: Snow Lion Publications, 2002).

Wisdom Publications' books are printed on acid-free paper and meet the guidelines
for permanence and durability of the Production Guidelines for Book Longevity
of the Council on Library Resources.

Printed in Canada.

Contents

Appendices

Meditations

Preface

AT THE HEART of this book you hold in your hands is a wish-fulfilling jewel. This gem has the power to manifest whatever one wishes, to fulfill the heart's deepest longings and desires. This wish-fulfilling jewel is none other than His Holiness Düdjom Rinpoché, the twentieth-century master chosen as the first supreme head of the Nyingma school of Tibetan Buddhism, who here guides us along the path of Dzokchen, the Great Perfection, toward freedom from suffering and the achievement of one's own perfect awakening in this very lifetime.

Düdjom Rinpoché was renowned for being among the foremost scholars in the Nyingma tradition. With his vast erudition, he wrote forty volumes of texts, which include classic scholarly texts as well as pith instructions, the latter of which you will find in this book. In addition to being a great scholar and contemplative, he was also a great bodhisattva, or *mahāsattva*, who inspired countless people to devote themselves to the practice of Dharma, with a special emphasis on Dzokchen. Like his predecessor, Düdjom Lingpa, Düdjom Rinpoché was also a great *tertön*, or treasure revealer, as illustrated in his root verses, which form the basis of his commentary in this volume. The treasures revealed by Düdjom Lingpa and Düdjom Rinpoché together form what is known as the Düdjom Tersar—the New Treasure tradition of the Düdjom lineage—which in turn was passed on to Gyatrul Rinpoché, as well as many other distinguished lamas who became disciples of Düdjom Rinpoché.

Within this book, you will find Düdjom Rinpoché's pith instructions in the form of root verses, entitled *Guidance Transmitted One-on-One to Those of Good Fortune*. These verses are actually part of a much larger cycle of treasure texts revealed by Düdjom Rinpoché on the wrathful manifestation of Padmasambhava known as Dorjé Drolö. Düdjom Rinpoché's autocommentary on these pith instructions, entitled *The Illumination of Primordial Wisdom*, forms the core of this volume. I have provided my own commentary on his root texts with the intention to help illuminate this path of the Great Perfection and inspire you to devote yourself to this greatest of all journeys. My own understanding, which I will share with you here, has been informed and inspired by the core teachings and guidance I've received from my lamas, who have led me toward this path of irreversible transformation—namely, His Holiness the Dalai Lama, Gyatrul Rinpoché, Yangthang Rinpoché, Drupön Lama Karma, and many others.

Throughout this book, you will find a series of interludes—separate chapters exploring topics related to the main text. Although they do not introduce new portions of Düdjom Rinpoché's root texts, they do provide a context within which to deepen your understanding of his pith instructions. At times, I have woven these profound teachings into a panoramic view of the evolution of the sciences and philosophy, which is then interwoven into modern-day life and reality as we understand it. This offers the opportunity to completely revolutionize the way you view yourself, your mind, and the world around you. As such, you can begin to debunk the widespread myths of modernity that once held together your fabricated view of reality, and so begin to see that things that seem inherently real and fixed are actually dynamic and changing, profoundly interrelated with our own perceptions and concepts about reality. By gaining insight into the emptiness of inherent existence of all objective and subjective phenomena, you can see clearly how your own views shape the reality you experience—and therein lies your key to freedom. Thus, by shifting your view in this way—and imbuing and sustaining it with authentic meditation and post-meditative conduct—you can determine with certainty that the actual nature of your mind and of the whole of reality is one that is unobstructed, unconditioned, clear, luminous, and nonconceptual, and is ultimately none other than the primordial consciousness that lies at the root of existence.

Further, in order to help bring these teachings into the realm of experience, you will find meditations interspersed throughout the book. These are equipped with links and QR codes that, when scanned, will allow you to access the audio recordings of the original meditations from the retreat on which this book is based. You can also access all the meditations at https://wisdomexperience.org/alan-wallace-dzokchen-meditations/ and the entire retreat at https://contemplative-consciousness.net/courses /illumination-of-primordial-wisdom/.

It is my sincere hope that the vast and profound teachings of His Holiness Düdjom Rinpoché will touch your heart and mind in such a way that you will feel inspired to embark on the courageous journey of reaching the Dzokchen path and moving swiftly along it to the culmination of your own perfect awakening for the benefit of all. Then, you will truly fathom your mind in order to heal the world!

Introduction

The Main Text

THE MAIN text translated in this volume, *The Illumination of Primordial Wisdom*, or *Yeshé Nangwa* in Tibetan, was the first Dzokchen text that Venerable Gyatrul Rinpoché taught me. In the summer of 1990, I drove from Stanford University to visit Rinpoché at the Tashi Chöling Center for Buddhist Studies near Ashland, Oregon, where he was its spiritual director. During that visit, one of his newer students came to him and asked for an introduction to Dzokchen. Rinpoché chose this text and requested that I interpret as he gave the transmission and oral commentary to both of us.

Although I had previously received public teachings on Dzokchen some months earlier from His Holiness the Dalai Lama, after twenty years of intensive study and practice of Tibetan Buddhism, this was the first one-on-one teaching specifically on Dzokchen that I'd received, consisting of pith instructions based on a classic text, a modern classic. In the tradition of pith instructions in Tibetan Buddhism, masters condense elaborate presentations of a given topic into its succinct essence, specifically for the sake of practice. The instructions in this manual are indeed pithy.

This main text focuses on three themes: First, a reference to preliminary practices up through and including *śamatha* within the Dzokchen tradition; second, on that indispensable basis, teachings on *vipaśyanā*, focusing on the actual nature of external, physical phenomena and internal, mental phenomena; and finally, an introduction to the view of the actual nature of reality from the perspective of pristine awareness.

These teachings are the seed. They are all expressions of and elaborations on the core teachings we will explore in this text. They also accord with the teachings I had received before, beginning in 1971, which always come back to the foundation: taking refuge, cultivating *bodhicitta*, the spirit of definite emergence (or a spirit of aspiring to definitely emerge *from* saṃsāra and *toward* nirvāṇa), the four immeasurables, śamatha, vipaśyanā, and guru yoga, all taught with an emphasis on reaching the Mahāyāna path—which means entering and proceeding along the path of irreversible transformation that culminates in the complete and total enlightenment of a buddha.

This is the way I've been educated and guided from the very beginning, validated by even the most recent teachings I've received from Drupön Lama Karma, for example, which emphasize śamatha, then vipaśyanā, then Dzokchen. This is the lineage and the path for me; I rejoice in this! I'm profoundly satisfied and grateful to have been shown this path.

The approach I've taken to my own practice—based on the lineages I've received from my own teachers—is a bit unusual, as I share with others this emphasis on reaching the path of irreversible transformation, in which neither in this nor in any future lifetimes will we fall back or lose our connection with the Dharma. In this way, in future lives we will never be lost, without any Dharma to guide us out of the cycle of *saṃsāra*.

The Translation

This isn't the first time Düdjom Rinpoché's *Illumination of Primordial Wisdom* has been published in English. Subsequent to my translating this text in 1990, it appeared as a section of a beautiful short book authored by Gyatrul Rinpoché, which also contains his marvelous oral commentary on Düdjom Rinpoché's text. First published by Snow Lion Publications in 1993, its first title was *Ancient Wisdom: Nyingma Teachings on Dream Yoga, Meditation, and Transformation*. When a second edition was published in 2002, it was titled *Meditation, Transformation, and Dream Yoga*.

Gyatrul Rinpoché, Sangyé Khandro (his principal student and translator), and I collaborated on the book; Rinpoché offered the oral commentaries, Sangyé Khandro translated the commentaries, and I translated the root texts. The word "Meditation" in that title referred to my original translation of the subject of this present book, *The Illumination of Primordial Wisdom* by Düdjom Rinpoché. "Transformation" in that title referred to the text *Transforming Felicity and Adversity into the Spiritual Path* by Jikmé Tenpai Nyima, the Third Dodrupchen Rinpoché. "Dream Yoga" referred to the text *Releasing Oneself from Essential Delusion* by Lochen Dharmaśrī.

In this current volume, I draw extensively from Gyatrul Rinpoché's commentary on Düdjom Rinpoché's text as contained in *Meditation, Transformation, and Dream Yoga*. I therefore encourage you to add a copy of *Meditation, Transformation, and Dream Yoga* to your library; you will not only be able to read the parallel passages of Gyatrul Rinpoché's commentary on Düdjom Rinpoché's work, you will also have the translations of the other two texts, not to mention the benefits from Gyatrul Rinpoché's marvelous oral commentary to each of the three texts.

In 2021, I was invited to lead a six-day virtual retreat on an "Introduction to Dzokchen" hosted by the Contemplative Consciousness Network in the United Kingdom. This occasioned a return to and careful review of my 1990 translation of Düdjom Rinpoché's *Illumination of Primordial Wisdom*, together with its root verses. Upon close examination, I realized that in the intervening thirty-one years since I last translated the text, my understanding had grown considerably, as I found a desire to revise and polish the earlier translation. I noted that virtually nothing in the original had been mistranslated, but there was room for numerous improvements. I then revised the 1990 translation in preparation for the 2021 retreat. I completed the current translation July 14, 2021, on Chökhor Düchen, the day commemorating the Buddha's first turning of the wheel of Dharma, and thereafter it was edited by Dr. Eva Natanya.

I wish to offer my heartfelt, reverent gratitude to the Ven. Gyatrul Rinpoché for opening the door to Dzokchen for me by granting his oral transmission and commentary on these pith instructions by His Holiness Düdjom Rinpoché. I am also deeply grateful to Sangyé Khandro for translating Gyatrul Rinpoché's oral commentary to this text on another occasion; to Martha Hanna for transcribing and lightly editing the recordings of my own commentary; to Virginia Craft for polishing those transcripts into a publishable form and for working extensively with Laura Cunningham, Chris Hiebert, and their colleagues under the leadership of Daniel Aitken at Wisdom Publications in further editing this manuscript; and finally to Eva Natanya for her invaluable editorial suggestions on the trans-lations of the root verses and main text. It is only with the expertise and insightful contributions of all these Dharma friends that we are able to offer the translation of these root texts and my commentary with the hopes that it may illuminate the depths of the view, meditation, and conduct of the Great Perfection in general and these sublime texts by Düdjom Rinpoché in particular.

PART 1

ROOT TEXTS

Guidance Transmitted One-on-One to Those of Good Fortune:

An Authentic Dharma Collection from the Profound Mind Treasure of Jikdrel Yeshé Dorjé Drodül Lingpa Tsel

HIS HOLINESS DÜDJOM RINPOCHÉ,
JIKDREL YESHÉ DORJÉ

For the profound stage of completion,
direct the spear of your entwined vital energies and awareness
solely at the red *hūṃ* at your heart.

Take as the path naked, empty awareness—
consciousness of the present moment,
in which the past has ceased
and the future has not arisen.[1]

All such things as *māras*, obstructive beings,
samaya-breaking demons, reifying demons,
and hatred-generated demons
are just appearing aspects of the mind.

Apprehend the mind, free of characteristics.

Emptiness and luminosity are the actual Drowo Lö.
Do not seek it elsewhere; just this naked,
self-emergent, pristine awareness
is the great, omnipresent lord of saṃsāra and nirvāṇa. [129]
Return to this great, primordial place of rest.

In this way, if you achieve stability through familiarization,
once all phenomena with characteristics have been overwhelmed,
Glorious Heruka will become manifest.

Samaya

Translated by B. Alan Wallace and edited by Eva Natanya

The Illumination of Primordial Wisdom

An Instruction Manual on the Originally Pure Stage
of Completion of the Powerful and Ferocious
Dorjé Drolö, Subduer of Demons

HIS HOLINESS DÜDJOM RINPOCHÉ,
JIKDREL YESHÉ DORJÉ

[424] *Namo Mahāguru Vajrakrodha Lokottarāye*

There are two parts to this instruction manual on the originally pure, profound stage of completion from the essential treatise on the accomplishment of the very secret, powerful, and ferocious Dorjé Drolö Tsel, subduer of demons: (I) the preparation: establishing the basis of śamatha, and (II) the main practice: generating the primordial wisdom of vipaśyanā.

I. The Preparation: Establishing the Basis of Śamatha

From the root text [*Guidance Transmitted One-on-One to Those of Good Fortune*]:

> For the profound stage of completion,
> direct the spear of your entwined vital energies and awareness
> solely at the red *hūṃ* at your heart.

In a solitary place free of human distractions and without disturbing noise and so on, regarding the vital point of the body, firmly compose yourself on a comfortable cushion in an erect, straight, cross-legged posture with the seven qualities of Vairocana. Regarding the vital point of your speech, [425] let your vital energies be just as they are. Regarding the vital point of your mind, without disturbing your mind through any activity, such as reflecting on the past or anticipating the future, cut off conceptual elaborations concerning the three times and rest your mind in an unstructured, undistracted state.

If you can remain there, that is enough. If you cannot, imagine at your heart a red syllable *hūṃ* about an inch in height, or any size that you find appropriate. Let this image arise vividly, without forcefully grasping it with your mind, and steadily focus on this clear image by naturally letting your awareness loosely settle upon it.

If you also find it difficult to rest there, place a small or large object—such as a seed syllable, a stick, or a pebble—in front of you. Then direct your visual gaze upon it, without moving your eyes or fluttering your eyelashes [426]. Without bringing anything to mind—such as judgments about good and bad mental states—and without thinking about or meditating on anything, release your awareness into utter ease.

From within that state, whatever conceptual appearances arise, do not follow after them, but, applying yourself to the meditative support, bear it in mind nonconceptually, vividly, and undistractedly.

If laxity arises, lift your gaze, firm up your posture, arouse your consciousness, invigorate your awareness, and focus single-pointedly. If scattering and agitation occur, lower your gaze, relax your posture, relax deeply, and rest in your natural state. Similarly, without thinking about anything apart from simply directing your consciousness to a distinct sound, a pungent smell, and so on, or else the natural exhalation, inhalation, and pauses of your respiration, you may place your attention on one of these in a relaxed way. Alternatively, you may place your attention by resting vacantly without any basis. It is permissible to settle your attention in any of these ways.

By meditating in this way, at the beginning you may think there are many appearances of conceptualization. Nonetheless, you should continue to meditate without regarding these appearances as either faulty or favorable; by so doing, they will gradually subside. Then, well-being will arise in your body and mind, and your mind will be unable to rise from this nonconceptual state. By proceeding gently, as if you have no desire to move, you will remain single-pointed. [427] These are the signs of familiarization with śamatha.

II. The Main Practice: Generating the Primordial Wisdom of Vipaśyanā

This section has four parts: (A) coming to conviction by means of the view, (B) practicing by means of meditation, (C) sustaining continuity by means of one's conduct, and (D) realizing the fruition.

A. Coming to Conviction by Means of the View

This section has three parts: (1) determining external apprehended objects, (2) determining the internal apprehending mind, and (3) identifying the view of the nature of existence.

1. Determining External Apprehended Objects

> All such things as māras, obstructive beings,
> samaya-breaking demons, reifying demons,
> and hatred-generated demons
> are just appearing aspects of the mind.

As exemplified by obstacles that are designated as māras and obstructive beings, everything that appears as oneself and others, as physical worlds and their sentient inhabitants, seems to be truly existent, yet, apart from being the delusive appearances of one's own mind, in actuality, nothing whatsoever is determined to exist. Appearances do indeed appear, but real things are not real. Regard these simply as illusory apparitions, which, like the appearances of a dream, appear vividly and randomly, even though they do not exist.

Moreover, apart from being mere designations, their nature is beyond being an object of the conceptual elaborations of existence and nonexistence. Thus, in actuality, by not even regarding them as objects to be apprehended as illusions, you will come to a conviction in the primordial wisdom that uniformly views all phenomena, all of which are one's own appearances, as being like an illusion. [428]

2. Determining the Internal Apprehending Mind

Apprehend the mind, free of characteristics.

Regarding the vital point of the body, adopt the seven qualities. Regarding the vital point of the speech, let your vital energies settle naturally. Regarding the vital point of the mind, let it be neither tight nor slack. Without bringing anything to mind, rest your awareness in an unmodified, relaxed way. With your consciousness directed inward, gaze steadily upon the mind's own nature. By so doing, there will arise a natural luminosity that is without any object, free of the extremes of conceptual elaboration, and free of any sense of apprehender and apprehended, whether as an observer and observed, an experiencer and experienced, or a subject and object. Freshly rest right there in meditative equipoise, without modification, contamination, or transformation.

This is a way of meditating for those of superior faculties, who are anointed by total immersion in pristine awareness. Most people find such awareness difficult to identify due to their minds being disturbed by conceptualization. So in that case, search for the mind by relying upon the practice of chasing solely after awareness.

Moreover, if fleeting, discursive thoughts flow forth unimpededly, closely observe by chasing down the origin from which they first arose, where they are now, and where they finally cease. Not only that, but who is the agent that experiences joys and sorrows? Who is the one who ascends to enlightenment? Who descends to wandering in saṃsāra? If you think that agent is the mind, ask yourself, Does that mind have a beginning, [429] an end, and an interim? Is the mind itself something real or unreal? If it is real, what kind of shape, color, and so on does it have? If you think that it is unreal, repeatedly ask yourself, Does it not exist at all, or what? Inquire again and again, without forsaking the task at hand.

If you think there is a real thing such as this, you have fallen into a heavily fortified grasping to true existence. If you think it is empty in that it does not exist at all, you are simply speculating. If, as a result of not finding the mind, you conclude that it has never existed, or if you feel that it must exist but can't decide whether you have found it, continue investigating and questioning.

If you do not see anything at all, whether the observed or the observer, the seen or the seer, and so on; if by seeking and investigating you find nothing, just as you don't see anything by looking into space; and if awareness appears nakedly and serenely, free of any recognition of an essential nature of appearances and awareness—unmediated, inexpressible, inconceivable, unobservable, empty and luminous, without an object—then you have internalized the instructions.

3. Identifying the View of the Nature of Existence

> Emptiness and luminosity are the actual Drowo Lö.
> Do not seek it elsewhere; just this naked,
> self-emergent, pristine awareness
> is the great, omnipresent lord of saṃsāra and nirvāṇa.
> Return to this great, primordial place of rest.

[430] In this way, one recognizes that which is free of all characteristics elaborating an apprehender and apprehended objects; one recognizes the primordial character, empty of any inherent nature of its own, the place of rest that is originally pure and inexpressible by thoughts or words; one recognizes the natural display of primordial consciousness, which is luminous, radiant, and unimpeded—spontaneously actualized as the great, omnipresent lord of saṃsāra and nirvāṇa. Moreover, one recognizes the mode of existence of the unconditioned place of rest, the primordially inseparable union of the two. Primordially awakened and naked, this self-emergent primordial consciousness rests in itself. The recognition of this enlightened view of the extinction of all phenomena is the view of the Great Perfection, which transcends cognition. Manifestly realize this by identifying it just as it is.

B. Practicing by Means of Meditation

> Take as the path naked, empty awareness—
> consciousness of the present moment,
> in which the past has ceased
> and the future has not arisen.

Recognize for yourself that the *dharmakāya* is none other than this great, empty, luminous, self-emergent pristine awareness, which transcends cognition. Do not construct or alter anything in the momentary consciousness of the present, in which past thoughts have ceased and later ones have not arisen. By so doing, settle your ordinary consciousness in its natural, unmodified state, uncontaminated by thoughts concerning the three times, resting in the fourth time that transcends the three times. [431] Come to the firm conviction that apart from this there is nothing whatsoever upon which to meditate.

Come to the indwelling, confident freedom of nakedly realizing that whatever arises and everything that appears is a display of the dharmakāya, empty awareness, free of cognition. Upon this basis, settle your consciousness in a state of effortless relaxation, like space, free of extremes. At that time, [outwardly,] even though the objects of the six senses do appear, let your awareness be self-illuminating, utterly naked, and free of grasping. Inwardly, let your mind be devoid of conceptual, analytical excursions and withdrawals, nakedly self-awakened. In between, awareness rests in its own place, and without being bound by antidotes, awareness remains uninterruptedly with the gaze straight ahead, uninfluenced by good or bad objects, and uncontaminated by grasping. Without letting cognition intrude with its remedies for countering obstacles, directly recognize the vividly clear aspect of cognizance. Sustaining awareness in this way—unobstructedly and nakedly—is a distinctive characteristic of the Great Perfection.

C. Sustaining Continuity by Means of One's Conduct

In this way, if you achieve stability through familiarization,

While in meditative equipoise, utterly release into this self-illumination, without contaminating the primordial consciousness of naked, empty awareness with grasping or clinging. During the post-meditative state, without grasping, decisively ascertain everything that appears as being luminous and empty, like illusory apparitions or the appearances of a dream. [432] By taking this as the spiritual path, periods of meditative equipoise and post-meditative states will merge indivisibly. As all appearances will manifestly release themselves, thoughts will arise as aids to meditation. If you are afflicted by thoughts, piercingly focus your attention on whatever roving thoughts arise. By so doing, thoughts will vanish without a trace, just as waves disappear into water. Once the certainty arises that thoughts have no basis or root, your practice will proceed joyfully. In short, during all your activities, do not succumb to the delusive proliferations of your ordinary cognition, but, like the current of a river, continuously practice this yoga that is free of distraction and of grasping. In this way, you will come to the culmination of familiarization with the practice.

D. Realizing the Fruition

> once all phenomena with characteristics have been overwhelmed, Glorious Heruka will become manifest.

The spontaneously actualized awakening of your own pristine awareness, which has never been deluded, is obscured by the addiction of grasping to the signs of delusive thoughts regarding adventitiously arising appearances that do not in fact exist, and you are trapped by the view of seeking to achieve enlightenment elsewhere. Then, due to the kindness of your guru, you identify your own face as the naturally present dharmakāya, and you continuously rest in the realization of primordial freedom. Thus, without conjuring up some new attainment, your primordial character manifests as it is, [433] and this is conventionally known as the fruition of the practice. Having mastered the state of the blood-drinker Heruka, the omnipresent lord of the whole of saṃsāra and nirvāṇa, you spontaneously actualize effortless, boundless, enlightened activity.

Colophon

Due to the encouragement of Tsewang Paljor, the teacher from Nyö, and many other aspirants to this path, I, Jikdrel Yeshé Dorjé, have composed these concise, clear instructions so that they can be easily understood firsthand. May there be victory!

Translated by B. Alan Wallace and edited by Eva Natanya

PART 2

COMMENTARY

Outline and Foundation

The Meanings of the Title and Subtitle

Turning now to an analysis and explanation of the updated and revised translation of the extraordinary root and main texts, we begin with the meanings of the title and subtitle. In the Tibetan language, the title of the main text is *Yeshé Nangwa*. Although I have previously translated *yeshé* as "primordial consciousness," in this context, *yeshé* means "primordial wisdom"—wisdom is something to be cultivated and developed. Within the teachings of Dzokchen, you do not cultivate, develop, or purify primordial consciousness, or buddha-mind. Instead, it is only to be revealed, to be made manifest, and to be identified. The same is true for its synonyms, such as pristine awareness, buddha nature, and, in Sanskrit, *sugatagarbha*. As we will see in the vipaśyanā section of this text, however, the author, Düdjom Rinpoché, says, "generating," so *yeshé* in this case translates as "primordial wisdom." This will be more fully addressed later in the text.

The subtitle of the text is "An Instruction Manual on the Originally Pure Stage of Completion." The Nyingma tradition identifies nine successive *yānas*, or vehicles, which form a single comprehensive path to enlightenment. The highest or most advanced of the nine are the three inner classes of tantras: *mahāyoga*, *anuyoga*, and *atiyoga*—mahāyoga corresponding to the stage of generation, anuyoga corresponding to the stage of completion, while atiyoga, or Dzokchen, being the ultimate vehicle. The stage of completion that normally corresponds to the anuyoga level of practice brings about a transformation in the subtle body and mind, which opens up and reveals the very subtle mind. This subtlest mind is called *vidyā* in Sanskrit and *rikpa* in Tibetan, and is what I translate as "pristine awareness," which is primordial consciousness. Note that within this commentary, you will see *rikpa* and pristine awareness used interchangeably. The teachings in this text, when practiced effectively and to their fruition, will bring about the same profound changes in your body and mind that could be accomplished in the classic anuyoga practices of the stage of completion, which entail the highly detailed and demanding practices involving the channels (*nāḍi*), the vital energies (*prāṇa*), and the vital essences (*bindu*) within the body. Those specific practices are not explicitly part of Dzokchen but are part of the stage-of-completion practices in Vajrayāna. However, Dzokchen is a straight, unelaborated approach without the need for visualization that, as mentioned, generates the same fruition as the more effortful and advanced practices of the stage of completion. The Dzokchen approach is the progression of śamatha, vipaśyanā, and *tekchö*, or "cutting through" to the original purity of pristine awareness.

Moreover, it is important not to be overwhelmed or intimidated as you venture into Vajrayāna, thinking that you have not become accomplished in the stage of generation or have not already gained realization of emptiness, for example. I recall a statement by the Lake-Born Vajra, who is a more gentle, only slightly ferocious manifestation of Padmasambhava, is the root guru of Düdjom Lingpa, and who revealed sublime Dzokchen teachings to Düdjom Lingpa. At the beginning of *The Vajra Essence*, the Lake-Born Vajra states,

> If you arrive with that aspiration at the gateway of secret mantra—and you have firm faith and belief in it and strong, unflagging enthusiasm—the time has come to practice. . . . Once you have obtained a human life and encountered a guru and the secret-mantra Dharma, if this is not the time to practice the Great Perfection, then there will never be a better time than this in another life—this is certain.[2]

Do you have faith? Are you drawn to these practices? Do you have trust in them? Do you have an aspiration to put them into practice? Do they inspire you? If your answers are yes, then you can stop questioning your readiness—

you are qualified. Have no qualms, no uncertainties; just continue. As that is true for *The Vajra Essence*, so is it true for these teachings here.

The subtitle identifies this text as "An Instruction Manual," implying that these are all pith instructions that are ready to be assimilated and internalized—guidance we can put into practice right now. This approach is not concerned with developing erudition or becoming a scholar or teacher; instead, it meets us where we are in this moment.

In the next part of the subtitle—"Originally Pure Stage of Completion"— the term "originally pure" refers to pristine awareness itself, which is primordially pure and never tainted. The second half of the subtitle—"of the Powerful and Ferocious Dorjé Drolö, Subduer of Demons"—could come as a surprise in a quintessential Dzokchen text that focuses on śamatha, vipaśyanā, and cutting through to pristine awareness. Dorjé Drolö was one of the eight manifestations of Guru Rinpoché, Padmasambhava. Dorjé Drolö is an archetypal wrathful manifestation of Padmasambhava and is depicted riding upon a pregnant tigress. He assumed this manifestation in a beautiful and renowned monastery perched on the edge of a cliff in Bhutan called Paro Taktsang, or Tiger's Lair. Padmasambhava manifested in this sacred site in order to bring the unruly local demons, guardians, and spirits under his control. Dorjé Drolö, who possessed extraordinary abilities to subdue these beings without harming them, turned them into allies who would no longer obstruct the Dharma practitioners in that region.

What does this powerful, ferocious, archetypal *yidam* manifestation of Padmasambhava have to do with Dzokchen? The demons who are being ferociously subdued in these practices are the afflictions of our own minds—they are not external demons. Demons and obstructive forces are exactly those impulses and tendencies that manifest in our minds and derail us, obstruct us, and torment us in the practice. This is the meaning of the subtitle.

Homage to Mahāguru Vajrakrodha Lokottarāye

Before entering the main body of a Buddhist text, there is an homage. In this case, Düdjom Rinpoché's homage in Sanskrit is as follows: *Namo Mahāguru Vajrakrodha Lokottarāye. Namo* can be translated in English as "homage to," or "I bow to." *Mahāguru* means "great guru." The name *Vajrak-rodha* simply means "the wrathful [or ferocious] vajra." A vajra is defined as something immutable, a symbol of pristine awareness, of primordial consciousness. *Vajrakrodha* can refer to any number of powerful wrathful deities—transcendent beings who display ferocious enlightened activity. In this case, *Vajrakrodha* refers to the powerful and ferocious Dorjé Drolö. Interestingly and notably, within this text, there is no reference to any kind of flagrant ferocity or violent activity.

However, if we think back to the Buddha's own account of the night of his enlightenment, we may remember that just before he crossed the threshold into the perfect nonabiding nirvāṇa of a buddha, he was assaulted by hordes of māras, obstructive beings who are personifications of mental afflictions. The obstructive beings saw that this was their last chance and mounted a final attack, trying to prevent him from achieving perfect awakening. Amid this onslaught, the Buddha did *not* respond by displaying ferocious paranormal abilities. Because the māras, or the obstructive forces, are within one's own mindstream and are not actually coming from the outside, the most ferocious way to overcome, subdue, control, and transmute them when they arise is simply to rest in pristine awareness. During those final moments before the Buddha's enlightenment, he was not operating as a sentient being; he was resting timelessly in his own buddha nature, and that was the fiercest response, rebuttal, and counterattack to all these māras. Attacking a person who is dwelling in pristine awareness is like trying to attack space. The most powerful way to overcome, subdue, control, and transmute all mental afflictions—the quintessential māras—is to dwell in the primordial purity of your own awareness such that when these māras arise, they release themselves without the need of a single antidote.

Moreover, from a Vajrayāna and Dzokchen perspective, the māras are not annihilated or transformed into nothing; rather, they are transmuted and then dissolved back into their ultimate ground. The māras of anger and hatred dissolve back into the ground of *mirror-like* primordial consciousness. In the case of the māras of craving, lust, greed, and attachment, nothing has to be done to transmute them when resting in awareness, as they release themselves into their ground as the primordial consciousness of *discernment*. The māras of ignorance and delusion—the most destructive of all mental afflictions, which are based in the grasping at a self and the reification of all phenomena—are transmuted by simply resting in pristine awareness. The māras of delusion arise, release, and melt into the ultimate ground of the primordial consciousness of *dharmadhātu*, the absolute space of phenomena. The pinnacle of ferocity does not entail bringing out a bigger weapon than the opposing forces, but simply resting in the utter inactivity of sublime primordial purity and luminosity. When this happens, the māras release themselves, and then the battle is over. One of the epithets of a buddha is a *jina*, a "victorious one." It is only by resting in pristine awareness that we gain final victory over all the mind's afflictive and cognitive obscurations, as well as everything that prevents us from manifestly recognizing our own nature.

Furthermore, this is the homage to the *mahāguru*, the great guru, Dorjé Drolö. The last part of the homage gives *Lokottara* as another epithet of Dorjé Drolö. *Lokottarāye* means "to the one transcending the world," who is "supramundane," "transcending space and time," or "transcending saṃsāra." The fierceness of the Great Guru Dorjé Drolö, or Vajrakrodha, who is Lokottara, causes all obstructions to enlightenment to release themselves. What greater weapon could there be than that: simply resting in the purity and stillness of awareness without the need to retaliate or respond, so that the māras release themselves.

The Outline of the Text

In Tibetan, the outline of a text is called the *sabché*. It is like the scaffolding for the entire text. Using the sabché as a guide as you move through the text, you can maintain sight of the overall framework of the text, enhancing your depth of clarity and understanding.

There are two parts to this instruction manual on the originally pure, profound stage of completion from the essential treatise on the accomplishment of the very secret, powerful, and ferocious Dorjé Drolö Tsel, subduer of demons: (I) the preparation: establishing the basis of śamatha, and (II) the main practice: generating the primordial wisdom of vipaśyanā.

Here again, we see a reference to the stage of completion, or *dzokrim*—a word that is very similar to *Dzokchen*, the Great Perfection. Dzokrim represents the culminating phase of the entire path to enlightenment and is delineated in these few pages. When one has achieved śamatha and vipaśyanā, understood the actual nature of reality, and identified the view of the nature of existence from the perspective of pristine awareness, this is the culmination of that path. His Holiness Düdjom Rinpoché's sabché text provides us with a framework that condenses this path down from a great mass of teachings into a wish-fulfilling jewel.

These teachings are designed to enable us to actualize ourselves as this enlightened manifestation of Padmasambhava for the sake of skillful means. In other words, we manifest ferociously in order to subdue our own obscurations and inner demons, and then—when it is suitable—to help subdue the demons in other people's minds. These teachings are designed to help us actualize ourselves in the identity and nondual form of Padmasambhava himself.

The first of the two main sections of this quintessential text deals with the preparation—establishing the basis of śamatha—a topic upon which Düdjom Rinpoché will elaborate and I will further expound. If you possess the sufficiently sharp faculties needed to set out on such a concise, unelaborated, direct, and simple path that can bring about the realization of perfect enlightenment in one lifetime, this text is enough to take you there. In order to travel swiftly along this path, an extremely well-tuned mind is necessary. It is through the diligent practice of śamatha—"calm abiding" or "quiescence," in English—that the mind is tuned, refined, and made serviceable for the more advanced practices of vipaśyanā, tekchö, stage of generation, stage of completion, and *tögal* (the direct crossing-over into spontaneous actualization). A well-tuned, stable, and clear mind is needed in order to effectively engage in the advanced mahāyoga and anuyoga practices of stage of generation and stage of completion. Düdjom Rinpoché makes this point unequivocally in this brief text. By labeling this section "The Preparation: Establishing the Basis," he is making clear that the indispensable foundation for everything else in this text is the practice and achievement of śamatha.

The second section of the text is entitled "The Main Practice: Generating the Primordial Wisdom of Vipaśyanā." There is an emphasis here on *generating* the primordial wisdom of vipaśyanā, which is why I translate *yeshé* here as "primordial wisdom," as opposed to the alternative "primordial consciousness." Again, wisdom is to be generated, developed, and cultivated, whereas primordial consciousness needs only to be unveiled.

Laying the Foundation for the Basis

Although it all begins with śamatha, we first need to recognize that establishing the basis of śamatha in the Dzokchen tradition requires preparation. Düdjom Rinpoché has stated that śamatha is the basis for vipaśyanā, and the union of the two is the basis for Dzokchen. The sabché, being a concise text of pith instructions, does not explicitly describe the bases for efficiently achieving śamatha. This is why Gyatrul Rinpoché's commentary on the preparation for śamatha in the Dzokchen tradition—included in the book *Meditation, Transformation, and Dream Yoga*—is indispensable. There, Gyatrul Rinpoché says,

> Although this subject is the essence of the pinnacle instructions on the Buddhist path, it is important to understand that [Dzokchen] must be preceded with a foundation. You cannot expect to be able to actualize that which is so profound if there is no basis or ground. There must be an entranceway before you can enter a building; before you reach the highest step, you must step upon the steps that precede it.[3]

What are the steps to the entranceway of the building, the foundation for Dzokchen? Gyatrul Rinpoché advises going step-by-step.

Some of you may have already established a regular śamatha practice. You may intimately know the multiple benefits that accrue from settling the mind in its natural state, practicing mindfulness of breathing, or other forms of śamatha practice. These benefits include increased self-awareness, being more present and grounded in your life, and being less reactive and more emotionally balanced. Nevertheless, making a commitment to *practice* śamatha, and actually *achieving* śamatha, are two very different things.

A full-time, single-pointed retreat provides the ideal set of circumstances—and the most efficient and effective way—to practice and achieve śamatha in a timely fashion. Practicing effectively in retreat requires a specific set of conducive outer and inner conditions. Although śamatha is the first practice explicitly addressed in this concise text, śamatha is not the first teaching or the very first practice one should venture into, for one simple reason: if you do not have a deep, earnest aspiration and commitment to practice śamatha in strict retreat and do not appreciate the enormous significance of achieving śamatha, you may merely practice a bit of śamatha here and there, like a hobby. Sitting for half an hour a day is good for your health and well-being, but it will not generate the momentum to make life-altering choices in this lifetime to search for a conducive environment and make spiritual practice the primary focus of your life.

The conducive outer conditions for the full-time practice of śamatha are not easy to find. You need a secluded, quiet, peaceful, and safe environment with access to food and support. Optimally, you need to have good spiritual friends who share your aspirations and engage in similar practice. Further, it is important to have the guidance of a qualified teacher in order for practice to be effective. It is difficult to make much progress in śamatha all on your own. His Holiness the Dalai Lama was once asked whether you need a guru to achieve enlightenment. After a brief pause, he said, "No, but it can save you a lot of time."

As for conducive inner conditions, it takes a powerful motivation to develop the kind of commitment and irreversible resolve necessary to achieve śamatha. You must have the mindset that says, "I *must* reach the path of irreversible transformation. I wish and resolve to achieve the perfect enlightenment of the Buddha for the sake of all sentient beings—and for that, śamatha is indispensable; otherwise, I will never reach the path. If I do not reach the path of irreversible transformation, I will never proceed along that path. Therefore, whatever it takes, and however long it may take, I will find a conducive environment with congenial companions, fellow voyagers, and spiritual friends. I will find a qualified instructor and cultivate the outer and inner conditions to enable me then to commit myself for as long as it takes to achieve śamatha."

How many people do you know who have that aspiration and are willing to make that kind of sacrifice? This means you are not doing anything else while in such a retreat; you are not raising a family; you do not have a job; you have given up everything to do this—you need to be very focused. You cannot dabble at it by going in and out of retreat, leaving in order to do other things, then returning to retreat, going back out, and so forth. The great master Atiśa (982–1054 CE)—a major figure in reviving Mahāyāna and Vajrayāna Buddhism in Tibet in the eleventh century—said, "As long as the conditions for śamatha are incomplete, *samādhi* will not be accomplished even if you meditate diligently for a thousand years."

The motivation required to achieve śamatha is more than just an intense desire, for desire itself is neither virtuous nor nonvirtuous. There are many types of desires that are not suitable for the practice of śamatha—such as the desire to become famous or to develop paranormal abilities for your own gratification. There can be many motivations for achieving śamatha, but if your practice of śamatha is for the sake of reaching the Mahāyāna path to irreversibly become a bodhisattva so that in all future lifetimes you will always be a bodhisattva until you are a buddha, then the only motivation for that is bodhicitta—the mind resolved to achieve perfect enlightenment for the benefit of all sentient beings. Likewise, if your aspiration for practicing śamatha is motivated by a wish to achieve your own individual liberation—to become an *arhat*—then you must have a very powerful, constant "spirit of definite emergence," which entails an emergence away from all the allures of saṃsāra, recognizing they are, at best, transient and empty; they will never satisfy. If you think about it, even the most famous and powerful people on the planet are not satisfied, and they will never be satisfied by having greater wealth, greater fame, or greater power. I have known some rich, famous, and powerful people and have not found them to be happier than people with only modest degrees of wealth, influence, and status. You must see through the veils and enticements of saṃsāra if your practice of śamatha is going to lead to your own liberation.

If you are seeking enlightenment, then the little sprout of your motivation for śamatha must also have four roots of the four immeasurables going down into the fertile, moist soil of this aspiration: loving-kindness, compassion, empathetic joy, and impartiality. For those committing themselves to this path of śamatha-vipaśyanā as revealed by the Buddha, these four immeasurables are the quintessence of Buddhist meditation. This fourfold practice was one of the Buddha's great innovations, which he introduced twenty-six hundred years ago to the already rich contemplative heritage of India, where samādhi had been deeply explored, many schools of complex philosophical speculation had developed, and advanced yogis had learned how to achieve a wide array of paranormal abilities (*siddhis*) and modes of extrasensory perception (*abhijñās*). It is quite clear that he was born into the most contemplatively advanced civilization on the planet. As far as we know, no other civilization at that time—not the Greeks, Jews, Chinese, or Mayans—had developed anything even close to the systematic theories and advanced practices of samādhi present in India during the time of the Buddha Gautama. It was certainly not a coincidence that he chose to be born in such a place.

Gautama gave up a lot when he left home at the age of twenty-nine. He renounced everything to become a homeless beggar and went through tremendous austerities and hardships. But, despite this, he would not turn back; he did not back down after it seemed like he had wasted his time and destroyed his health by struggling through six years of austerities. Imagine how delighted his wife, father, and child would have been if he had said, "I tried it, but it didn't work out; I'm ready to come home." His resolve to find the path to irreversible and complete freedom from suffering and its causes was stable and immovable.

The technical term in psychology for this kind of resolve is *conation*, which includes the mental faculties of motivation, desire, and intention. You must begin with conation—a desire, an aspiration, a shifting of values, ideals, and goals. You must ask, What do I want to do with my life? There are an inconceivable number of ways to pursue your aspirations for freedom from suffering, for finding a sense of truth, sustainable fulfillment, satisfaction, joy, and happiness. There are many options, so why choose śamatha? Why make all the sacrifices necessary to achieve śamatha? Your aspirations can be fulfilled if, and *only if,* you have become thoroughly disillusioned with saṃsāra and with a lifestyle that is rooted in self-centeredness. As for myself, in my early years before I encountered Dharma, undoubtedly my top priority was my own well-being and an "I, me, mine" mentality. In my late teens, I wanted to devote my whole life to ecology and environmental activism because I thought that would bring me happiness and the greatest fulfillment.

As we look more deeply into the very nature of our self-centeredness, of prioritizing our own well-being over that of others, we see that this is a dead end rooted in delusion; whereas altruism, the four immeasurables, and bodhicitta are rooted in reality, in exchanging self for others. We shift our priority from "me first" to "everyone else first." It is this shift in motivation, or conation, that forms the bedrock of the "foundation" that Gyatrul Rinpoché is advising us to develop in order to enter the door of practice.

As mentioned above, these teachings on śamatha and vipaśyanā go back to the Buddha. Are these teachings authentic? Have they proven themselves to be useful? Do they lead to liberation, to enlightenment? We return to the historical Buddha, who turned the wheel of Dharma almost twenty-six hundred years ago, and to the four noble truths. Regarding the fourth noble truth—more accurately translated as the fourth ārya reality, which is the reality of the path that leads to the end of suffering—the quintessence of the path is that we first develop and deepen our concentration through the practice of śamatha for the sake of wisdom achieved through vipaśyanā. When we learn about the foundational teachings of the Buddha—the first turning of the wheel of Dharma, the four noble truths, and the practices of ethics, samādhi, and wisdom—we might ask ourselves, Do they inspire faith, confidence, and trust in the Buddha who claimed to have achieved perfect awakening? As we encounter the life and teachings of the Buddha, do we feel a deep sense of faith and reverence, of commitment and trust? Likewise, are we inspired by the teachings that he revealed and that can be conveyed in the Dharma of words and expression, as well as in the Dharma of realization? These are two types of Dharma: that which can be expressed in words, and the realization to which the words point. Do we have trust and faith in the Buddha and the Dharma? Do we take refuge in them?

Following the Buddha, of course, we have had a hundred generations of Buddhist practitioners, monastic and nonmonastic, who have kept this a living tradition for many centuries right to the present day. Are there people today who are achieving śamatha and vipaśyanā? Is anyone still gaining a direct identification of pristine awareness? Undoubtedly, yes! We are not exhuming a corpse here; we are not digging up old texts, the meanings of which have been forgotten and are irrelevant. This tradition is alive; it is living right now. The torch burns because of the continuance of the Saṅgha since the time of the Buddha, especially those authentic holders of the Dharma and its lineages. Do we have faith, confidence, and trust in such people? For myself, such people include His Holiness the Dalai Lama, Gyatrul Rinpoché, Yangthang Rinpoché, and Penor Rinpoché, as well as many other lamas.

The place to begin is to aspire to be free of suffering and to find happiness. But whom do you trust? Are you going to try to make it up as you go and figure it out all by yourself? In countless lifetimes, that is exactly what you have done. In countless lifetimes, you have not had qualified spiritual mentors, not encountered the Dharma, not devoted yourself to ethics, or to śamatha, and so on. You have "been there and done that," and where has it taken you? Where are you right now? You *do* have some momentum, and so the question is, Do you ride that wave of momentum and build it even further, or do you find something else to do because you feel the short-term gratification is greater or easier?

Revolutions in Outlook

As Gyatrul Rinpoché emphasizes in his commentary, you must go step by step. He then gives a beautiful, short discourse on the four revolutions in outlook in order to explain how to arouse this aspiration to be free of suffering and to find happiness. As he explains, the first of these revolutions in outlook involves reflecting on the rarity and preciousness of gaining a human rebirth, replete with all the "freedoms and endowments,"[4] all the outer and inner conditions that provide us with the opportunity to achieve enlightenment in this very life. In brief, these include being born in the human realm: in a land where you have access to authentic Dharma, your faculties are intact, you are able to adopt a lifestyle where you are not harming others or engaging in nonvirtue, and you have faith in the Three Jewels. When all of those freedoms and endowments are assembled in one life, you have everything; all the requisites are there to at least reach the path—and even, in principle, to achieve perfect enlightenment—in this lifetime. There are eighteen qualities of such a fully endowed human life, and you need all of them to do so. Some people in the world have three, some have two, and many others have none. Chances are, if you are reading this book, you have all eighteen.

Having all of these requisites is like planning to cook a banquet. You have not yet begun cooking, but you go into a master chef's kitchen, look at all the ingredients, and see that everything is there to prepare the meal, including the stove, oven, cooking utensils, pots, pans, and ample space to do so. All you need to do is put everything together, give yourself some time, and you will serve a banquet unlike anything you've seen before. In this way, we are preparing a banquet of Dharma; all the requisites are here.

Recalling the analogy His Holiness the Dalai Lama gave me during my first audience with him, he said that I was like a homeless beggar who had come to Dharamsala seeking spiritual nourishment. Sitting down with a feast of Dharma in front of me, there was the invitation to dine well. "Now you have the opportunity to cook your own feast," he told me. "The more you are nourished by this feast of Dharma, the greater your strength and vitality will grow, and the more capable you will become to share this feast with others."

Gyatrul Rinpoché comments here on the preciousness of obtaining a human rebirth with freedoms and endowments, saying, "With these freedoms and endowments, you are then in a position to achieve freedom or ultimate, permanent happiness in this very body, in this very lifetime."[5] All the requisites, outer and inner, are already assembled, thanks to powerful merit accrued over past lifetimes. Having a precious human rebirth is not random; it does not happen out of luck. There is no such thing as luck when it comes to actions and their consequences—there are simply actions and the fruition of those actions. Without developing a sense of pride or superiority, you should feel grateful for these precious opportunities. Considering the eight billion people on the planet, your current situation is extremely rare. When you look into these qualities of a life replete with all the freedoms and endowments needed to achieve enlightenment in one lifetime, notice how remarkably uncommon this opportunity is—*uncommon*, but not mysterious. With these endowments, you are, as Gyatrul Rinpoché says, "in a position to achieve freedom or ultimate, permanent happiness in this very body, in this very lifetime."

"On the other hand," Gyatrul Rinpoché continues, "if you misuse such an opportunity, through this very body you can accumulate karma that produces the result of a lower rebirth."[6] You should have overwhelming gratitude for all who have enabled you to be where you are right now. You have survived; perhaps you are in good health; you are clothed, sheltered, and even have the Dharma. You are here and wouldn't be alive right now if it were not for the kindness of others who provided you with food, clothing, transportation, education, and so forth.

In my case, virtually all the education I've received—the inexpressibly precious teachings I received in India over the last fifty years from lamas, as well as the educations I received at Amherst College and Stanford University—has been for free. I never could have received this Western education if I had to pay the tuition; it is only because of the kindness and generosity of others that I was able to attend these institutions. With that comes a solemn responsibility, a sense of gravitas. I have received an enormous amount and feel so wealthy when it comes to the Dharma; it is therefore my responsibility to selflessly teach when it is requested. In so doing, I am given the opportunity to repay the kindness of my gurus and of sentient beings. I firmly believe that I will not have fully repaid their kindness until every sentient being is free—that is the bodhisattva's aspiration.

The path starts with motivation—recognizing the preciousness and the rarity of this opportunity, and knowing that this life is a time of enormous potential. However, if you misuse it, treat it casually, disregard it, or distract yourself with mundane pursuits driven by attachments and self-centeredness—wealth, success, and so forth—then obstacles are going to arise. Saṃsāra is an ocean of adversity with glimpses of felicity here and there. As long as you are driven by mundane desires and self-centeredness, then undoubtedly you will encounter a myriad of impediments that will easily arouse jealousy, anger, hatred, resentment, anxiety, fear, and subsequent retaliation. The story of saṃsāra is not a happy one; it is a chronicle of variations on misery, with a few people getting the cream, and most people getting the mud.

You have this opportunity, and the question is, Do you take full advantage of it? Do you fully recognize what you have received? It is not because God, Buddha, or anybody else favors you or thinks you are elite. It is simply that by the great merit you have accrued in past lifetimes along with your motivation, ethics, purity, and dedication to practice, that you have these rare and precious opportunities. What will you do with these opportunities? Will you recognize them fully? If you do, then your priorities will shift radically, and you will develop conative intelligence.

In my case, that priority shift occurred to some extent by the time I was twenty-one years old. I had no outside financial support but had enough savings to buy a one-way ticket to India without extra money for a return ticket. If any sacrifices needed to be made, I was willing to make them, although I didn't feel they were even sacrifices in the first place. In every case, those great beings who have achieved profound states of realization have turned their minds away from mundane desires, priorities, and goals. Whether as monastics or laypeople, they completely oriented their aspirations toward the liberation of perfect awakening for the sake of all sentient beings. They are the ones who became the mahāsattvas, the great beings, yogis, scholars, teachers, and realized ones. Motivation starts by recognizing our current opportunities.

Gyatrul Rinpoché continues by commenting on the importance of facing and accepting the reality of impermanence and mortality and, in particular, of recognizing the vulnerability to suffering that is found in all realms of saṃsāra. As Gyatrul Rinpoché explains, "Contemplating the suffering of cyclic existence and the precious human rebirth, which is so difficult to obtain inspires you to seize this rare and precious opportunity."[7] We don't even need to look beyond the human realm to get a sense of the horrors of the lower realms. There are the hellish realms people find themselves in as human beings; many people exist in a *preta*-like realm of starvation, poverty, and the like. The many people who are enslaved, or who are trying to eke out an existence for a minimum wage under the domination of tyrants, bosses, or a poor economy, are living in a facsimile of the animal realm, where they are treated like human animals. In such conditions, many people don't have any higher or loftier aspirations beyond simply getting by and having enough food, shelter, and clothing to survive.

You now finally have the opportunity in this lifetime to realize what you have always wanted. Your desire to be happy and to have sustainable well-being did not come from the Buddha or from any other great spiritual leader or teacher. You have always wanted to be free of suffering; yet, here you are, still vulnerable. However, now in this lifetime, you can irreversibly change all of this so that you are never in that same condition ever again. Gyatrul Rinpoché describes the next step once you have developed and sharpened the proper motivation, saying, "it is the contemplation of impermanence that truly motivates you to begin practice immediately."[8] By "impermanence," he means the impermanence of your own mortality and of everything around you.

Everything that is born then dies or vanishes. Within saṃsāra, whatever goes up must come down; whether it is wealth, prestige, or any number of transient attainments. Where there is a meeting with your loved ones, friends, pets, and so forth, there is also a parting. Whatever you acquire will be lost. Recognize that within saṃsāra you will never find the satisfaction you seek, even if you could live for a hundred thousand years and acquire all the wealth imaginable. Now, however, this precious human rebirth provides for you the opportunities to attain true satisfaction—and yet, these opportunities could vanish at any time. You are never too young to die—not in your mother's womb, childbirth, or infancy. You are never too healthy or too safe to die. You will never have enough insurance such that you couldn't die at any time. Factor all of this into your pursuit of happiness, and it will fundamentally change your priorities. It is an inexorable fact that you *will* die—you do not know when, but your life is going to be over, and you will no longer have this body, mind, and identity of being this particular human being. However, you will not vanish. Many people wish and believe they will simply stop existing at death, but this is not how it works; consciousness is conserved like mass and energy—it cannot become nothing, and it does not originate from or turn back into matter or energy. You will be here in the reality of saṃsāra indefinitely unless you find the right combination of practices and ways of viewing reality in order to open the door to liberation.

If you can say in truth that you are pure, your mental afflictions are subdued, and you are living a life of constant virtue, then wonderful! Most people, though, have amassed an abundance of negative karma. Eruptions of anger and rage? Welcome to the hell realms. Flares of greed, lust, and selfishness? The preta realms will consume you. Spurts of stupidity and delusion? An animal existence awaits you. Bursts of jealousy? Be prepared for the asura realms. As for living a virtuous life while also reveling in mundane pleasures, you may get what you want, be born as a *deva*, and have a really enjoyable time for a while; but your karma will eventually exhaust itself, and then it's right back into the dump you go!

You need to recognize that this human life you have attained is an incredibly rare and precious opportunity—and it does not last. You are getting older, and time never reverses; you are never getting younger—though you can pretend you are. With a lot of "work," you can look like you are not aging as quickly or maybe even look younger, but it is all merely a façade. Your internal organs are getting older, and your brain is getting older. Becoming aware of and accepting the fact that you have the opportunity to practice *now* will fundamentally shift your priorities. It gives you a titanium grit, such that whatever hardships come along on the path of Dharma—and they will come, sometimes intensely or, it may seem, unbearably—will not be as intolerable as saṃsāra. What's oppressive is life without Dharma. This contemplation of impermanence is what truly motivates us to begin practicing immediately. There is no time to waste!

Further, with every volitional act, you are creating your future. Every moment has significance. These revolutions in outlook will change everything. When you see that śamatha is a direct route within the domain of saṃsāra to tapping into a sense of genuine well-being that is robust and sustainable, then you will view differently hedonic pleasures and the pursuits of them.

A Qualified Teacher, Guru Yoga, Refuge, and Bodhicitta

Gyatrul Rinpoché continues, "You also begin to realize that it is extremely difficult to consider getting out of saṃsāra without someone to guide you."[9] If you could do it without any external guidance, you would already be free since you have been intelligent and educated in countless past lifetimes, and have had varying degrees of wealth, power, and prestige. None of that has helped though. There are plenty of people offering advice, and a lot of it is good. Just pick up any newspaper and there will be good advice—albeit advice to make saṃsāra a bit more pleasant and to alleviate a transient amount of pain, discomfort, and anxiety in this lifetime. There is no end to good advice. But how many people can show you the way to complete and irreversible freedom in all lifetimes? How many can plant the roots of Dharma so deeply in your life that you will never be separated from Dharma in any future lifetime? Optimally, the greatest guide you could possibly hope for is to encounter a buddha and receive guidance from that person, as the direct disciples of the Buddha did. They were inconceivably fortunate; they had accumulated an enormous amount of merit to be able to walk the earth with the Buddha and receive his personal guidance. We do not have such an opportunity to study with the historical Buddha. Even so, there are people now who carry the Buddha's lineage and wisdom, people who have gained some understanding, knowledge, and perhaps insight and realization, and who can shed light on the path that Buddha Śākyamuni revealed—the same path that the historical individual Padmasambhava revealed, along with the many other great beings who followed—Nāgārjuna, Asaṅga, Śāntideva, Atiśa, and more. In order to have any chance of even finding this path, let alone proceeding along it, you need someone to guide you. Such a guide will save you a great deal of time.

Gyatrul Rinpoché echoes this point, saying, "Until now you have been unable to liberate yourselves without a guide. It's very important that you find a spiritual teacher who is qualified and willing to help you achieve freedom."[10] The importance of the guru is such that he or she points out your actual nature, to which you have been oblivious for countless lifetimes in the past. Note that in Dzokchen practice, there are many preliminaries, and these preliminaries are not finished until you are perfectly enlightened. As you devote yourself to and immerse yourself in this straight, unelaborated path of śamatha, vipaśyanā, and tekchö, there is one utterly indispensable and complementary practice that will enrich, adorn, support, sustain, and empower your practice: guru yoga. This is the relationship with a guru that is indispensably rooted in a clear understanding, and preferably some realization, of the emptiness of inherent nature of yourself. You are not intrinsically a sentient being and never actually came into existence as a sentient being—it is all delusive appearances.

Moreover, the guru is someone who you have ascertained to be qualified by way of his or her teachings being authentic and, in this case, truly representing the Dzokchen tradition. You have determined by observing this person that their conduct is very much in accordance with the teachings they are offering. To the best of their ability, they are embodying and enacting the teachings they are sharing, and you know this with confidence for yourself. You can see whether or not this is true by using your own sound, discerning intelligence. Relatively few people are qualified to teach Dzokchen. Ensure that the teachings are authentic and that the guru's conduct neither obscures the teachings nor their buddha nature as you see it. The guru's conduct must not be incongruous, incompatible, or dissonant with the sublime teachings, and you must know that directly.

Subjectively, it is important to have a personal connection with the guru. Is your heart touched? Do you feel blessings? Do you feel a resonance with the guru's way of teaching? Are you truly benefiting from the presence, the conduct, and the teachings of the guru? If you have ascertained so, using your own intelligence, then you may view a certain person as your guru.

That said, it is not enough simply to encounter a fully qualified teacher who understands how to reach the irreversible path and proceed along it; you must inquire into the teacher's *motivation* to teach. Again, just like with the aspiration to achieve śamatha, there are many motivations people might have for wanting to be a Dharma teacher. Some may like to teach Dharma because they want to have the respect and reverence of other people, to have followers and students, and to gain a reputation. That could be a motivation, though it is one more expression of ego-grasping and self-centeredness; it is the motivation that says, "I want to be somebody who people recognize and appreciate!" For some people, the motivation could be wealth; for others, it might be fame, power, and influence. Although there are many possible motivations one might have for teaching Dharma, there is only one *suitable* motivation, without which one should not teach. Whatever lineage one belongs to—Theravādin, Zen, Tibetan, and so on—the teacher should be teaching with at least an approximation of the Buddha's own motivation: *compassion*. With such compassion, you recognize that sentient beings around you are suffering, and most of them do not know the actual causes of suffering. They may know what outwardly contributes to their suffering, but they do not recognize the *actual* causes of suffering within. They can name heaps of things around them that bring temporary happiness; but how many people know what can be cultivated from within to create a sustainable sense of well-being? Such well-being is not achieved all at once but grows progressively, so that eventually your ground state is an ongoing sense of well-being.

Look at His Holiness the Dalai Lama, who seems to always be riding a wave of well-being! He emanates warmth, kindness, and laughter with such ease. It is not necessarily his inconceivable degree of realization, but simply his maturation in Dharma that leads him to ride such a current of well-being. Another beautiful example is Khandro-la—Rangjung Neljorma Khandro Namsel Drönme—a naturally self-emergent yogini and *ḍākinī*. Listening to her voice, looking at her facial expressions and body language, it is obvious that she embodies joy, wisdom, compassion, and kindness. Every part of her seems to be saturated by such contentment. In other lamas, this quality of well-being often manifests more as a profound serenity. Yangthang Rinpoché was a great flow of serenity, calm, peacefulness, and wisdom. For Gyatrul Rinpoché, it manifested as an ongoing stream of humility, humor, kindness, joy, and compassionate service. This is Dharma. It is deeply inspiring to encounter such people. They give us hope by letting us know that they have not always been this way; even the Buddha was not always that way—their realization has been cultivated. If His Holiness the Dalai Lama, Gyatrul Rinpoché, and other great beings can manifest in this way, then there is some hope for us too.

Within Vajrayāna there is still the foundational refuge of Buddha, Dharma, and Saṅgha, but additionally there is the outer refuge-taking in your lama. The lama is more than simply a spiritual friend, a spiritual guide, or a person who gives instruction. Within the context of Vajrayāna, the lama is your spiritual mentor. As you take the fruition as the path—for yourself, for your lama, and over time, for your vajra siblings—you develop pure vision in all directions. Then, the lama becomes an embodiment and an emanation of the Buddha. It is of utmost importance to choose a qualified lama, because if, out of lack of understanding or delusion, you choose someone who is not qualified, that person can turn into your worst enemy and even lead you astray. You must take heed and use caution. Having found a genuine teacher, seek refuge in the Sūtrayāna path, comprising the bodhi-sattva path and the path of individual liberation; take refuge in the Buddha, Dharma, and Saṅgha. From there, you may move to more advanced levels of practice in Vajrayāna. Still, you do take refuge in the lama and in your *yidam*.

Your yidam is that personification, archetypal form, deity, manifestation of the divine and of the Buddha, that most resonates with your heart and most stimulates your faith, trust, admiration, and worship. The yidam may be in a divine feminine form, like Tārā; in a divine masculine form, as in Mañjuśrī; or in the form of a historical figure, like Padmasambhava, Yeshé Tsogyal, or Jé Tsongkhapa. The yidam often emphasizes a particular quality of enlightenment—compassion in Avalokiteśvara and power in Vajrapāṇi, for example—and is the Buddha with whom you feel a strong heart connection. It is the manifestation of the Buddha—Mañjuśrī or Tārā, for example—that you would like to actualize. The yidam reminds you that you do, in fact, have that potential.

In Vajrayāna, in addition to taking refuge in the lama and the yidam, one also takes refuge in the ḍākinī—*khandroma* in Tibetan—the feminine principle and the feminine embodiment of enlightenment. The ḍākinī encompasses all the qualities of enlightenment, not just compassion or loving-kindness. She is peaceful, expansive, powerful, and even ferocious, all manifesting in feminine forms. Taking refuge in the feminine aspect of enlightenment and the feminine embodiments of the qualities of enlightenment allows you to embrace this yidam as an object of refuge. It is crucial in Vajrayāna practice to revere and honor the feminine manifestation of enlightenment with profound humility, regardless of your gender.

A further refuge is also found within the stage of completion in Vajra-yāna, where you go into the subtle physiology of the channels, the vital energies, the essential fluids, and the *cakras*. You are also taking refuge here because it is through the refinement of the subtle body that this profound inner transformation takes place. Accordingly, you entrust yourself to these inner aspects of your own being. Finally there is the culmination, atiyoga, which is synonymous with Dzokchen, or Mahāsandhi (Skt.)—the Great Perfection. It is here that you come to the pinnacle, and to the simplest, of all the spiritual vehicles. These vehicles start with the Śrāvakayāna and progress through the Bodhisattvayāna, to the outer tantras, inner tantras, and, ultimately, to the ninth yāna, or spiritual vehicle: atiyoga. In this final vehicle, you take the ultimate refuge, what all the other refuges—Buddha, Dharma, Saṅgha, lama, yidam, ḍākinī—are all pointing to. These objects of refuge all finally direct your attention inward to the *ultimate* source of refuge, that in which you can most essentially and profoundly take refuge and trust: your own buddha nature and pristine awareness. Hence the Dzokchen aphorism, "Do not look outside yourself for the Buddha." But until you are sufficiently matured for such a realization to become real, practical, meaningful, transformative, and to truly provide you with a sense of safety and refuge, it will serve you first to take outer refuge and then spiral inward, until you come to the very ground of your own being.

Atiyoga refuge involves taking refuge directly in the mind's essential, empty nature, in its luminous manifest nature, and in its distinctive characteristic of unobstructed, unconditional, all-pervasive compassion. These are three facets of pristine awareness. The first is the empty, essential nature, which is in fact nothing other than dharmakāya, the mind of the Buddha. The second characteristic is the luminous manifest nature, which is *sambhogakāya*, the subtlest, most rarefied manifestation of the Buddha's service for others. The third facet is the unobstructed, all-pervasive compassion, which is simply *nirmāṇakāya*. The central theme of the Dzokchen view is that all of the three *kāyas*, or embodiments—dharmakāya, sambhogakāya, and nirmāṇakāya—are already perfect and complete within. They are already there, so all you need to do is remove the many veils and obscurations that conceal your actual nature. For this reason, it is classically said in Dzokchen that the fundamental difference between sentient beings and buddhas is that sentient beings do not know who they are, and buddhas know. It is that simple.

In the face of internal or external adversities—when saṃsāra is rising up to meet you and negative karma is ripening, when you become ill, assaulted by enemies, face natural catastrophes, or personal tragedy ensues—then you will need refuge. There is no one who is so strong, bold, or courageous that they do not need a refuge—unless, of course, they are an arhat or a buddha. In the face of felicity—when everything is fine, fortune seems to be smiling on you, and things are going smoothly—you are still not immune to aging, sickness, and death. Adversity comes to everyone. Tragedy comes to everyone. When it does, it becomes evident what was always true: if we are to bear the adversity and transform it into Dharma, we need refuge.

Everybody has some sort of refuge. Some people call it their bank account; others call it job security; and for some, it may be food, drugs, or alcohol. There are many false or thin refuges that entail looking for refuge within saṃsāra. Only those who are sublimely free of even the differentiation between saṃsāra and nirvāṇa—that is, the buddhas—are the true guides, the true refuges. If you take refuge today, you can have these enlightened beings as your refuge starting today and until you become enlightened. They can provide this security in every lifetime—but only if you take refuge. If you are not seeking refuge, then they cannot be there for you in this way. Use discernment and beware of the innumerable false refuges and people who give misleading, superficial, or bad advice. Taking refuge is *your* responsibility. You should take care to choose an appropriate teacher and to take refuge in that which actually offers a true refuge from the sufferings of saṃsāra.

Coupled with this true refuge, you must develop bodhicitta to venture into Dzokchen and into Mahāyāna in general. Regarding bodhicitta, Gyatrul Rinpoché declares, "Developing the wish to liberate or enlighten all living beings is the initial stage of developing bodhicitta, the awakening mind. With that wish, you need to develop immeasurable impartiality, love, compassion, and empathetic joy for all beings and their deeds,"[11] taking delight in their deeds and their virtues. He continues, "Once these four immeasurables have been developed, you are ready to practice bodhicitta." Gyatrul Rinpoché is describing here the two main categories of bodhicitta: *aspiring* bodhicitta entails the profound resolve to achieve enlightenment for the sake of all beings, while *engaged* bodhicitta involves actualizing that aspiration by devoting yourself to the cultivation of the six perfections. Düdjom Rinpoché's quintessential commentary is focused on explaining stage-of-completion practices and does not explicitly mention the prerequisite of developing bodhicitta. But before engaging in such advanced practice, you first have to identify and take to heart all the preparations needed to come to this completion.

Gyatrul Rinpoché concludes his discussion of the preliminaries, stating, "This has been a brief overview of the meaning and importance of the preliminary contemplations, as well as the basic taking of refuge and generation of bodhicitta. These practices are essential prerequisites to the practice of śamatha, which is the main subject of discussion." Düdjom Rinpoché doesn't explain these preliminaries simply because he assumes you have read other Dharma texts before. But Gyatrul Rinpoché precedes the instructions on śamatha with these absolutely essential, indispensable points. People with no background in Dharma whatsoever can practice śamatha, of course. Anybody can watch their breath, observe thoughts, or rest in awareness, and they can do so with a multitude of motivations. However, śamatha in our context is for the sake of Dzokchen, and Dzokchen is for the sake of achieving enlightenment in this very lifetime. Gyatrul Rinpoché has provided us with the foundation of the foundation—the deep root system of the basis. The foundational preliminary practices just discussed form a support structure for śamatha, the basis of all the other higher practices.

Establishing a Healthy Baseline

The terms "baseline," "default mode," and "ground state" are terms used regularly in the realms of psychology and neuroscience. Your baseline is your mind in its ordinary mode. If you're like most people, your waking baseline is rumination. You generally sit there with a wandering mind, thoughts flitting about from this to that, and this state is your normal baseline. However, in the practice of Dharma, you are seeking to establish a baseline of dynamic equilibrium—not one of rumination, chaos, and the clustered confusion of thoughts and memories. This dynamic equilibrium is not rigid, but flows without any perceived chaos or disarray on the outside, without diverging from your firm yet spacious baseline.

In order to establish such a baseline, a good thing to do throughout the entirety of our Dharma practice is to reflect on and practice the bodhisattva way of life, in which the aspiration and ideal is that we deeply cultivate the four immeasurables of loving-kindness, compassion, empathetic joy, and impartiality. Then, on the basis of that fourfold root system, we cultivate bodhicitta so that it is the underlying motivation for our practice—in this way, what we fundamentally and continuously want more than anything else is to achieve perfect awakening for the sake of all sentient beings. Thus, you practice more and more deeply until bodhicitta arises more spontaneously and effortlessly, becoming the desire behind all other desires.

If you are hungry, then there is a desire to eat; but *why* should you eat? There are many reasons to eat, but how about eating to nourish your body so that you can continue to practice and achieve enlightenment for the sake of all sentient beings? You might want to go for a walk, but *why* go for a walk? Your body needs exercise in order to be healthy; but why does that matter? It matters so that you can practice Dharma and achieve enlightenment for the sake of all sentient beings. For any endeavor—eating, going to the bathroom, walking, sleeping, conversing, having occasional entertainment—the underlying motivation for every meaningful activity that is not clearly nonvirtuous and detrimental could be the motivation of bodhicitta. Cultivate that and, as many times as possible, season the day throughout with that and the four immeasurables. Like a homing pigeon that keeps returning to its roost, keep returning to this home. In this way, you will establish more firmly a baseline that is rich and replete with virtue and momentum for enlightenment—for the benefit of all.

As mentioned, another crucial element in every meditation session is taking refuge. You can even take refuge at the beginning of every meaningful endeavor: taking a class, doing homework, teaching, plumbing. You can take refuge every time you need someone's help. If a screen is torn or blinds are broken, you can take refuge in the people who replace and repair screens and blinds. When beginning all meaningful activities, return to the equilibrium of breathing and relaxing, settling in the present moment, and grounding your awareness. In this calm and balanced place, you are embodied. Return to settling your respiration, which can often be strained, restricted, and impeded by emotion, tension, anxiety, and so forth. These tensions can disturb the flow of the respiration and disrupt your nervous system. Keep coming back again and again to bodhicitta as a motivation for every meaningful deed. Even when having a sip of water, you can drink more water for the sake of all sentient beings. Your motivation right now is to cultivate bodhicitta in order to let the nectar of Düdjom Rinpoché's and

Gyatrul Rinpoché's teachings flow into, saturate, permeate, and purify your mind.

In terms of his own practice of vipaśyanā, His Holiness the Dalai Lama has commented that he meditates on emptiness and the Madhyamaka, or Middle Way, view about twenty or thirty times a day. By so doing, his ability to view reality from the Middle Way perspective permeates all that he does. Similarly, if you can cultivate the four immeasurables such that bodhicitta arises more and more effortlessly because you are so deeply familiar with it, then it will suffuse with meaning everything that you do. Śāntideva said that there is nothing bodhisattvas will not learn in order to be of service to the world. A bodhisattva might practice any trade that is an authentic livelihood in the service of others. This is because all sentient beings need to be served in all manner of ways. If you are going to spend three countless eons in the bodhisattva way of life, then you have time to learn plumbing, accounting, gardening, and everything else, and will be able to serve in a myriad of ways. However, if you are following the Vajrayāna or Dzokchen path, you might want to narrow down that skill set, because life is short, and this opportunity is precious and rare.

Preparation for Meditation

As part of your preparation for meditation, you take refuge. With the idea of taking refuge in the Buddha, Dharma, and Saṅgha, as well as the further layers of taking refuge completely, the culmination is in taking refuge in your own pristine awareness—the dharmakāya within. This means taking refuge from now until enlightenment. When you understand the significance of why you need to take refuge, what you are taking refuge from—the stormy ocean of saṃsāra—and that which you are taking refuge in—the light of freedom—then certainly in the bodhisattva context, taking refuge is taking refuge from now until your own perfect enlightenment. With this momentum going into a meditation session, your practice will be enriched, blessed, and infused with refuge, the four revolutions in outlook, the four immeasurables, bodhicitta, and guru yoga. In so doing, a meditation that could be viewed as a simple exercise can instead be seen as a step toward the path to perfect enlightenment.

❖Meditation: Refuge and Bodhicitta

https://wisdomexperience.org/alan-wallace-dzokchen-meditation-1/

Begin by finding a comfortable posture.

In the preceding introduction, there is an enormous amount of wisdom to be passed on, received, and assimilated. For this meditation session, focus on your motivation—your desires, aspirations, priorities, and your goals in this lifetime and in future lifetimes. What is your deepest longing? Make it very personal; you are not going through a routine, ritual, or a script. As a unique individual, what are your opportunities? What are your freedoms in this lifetime, right now, to effectively realize what you have always wanted and now have the opportunity to accomplish? Consider the nature of your human life, precious and rare, replete with all freedoms, endowments, and opportunities to become a buddha in this very lifetime. What is your situation, and is this precious human life true of your situation and life now? Pause here to consider this.

There is no value in having a treasure chest filled with jewels, gold, and silver right under your bed unless you know it is there and that you can use it in order to benefit from this wealth. Such a treasure is of no value if you do not recognize that it is there and how rare it is to have it so close at hand. Recognize it, treasure it, and use it.

Your life is passing inexorably every moment. Time is running out, and you don't know how much time you have left in this lifetime with this body. Death so often comes unexpectedly; suddenly, there is an accident, you are diagnosed with a terminal illness, or there is a tragedy, and then your life is over. Sooner or later, your life will definitely be over, and all that you identify with—your body, mind, friends, wealth, enjoyments, environment— will all be lost. For others, you will become only a memory, and though you will continue in a conscious flow of experience, you will no longer have the opportunities of this life—your karma will have ripened and exhausted itself. This life is so precious. Do you sense the urgency not to waste time, not to idle away the hours, not to kill time? People acquire wealth and spend it, but they can get more. Contrarily, you cannot get more life; you cannot add to your account. How shall you invest the moments and days of your life in order to reap the greatest benefit, the richest harvest? It is imperative not to waste time when time is so precious. Reflect on this.

Many of the events waiting for you in this lifetime will come as a result of the maturation of your actions in past lives; it is not chance or a matter of luck. You are crafting your life and your future by the decisions you make and the actions you perform. You are not in total control, but you have more control than anyone else. Recognize the significance of the long-term consequences of every action, for good or ill, and take responsibility so that you continuously devote yourself to virtue and to overcome, restrain, and counteract the tendencies for harm. In this way, devote your life to nonviolence and benevolence. This is the nature of karma: actions have consequences.

The blind faith of those who think there is only one life to live leads them to think, "Live your life to the fullest; fill it with as many enjoyable experiences as you can, for when you're dead, you're dead, and then you're nothing." Do not look to science for the answer here, because the scientific community has no idea what happens at death. They know that the brain dies and the body dies, but that's not news. They have no idea from where consciousness comes, what its nature is, and what happens to your own individual stream of consciousness at death; it is a mystery for them. But contemplatives throughout history and across all societies have discovered that consciousness continues. Call it "consciousness," "*jiva*," or "soul," but annihilation is not an option. It is foolish to believe that death is the end simply because many people hold unquestioningly to that faith. There is not such an easy escape from saṃsāra. Whether the suffering is blatant or implicit, the sheer vulnerability to suffering does not go away by itself. Saṃsāra is a vast ocean, and looking outward will never offer the happiness, safety, or fulfillment you seek.

Who can provide you with refuge, an island of safety in this vast, turbulent ocean, a vessel to cross to the farther shore? Only those who have gained such freedom themselves can. Thus, you take refuge in the Buddha, the Dharma, and the Saṅgha. As you venture into Vajrayāna, you take refuge in the lama, the yidam, and the ḍākinī—our true refuges. And coming to Dzokchen, you place your trust in your own pristine awareness, or rikpa.

Even if you have not yet clearly identified rikpa, you can affirm it intuitively by knowing its presence in your heart of hearts. This is your innermost refuge, the source of ultimate healing, the source of all virtue. The wellspring of all genuine well-being is already within. Everything and everyone else— teachers and Dharma friends, your true external refuges—lead you to this inner refuge from which you are never parted; it is who you are.

Then, open your awareness to everyone around you—perhaps those in the room with you or in the house, neighborhood, or community—and expand the field of your awareness out over the countryside, up into the sky, across the land, and into the oceans. Be aware of all of your neighbors—all of *our* neighbors—human and nonhuman, visible and nonvisible, on this planet and throughout countless other world systems in the universe. Here we are, all one family, all of us wishing to be free of suffering, always wishing to find a satisfying and sustainable happiness that frees us from discontent. Recognize that there are no real barriers or demarcations between self and other. We are all arising in mutual interdependence; we are all of the same family. These are our mothers, fathers, and siblings. Since we live in the very nature of interdependence, how can we then realistically aspire only for our own freedom? It is fundamentally unrealistic because we do not exist autonomously. With this awareness, expand the field of caring to embrace everyone around you and let your heart open with the following aspiration: May we all find the happiness we seek, our deepest aspiration, and cultivate the causes for such happiness. May we all be free of suffering and remedy the underlying causes. May we all take delight in everyone's virtues and their joys, and looking upon all with impartiality—as being equally deserving of our love, compassion, and care—take them all into our hearts. Aspire for their well-being just as you do your own.

Then, ask yourself, How can I be of service? How can I alleviate the suffering of others when I, myself, am suffering and perpetuating the inner causes of my own suffering? You can do what those who have gone before you have done: achieve freedom and the perfect awakening of a buddha. That is the highest thing you can do in order to be of the greatest benefit to those around you in the short and long terms, in this lifetime and all future lifetimes. Out of great compassion, arouse bodhicitta—not merely the aspiration, but the resolve to achieve perfect awakening for the sake of all sentient beings. Commit yourself to serving the welfare of others. For as long as space remains and there is a single sentient being remaining in this ocean of saṃsāra, resolve to remain, manifest, and be of service until all are free, until all have awakened to their own actual nature.

Further, resolve to devote yourself to practice and to follow this path of all the bodhisattvas of the past, present, and future, and to cultivate the perfections of generosity, ethical discipline, patience, enthusiastic perseverance, meditation, and wisdom.

Let your awareness venture into the realm of possibility through the power of imagination. Imagine now what *could* be. See yourself as a buddha.

With each in-breath, envision drawing in the light of the enlightened activities of all buddhas, which is filling your own being. With every out-breath, see rays of light emanating from your body, manifesting in whatever way is helpful for sentient beings in order to free them from suffering and bring them to full awakening. Breathe in the light of all the buddhas; breathe out the light of the buddha within. Next, release all imagery, aspirations, and objects and activities of the mind. For a moment, utterly rest, relax, and release. Rest in awareness itself—in its primordial purity, clarity, and stillness.

Bring the meditation to a close by dedicating the merit of this session to the realization of these aspirations, so that you may indeed achieve perfect awakening for the benefit of all beings. ❖

I. The Preparation: Establishing the Basis of Śamatha

M OVING NOW to the preparation: establishing the basis of śamatha. Düdjom Rinpoché's precise and concise root verses, *Guidance Transmitted One-on-One to Those of Good Fortune*, begins with the following seven lines:

> For the profound stage of completion,
> direct the spear of your entwined vital energies and awareness
> solely at the red *hūṃ* at your heart.

In this quintessential root text, every single word is absolutely core; therefore, every line—and, at times, every word—deserves to be read closely with due diligence. In the first line, what is the significance of "stage of completion"? In *The Vajra Essence*, the Lake-Born Vajra says,

> Only those who have stored vast collections of merit in many ways, over incalculable eons, will encounter this path. They will have aspired and prayed repeatedly and extensively to reach the state of perfect enlightenment, and they will certainly have discovered the path previously through other yānas. Thus, by seeking the path, they will have established propensities to reach this path. No others will encounter it.[12]

The vast majority of people will never hear about teachings such as this, because they are not ready for them. Indeed, most *Buddhists* will never hear about teachings like this. It is only those with tremendous momentum from past lives—those who have practiced the fundamental teachings of the Śrāvakayāna and the more advanced teachings of the Bodhisattvayāna and Vajrayāna, such as stage of generation and stage of completion—who will encounter this path. Those who have already achieved a high level of maturation along the path will have the karma and the fortune to encounter a text such as *The Vajra Essence* and other comparable quintessential texts. On this subject, the Lake-Born Vajra says,

> Although people lacking such fortune may be present where this yāna is being explained and heard, because they are under the influence of their negative deeds and the strength of the powerful, devious māras of mental afflictions, their minds will be in a wilderness five hundred *yojanas* away.[13]

That is, they will be looking at the text, their bodies will be in the same space, yet they will not comprehend it, as if their minds are thousands of miles away. In this way, the stage of completion is only for those who are ready to enter into this practice.

"**Stage of completion,**" here, is not meant as a technical phrase identifying the more advanced stage of highest yoga tantra—namely, anuyoga—but rather it denotes that one is coming to the stage of completion of one's spiritual journey, which may have extended back countless lifetimes. It could be in this lifetime that you finish what was begun many eons ago and finally realize an aspiration you had throughout all lifetimes. For what do we and all other sentient beings always wish? The great Tibetan master Jé Tsongkhapa identifies our "eternal longing"—what sentient beings have always been seeking—as freedom from suffering, pain, fear, and anxiety. We wish to realize a quality of well-being that is sustainable and is not merely a pleasant episode that turns into a fleeting memory that then tumbles right back into the ocean of saṃsāra. We long for a sense of satisfaction and a fulfillment of our deepest yearning. Catalyzed by concise texts such as this, this very lifetime can culminate in the completion and perfection of our eternal longing—and it all begins with śamatha.

This is the stage of completion of the powerful and ferocious Dorjé

Drolö, subduer of demons. Dorjé Drolö is not simply a wrathful manifestation of the historical figure Padmasambhava, who lived some twelve hundred years ago. Dorjé Drolö is a wrathful manifestation of our own pristine awareness. Pristine awareness can manifest in peaceful ways, enriching ways, powerful ways, and ferocious, wrathful ways. Dorjé Drolö, powerful and ferocious, is a warrior.

This "**profound stage of completion**" involves directing the spear, a sharp weapon. This brings to mind *The Sharp Vajra of Conscious Awareness Tantra*, one of the five principal treatises on Dzokchen revealed to Düdjom Lingpa by Padmasambhava manifesting as the Lake-Born Vajra, on which Düdjom Lingpa wrote a commentary. Metal vajras are hard with a point and could be used as a weapon. *Vajra* means an object that is adamantine and impenetrable; it can pierce anything and is immutable. Its purpose is to shatter, split, and cut through the reification and crystallization of your own sense of who you are. It cuts through the hardening and contraction of minds that are ossified by self-grasping, frozen by reifying a sense of identity that insists *I am*: *I* am autonomous! *I* am separate! *I* am in charge! *I* am *me*! This tendency of reifying all objects and appearances is connate. This tendency of dualistic grasping leads us to see others as radically other. Whether it is in relation to other persons, places, or things, this habit of *othering* makes us perceive people and objects as radically "over there," as existing independently from their own side, and—based on the prior, connate assumption—*we* exist independently "over here." With such dualistic grasping, when I point my finger to me, it feels that I am really pointing at someone. Interestingly though, when people say, "me," they usually don't point to their head; they point to their heart.

What is the nature of this spear? Düdjom Rinpoché's root text describes it as "**the spear of your entwined vital energies and awareness.**" The Tibetan word for "entwined" here is *drilwa*. If you have two strands of hair and you braid them, they are drilwa; that is, they are merged, blended, or coiled together. Here, it is the stream of vital energies that is entwined with awareness. Vital energies are physical, but very subtly physical. These vital energies are so subtle that they are not measurable with mechanical instruments. As for awareness, it is nonphysical; it is pure mind.

All plants grow from a seed. They may become ill and die because of illness, or get old and then die. This is true for all plants. The Buddha did not include plants among the six classes of sentient beings. If you pluck a carrot from the ground, wash it off, and bite into it, you can do so without having a bad conscience that it is screaming as you are biting off its bottom. However, in the Buddhist worldview, all plants can be the *abode* of sentient beings; in which case, you could argue that killing a tree, the home of sentient beings, is not all that different from killing the sentient being directly. In a similar way, you could say that this body is like the shell of a hermit crab; it is not a person; there is no part of this body, flesh, bone, blood, and so forth, that is actually *yours*. It is a product of your parents' egg and sperm that conjoined and then combined with food for nourishment in order to produce a body. Your parents' egg and sperm are not *you*, and nothing else that came later that contributed to the formation of "your" body—food, water, nutrients, and so forth—is you either. Your continuum from past lives is composed of the *substrate consciousness* (*ālayavijñāna*) and the subtle continuum of vital energy from the previous life. These two—the substrate consciousness and the subtle continuum of vital energy—are drilwa; they are entwined, interwoven, and blended. These two are not identical—in the way that your own pristine awareness, or buddha nature, is of the same nature as your ordinary flow of mental consciousness—though they are closely, inextricably conjoined.

What came from your prior life was this entwined awareness and vital energy, with the former being nonphysical, mental, and purely consciousness, and the latter being of a subtle physical nature. It is the continuum of these two that flows into and conjoins with the egg and sperm at conception. In the Buddhist view, only if that happens will the egg and sperm conjoin and transform into an embryo. Without that, they will simply be an egg and a sperm that will eventually decay without creating an embryo. His Holiness the Dalai Lama once spoke with medical doctors in the field of embryology and asked them whether it is the case that any egg and sperm that become conjoined always transform into a fetus. The doctors responded that that is "not always" the case. His Holiness concluded that the conjoining must rely on something more besides the biological factors—egg, sperm, and their union. Buddhism asserts that the "something more" is the entwined continuum of subtle vital energies and mind.

In this practice of śamatha, you "**direct the spear of your entwined vital energies and awareness solely at the red** *hūṃ* **at your heart.**" There is no vital energy of this kind that is independent of the mind. In other words, these two neither conjoin nor separate. It is an indivisible alloy of vital energy and mind. Right now there are coarse vital energies flowing through the body correlated with mental processes of the coarse mind as it gets excited, agitated, bored, angry, compassionate, and so forth. The fact that the seed syllable *hūṃ* is red is interesting. In the triad of syllables *oṃ āḥ hūṃ*, the *oṃ* is typically white and sits at the crown cakra, the *āḥ* is red and sits at the throat cakra, and the *hūṃ* is blue and sits at the heart cakra. Here, however, the *hūṃ* is red. Red is the color associated with power and, more specifically, the powerful enlightened activity of buddhas and bodhisattvas.

The phrase "**direct the spear,**" indicates that one is wielding a single-pointed object, or a spear. So, here, your energy-mind is being directed in a very single-pointed way. Your *energy-mind* refers to the continuum of the close coupling of your vital energy and mind. As an analogy, the immaterial mind is said to be like a rider on the mount of the vital energy, which is a subtle kind of physical phenomenon unknown to modern science, but detectable through first-person experience. You direct this spear, this single-pointed flow of mind and awareness conjoined with energy, right into your heart. How do you find the center of the target? If you're a marksman, you put up a target and then you try to hit the bullseye. Your heart cakra is the target, and you create a bullseye by visualizing or imagining a red *hūṃ* right in the center of the heart cakra, which is located in the center of your chest, not off to the left, the location of the heart organ.

This is all a bit ferocious and powerful. Why would you ferociously direct the flow of your mind and awareness at the red *hūṃ* at your heart, like a spear piercing a bullseye? If you are an accomplished yogi, you have already deeply balanced your body, speech, and mind and have refined your intelligence and the flow of your attention. Because of this, you will be able to focus and clearly visualize the red *hūṃ* right in the center of the heart cakra. Start by steadying your focus without contraction, tightening, stress, or exhaustion—lightly and gently releasing these modes of grasping—and let your awareness loosely settle upon the syllable. To do so in a relaxed and gentle way is of utmost importance and will be discussed more a bit later in this commentary. If you can hold the visualization right in the center of your heart in this way, then the indivisible union of mind and vital energy will cause your mind and awareness to become concentrated right into the *hūṃ*. The smaller the syllable, the more intense and powerful will be your samādhi. Standing with a spear a few feet away from the target is easy. What if the target were ten feet away and only three or four inches across? What if it's only one inch across? Then your aim would have to be pinpoint precise to strike the bullseye. If you are an accomplished yogi and your samādhi is well-honed, you will be able to visualize the red *hūṃ* at your heart and then piercingly focus the flow of your attention right there, single-pointedly. As you do so, you are also necessarily drawing the vital energies related to the mind into the heart cakra—*if*, that is, your samādhi is both powerful *and* relaxed. This is an incredibly important point: if you are tense, you will become more and more exhausted, stressed out, and irritable the longer you practice. However, if you are relaxed and quite familiar with samādhi, your awareness will naturally, loosely, and vividly settle on the seed syllable.

I was trained in this kind of practice years ago by His Holiness the Dalai Lama, who instructed me to visualize as clearly as I could a seed syllable in the navel cakra as a śamatha practice. When I felt I had progressed somewhat, he instructed me not to focus mentally upon the seed syllable as if from my head—like being in the penthouse suite, gazing down five or ten stories below at one of the lower cakras. Basically, he encouraged me not to look down upon the seed syllable as if from above—or as if maybe from outside looking at the face of the seed syllable—but to let my awareness descend *into* the seed syllable and take on the form of that syllable. In this way, I was to visualize it as my own form, and then develop my samādhi there.

This instruction emphasizes that there is no separate observer—up here, over there, or anywhere else. In this practice, the observer merges with the observed; you are visualizing the form of your own awareness. Awareness has no form per se; it can take on any form by the power of imagination. In this way, your samādhi can develop and strengthen. If you can do the above practice in a relaxed, calm, and composed way, then your visualization, with increasing clarity, vividness, acuity, and focus, will be like a powerful magnet drawing the vital energies related to the mind into the heart cakra.

When you fall asleep, the vital energies converge in the heart cakra. When you die, they converge in the heart cakra. At conception and during the development of the embryo, they emerge, differentiate, and expand from the heart cakra. When you achieve śamatha, your coarse mind dissolves into the subtle mind, and the vital energies related to the mind converge into the heart cakra. Visualizing this bright, vivid, brilliant, ruby-red *hūṃ* at your heart as your own form—which your mind's eye can see with great clarity and precision—will provide a subtle physiological boost for swiftly achieving śamatha.

It is important to understand that these texts by Düdjom Rinpoché are Dzokchen stage-of-completion texts. The stage of completion in anuyoga, by contrast, entails the direct utilization and refinement of your channels, vital energies, vital essences, and cakras. The Dzokchen stage-of-completion practice detailed here already has the taste of the classic anuyoga stage-of-completion Vajrayāna practice, wherein you are drawing the energies into and up through the central channel and into the heart cakra, such that the coarse vital energies dissolve into the more subtle vital energies at the heart. When this happens, the coarse mind concomitantly dissolves into the subtle continuum of mental consciousness, and you have thus achieved śamatha. Whereas that is an advanced practice, in this text Düdjom Rinpoché teaches it as the very initial stage—though he is giving these specific instructions as only one of a few options, which he will discuss later. Hopefully this commentary clarifies more fully the significance, depth, beauty, and profundity of this initial practice.

Returning to Düdjom Rinpoché's commentary on his root text, we read:

> In a solitary place free of human distractions and without disturbing noise and so on, regarding the vital point of the body, firmly compose yourself on a comfortable cushion in an erect, straight, cross-legged posture with the seven qualities of Vairocana.

There is a lot packed into the phrase, "In a solitary place free of human distractions." For almost everyone practicing śamatha, it is indispensable to retreat from the myriad activities, social engagements, and concerns of the mind; to retreat into simplicity, solitude, and a place where you may enjoy the beauty of nature—which can be very helpful for your practice—that is also free from human distractions. Regarding outer solitude, this can simply be anywhere you can get away and be by yourself. It could be a room with a closed door and no noise, a quiet room in a house, or it could entail going out to the desert, like the Desert Fathers of early Christianity or the great yogis of India and Tibet who retreated into solitude in the Himalayas. I have spent years in solitary retreat on three different continents, and finding a conducive external environment where there is solitude—a quiet, safe place with easy access to food, sufficient clothing, and shelter—is not easy. With this in mind, I have sought to acquire and establish the Center for Contemplative Research, with branches in several locations, so that practitioners can have a conducive environment of outer solitude.

However, at least as important as outer solitude, is *inner* solitude, which is far more difficult to achieve. Inner solitude has nothing to do with where you are spatially. Rather than simply retreating from a *place*, you withdraw and retreat from the myriad activities, concerns, hopes, and fears of your worldly existence—you simplify. Such inner retreat involves detaching from the eight mundane concerns, which are comprised of four pairs of related attachments and aversions: (1) The attachment to acquiring wealth and material goods, and the aversion to losing what you have; (2) the attachment to mundane, hedonic, and stimulus-driven pleasures of all kinds, and the aversion to experiencing discomfort, pain, and stimulus-driven unhappiness; (3) the attachment to praise, and the aversion to being ridiculed; and (4) the attachment to a good reputation that generates other people's admiration and respect, and the aversion to how others may look down upon you, speak badly about you, and that you may lose your reputation and fall into disgrace. These eight mundane concerns act as the central framework of many people's whole lives. If you wish to achieve śamatha, then your mind cannot continue to be caught up in these mundane concerns, let alone activities to pursue them.

Inner solitude is distancing yourself from all these mundane hopes and fears, attachments and aversions—going into an inner solitude, inner silence, inner simplicity. If you do not have that inner retreat, even if you go to the most remote place on the planet, you will still have a lot of company and many distractions, all generated by your own mind: wishing for things you don't have, not being satisfied with what you do have, hoping and fearing for the future, lingering in the past, and so forth. If you have not truly gone into retreat from your attachments and aversions, you will be in a Grand Central Station of the mind.

This is why the "spirit of definite emergence"—the complete disillusionment with saṃsāra and the single-pointed focus on liberation or freedom—is so important. The desire to attain freedom for yourself and for all sentient beings has to overwhelm and outshine all of your other desires and priorities. If there is still competition—"I want to achieve śamatha, but I also want to have a nice girlfriend or boyfriend, financial security in the future, and I also want this and that"—then it is like a horse race in which the horse of śamatha is probably going to come in last or maybe not even get out of the starting gate. In order for you to achieve śamatha, you need to make it a one-horse race. Whether it takes a long or short time, the horse will not stop until it reaches the finish line. That is solitude; that is going into retreat. The inner retreat, the inner solitude is far more difficult to achieve than the outer.

When Düdjom Rinpoché describes a solitary place "free of human distractions," he is referring to the presence of other people: visitors dropping in, or people contacting you on the internet, by telephone, by sending smoke signals, or anything else. Interacting with people is a distraction because everyone else around you is almost certain to be prioritizing something besides śamatha—otherwise they would be in retreat with you. This means they want to do things other than practice śamatha, and they would rather draw you out of your practice as well. People like family and friends can be some of the greatest hindrances to achieving śamatha because they probably will not understand what you are doing—"Why are you going into solitude? Why are you not raising a family? Why are you not getting a job? Why are you not succeeding at something? What are you doing? You are merely following your breath or watching your thoughts? Oh, come on! Get up and do something useful!" They will not understand, and it is likely futile to try to persuade them. Regardless, it is not your job to get up on the rooftop and say, "Hey, everybody, what I'm doing is really worthwhile—believe me!" You have to go against the flow. During the time of the Buddha, he went against the flow by leaving home. Most likely, not one person in the palace wanted him to leave or agreed with his decision. That is why he had to slip out in the middle of the night.

Regarding "disturbing noise," a quiet environment is vital, particularly during the early stages of practice when you are still in the śamatha incubator. If there is noise—construction clamor, people making commotion, dogs barking—it will puncture your concentration. Yogis have been saying for centuries that noise is "the thorn for samādhi." Nowadays, double-paned windows, noise-canceling headphones, and earplugs can be helpful. Generally, it is preferable to find a peaceful and quiet environment, so that technological aid is not needed to create such an atmosphere. This is an important point.

In Düdjom Rinpoché's instructions that say, "In a solitary place free of human distractions and without disturbing noise and so on," "and so on" refers to anything else that could divert you from your practice. This is why in śamatha retreat, simplicity is the goal. Having a space where you don't have to fuss with a refrigerator that breaks down, plumbing that goes awry, a leak in the roof, or having ants or mosquitoes, helps to create a conducive environment. In one retreat dwelling I was living in, many bed bugs chowed down on me every night. Bed bugs don't make a lot of noise, but they certainly are distracting.

Düdjom Rinpoché packs an enormous amount of instruction into the phrase just quoted above, and this instruction is of critical importance. If you are in an unconducive environment, or your mind is still clinging to other people, places, activities, entertainments, or hedonic pleasures, then your efforts to achieve śamatha will be unsuccessful. Remember Atiśa's statement that if you do not have the outer and inner prerequisites, then even if you have a very strong desire and powerful renunciation, you could practice for a thousand years and never achieve śamatha. Whether you enter full retreat efficiently or *in*efficiently depends almost entirely on whether you have the necessary prerequisites: good companions who are there for mutual support, and a spiritual guide who can give you experiential guidance on the path.

Settling Body, Speech, and Mind in Their Natural States

Düdjom Rinpoché's commentary says, "regarding the vital point of the body, firmly compose yourself on a comfortable cushion in an erect, straight, cross-legged posture." This means to sit upright and not to let your back be crooked or hunched over. The legs can be in the bodhisattva position, where they are both flat on the ground; they can be in what is often called the half-lotus position, where one leg is up with the foot resting on the thigh; or they can be in the full-lotus position—more technically called *vajrāsana* (*vajra* + *āsana*, "indestructible posture")—where both feet are up resting on the thighs. All of these options are in line with the instructions in the commentary of being "cross-legged."

We should clarify what is meant by a "comfortable cushion" here. If you are sitting on a cushion but are uncomfortable because your knees, back, or bottom hurt, then it is not a comfortable cushion. The point here is not trivial; that is, when you are practicing śamatha, it is crucial that your body is in a comfortable posture. Gyatrul Rinpoché has commented repeatedly that when you adopt a posture for meditation, you should be comfortable, and if you cannot be comfortable sitting cross-legged, then there is no comfortable cushion for you to sit cross-legged. In this case, do not sit cross-legged on a cushion. Instead, find a comfortable chair that lets your spine be erect, straight, and gives you good support. However, some people cannot sit comfortably even on a nice chair for a sustained period, maybe due to age, injury, scoliosis, or other conditions. Gyatrul Rinpoché says to find a posture that is comfortable for *you*. Your spine should be straight, but it does not necessarily have to be vertical or erect. One classic posture in yoga is called the *śavāsana*, the "corpse" position, where you lie flat on your back with a straight spine and legs, with arms out to the side. Hopefully, unless you have severe spinal problems, you can be very comfortable emulating a corpse in terms of your posture, perhaps even with a pillow under your knees to flatten your lower back. Some people have back problems such that lying in the *śavāsana*, or supine, position is also not comfortable. If this is the case for you, a variety of designer chairs are now available that may work better for you.

Along with being comfortable, all that is really necessary is that your spine is straight. This is because the spine is closely related to the central channel through which the vital energies flow, and you want the vital energies to be able to flow unimpededly, without being blocked or meeting a fork in the road; this is why the spine must be straight. If at first the supine position is comfortable for you for only twenty-four minutes (a suggested duration for beginners)—increasing slowly over time, eventually allowing for a more sustained period of meditation—then that is enough. The supine position is a legitimate, suitable, and—for some personality types—optimal meditation position. It has been referred to by some of the great arhats of India, such as the Arhat Upatissa (c. first century CE), who advised, "The standing and walking postures are particularly suitable for lustful-natured personalities, while sitting and reclining are more appropriate for anger-natured personalities." Similarly, on the topic of postures, the great Theravāda master Buddhaghosa (c. fifth century CE) wrote, "Walking suits one; standing, sitting, or lying down suits another. So one should try them, like the abode, for three days each, and that posture is suitable in which one's unconcentrated mind becomes concentrated or one's concentrated mind becomes more so. Any other should be understood as unsuitable."

The primary challenge you may soon encounter here with the supine posture is not to fall into the old habit of lying down and letting your mind float off into rumination, become spaced out, or fall asleep. Any tendency of slipping into laxity and dullness must be overcome. As you relax more and more deeply in the supine position, it is important to sustain your initial clarity and to continue to exert the amount of effort required to maintain the continuous flow of attention. The second challenge is to apply just the right amount of effort—too much, and you get stressed out; too little, and you will be sloppy and end up mindlessly ruminating.

In summary, first, you must relax in order to develop sustainable stability, or continuity of attention. In the second phase, it is crucial to develop greater and greater stability, coherence, composure, single-pointedness, and continuity of attention, without losing the underlying sense of relaxation—in fact, you may become increasingly relaxed as your mind is calmed and stabilized. Then, on that basis, you start enhancing the clarity, vividness, acuity, and focus of your attention, without losing the underlying stability and composure of that attention. In the preceding sketch of how you develop and achieve śamatha, you may have noticed that it is all based on relaxation—if you are not relaxed and comfortable, then your body is going to be a source of distraction that hinders the mental discipline of training attention. Your body will start grumbling at you, then grumbling louder, then shouting, and then shrieking at you, "I'm in pain! I'm in pain!" This will definitely distract you from your śamatha practice. Many people skip this initial part and, therefore, do not develop relaxation. Without developing a deepening sense of ease as practice continues, sooner or later you will run out of gas. Tightness will intrude, tension will appear, and you will become exhausted, stressed out, and irritable.

Reference to the posture is described as being "with the seven qualities of Vairocana." These are also known as the "seven points of the posture of Vairocana." Buddha Vairocana is a personification of one of the five facets of primordial consciousness; namely, the primordial consciousness of the absolute space of phenomena. The seven qualities are the seven attributes of an optimal posture for meditation, in general, and for śamatha, in particular. All the elements of the posture are there to give you a subtle physiological basis for being able to stabilize and refine your attention. The seven points are as follows: (1) The legs are crossed. As mentioned, it is important to cross the legs in such a way that you can be comfortable for a sustained period of time, if at all possible. (2) The hands are in the *mudrā* of meditative equipoise: the palms are up, the right hand resting on the left hand in your lap under the navel, the tips of the thumbs touching each other. The left hand symbolizes wisdom, and the right hand symbolizes skillful means or compassion; this gesture is symbolic of their union. There are also subtleties in the movements of vital energies in the body such that this gesture is conducive for creating something like a closed circuit. Cycling these energies, even through your fingers, will help to stabilize the mind. (3) The spine is erect and the torso is straight. (4) The neck is naturally in alignment with the spine, albeit somewhat inclined, with the chin tucked slightly; this proves to be optimal over the long term. (5) The shoulders are pulled back, opening the torso, while the chest is relaxed. Here, your elbows are slightly extended to the sides, like the outstretched wings of a vulture. This provides a bit of breathing space and more openness to your posture. (6) The eyes are open in a soft gaze down *toward* the tip of the nose. Do not read it literally that you should actually be focusing on the tip of your nose because that could turn out badly. Sitting cross-eyed is not a good habit, and it can create headaches and migraines, among other things; so do not gaze at the tip of your nose. What is intended here is that your gaze is totally relaxed and loose, the direction of your gaze following the line of your nose. This means that you are gently gazing downward but not focusing on anything; without locking on to some visual target in front of you, your gaze is resting vacantly in the space in front of you. The eyes are relaxed and soft, blinking when needed. It is important to note that this is a very natural and soft gaze that is not straining the eyes in any way. (7) Finally, the tip of the tongue should be lightly placed against the roof of the mouth behind the upper teeth.

There is good reason for the specificity of this last instruction—that the tip of your tongue should be lightly pressed against the roof of your mouth behind the upper teeth. It is not so pertinent in the early phases of developing samādhi, but when you go into deeper and deeper levels of samādhi with a very focused attention for hours at a time, your senses will implode. Your eyes can be open, but you won't see anything. Your ears will have no noise-canceling earplugs, but you won't hear anything. As you go deeper, your awareness is being immersed in the space of the mind and, thereby, withdrawing from all of the five sensory fields; your body is on autopilot. This is why you want to have a posture that is very balanced and stable, like a fortress, so that you will not fall over. With good balance, you can achieve that even when you are not consciously aware of your body. It is not an untested hypothesis and has been done many times. When you are in deep samādhi, quasi-oblivious or entirely oblivious of your body and the surrounding environment, then your mouth might open a bit. Yogis have found sometimes that they start to drool because they are so unaware of the body that the drool coming down the cheeks or the chin is unnoticed. If somebody were to photograph you in deep samādhi, it wouldn't be a pretty picture. It is all the worse up in Tibet when it's freezing and you end up with a beard of icicles coming down your chin! Thus, the reason for having the tip of your tongue lightly touching your palate is simply to keep in the saliva.

Traditionally, the Vairocana posture is considered the optimal posture for sitting comfortably in meditation, which is why it is mentioned many times. If you succeed in maintaining that posture, and find that it is really comfortable, śamatha can be achieved here. You are encouraged to start young, when the body is quite flexible, malleable, and pliant, so that you can feel relaxed in the posture for sustained periods.

Regarding the full-lotus position, or vajrāsana, I suggest you find either an experienced meditator who is deeply familiar with the posture and has mastered it, or go to a competent yoga teacher. I practiced for years in that posture, though I do not anymore. When your legs are in full lotus with your feet up on the thighs, you have a rock-solid foundation that is locked in and supportive of going deeper in samādhi while maintaining a straight spine. But if you are not skillful in learning how to get into that posture and maintain it, then you risk pulling muscles, tendons, and ligaments in your knees. I will give you an additional word of advice that I learned the hard way: If you want to save yourself some time and not deform your feet or ankles, then practice symmetrically. In the thangka depictions of the buddhas, you will invariably see the left foot is up on the thigh, and the right calf is on top of the left one. Instead of emulating this every time when in vajrāsana, it is important to alternate legs so that the right foot is up on the thigh with the left calf on top of the right, and then repeat this on the opposite side. In such a manner, you will be symmetrically extending and stretching the muscles, ligaments, hips, joints, and knees on both sides, thereby creating more balance within the body.

In short, the vital point of the body is to find a comfortable posture—optimally, with the "seven qualities of Vairocana"—that allows you to meditate in a way that is comfortable while ensuring a straight spine. This is a very gentle and motherly approach that provides the grounds for the relaxation and stability needed to achieve śamatha. There is a posture for you, so take time to experiment and see what works.

The next topic that Düdjom Rinpoché addresses is the "vital point" of speech, saying,

> Regarding the vital point of your speech, let your vital energies
> be just as they are.

The term "vital energies" is a translation of the Sanskrit term *prāṇa*. These vital energies have not been measured using instruments of modern science, so people who rely solely on science think that vital energies do not exist. Such a view is about as open-minded and intelligent as religious fundamentalism, which declares, "If it is not in our holy book, it must either be untrue or irrelevant!" Thinking that science is the *only* method for understanding reality is very similar—it is simply *scientific* fundamentalism. Vital energies *do* exist, and their existence has been confirmed innumerable times over thousands of years. In India, they call it *prāṇa*; in ancient Greece it was called *pneuma*; in China, *chi*; in Japan, *ki*; and in Tibet, *lung*. Many traditional cultures around the world have recognized that there are flows of subtle "energies" in the body, and they have an enormous bearing on one's health and on the quality of one's awareness and state of mind.

In the practice of śamatha, your posture and breathing can ensure the vital energies are flowing smoothly, unimpededly, and in a healthy way. The flow of the vital energies is closely related to the respiration, or the flow of the breath, as oxygen moves in and out of your lungs. The connection between the breath and the vital energies has been known in Tibet for at least the last twelve hundred years, and in China and India for thousands of years. They knew that regulating your breathing also regulates your vital energies. There are plenty of systematic methods aimed at such regulation—*prāṇāyāma* and other yogic exercises that developed in India; *qigong*, in China; and the stage-of-completion practices in Vajrayāna are some examples. It is interesting to note, however, that there is no mention of regulating your breath here in Düdjom Rinpoché's texts, nor in the classic Buddhist texts that describe the practice of mindfulness of breathing. For our purposes here, without interfering with the breath, exerting effort to breathe, or impeding the flow of the breath in any way—whether due to a crooked or hunched-over posture, or from intentionally trying to control the breathing—see that the breathing flows unobstructedly and effortlessly, as in deep sleep. By so doing, the respiration will settle in its natural rhythm, and the corresponding vital energies will naturally and gradually start to flow into the central channel. It is best if the flow of vital energies is *not* directed through the subsidiary left and right channels—as these are associated with attachment and hatred—but, rather, through the central channel, the channel of wisdom.

As you progress along the path of śamatha, do not try to visualize or modulate your breathing in any way. Overall, aim to develop the foundation of a proper posture coupled with the vital point of speech, which corresponds to the breath and the vital energies. By so doing, and by precisely adopting the quintessential Dzokchen methods of śamatha discussed in this text, gradually your respiration will settle into a natural and unforced rhythm—a smooth, sinusoidal type of wave, whereby the undulations of the in-breath and out-breath become calmer and calmer. The need for oxygen decreases as your whole body-mind becomes more relaxed. With a tranquil mind, your brain is not working as hard, so you will need less air. Your breath will become very subtle and shallow, even to the point where you cannot hear it anymore and it becomes imperceptible. When the breath relaxes into such tranquility it means that the flow of your respiration has settled in its natural state—an ongoing flow, like a current that will take you all the way to śamatha. The breath becomes short—about two seconds for each inhalation, two seconds for each exhalation. And, although it is also shallow, you are in no way depriving yourself of the oxygen you need; your body simply does not need very much. The further you go along this path of samādhi, the more finely tuned your whole nervous system becomes, which means that your need for oxygen will decrease; the breath will become more and more superficial, though the frequency of the respiration remains the same.

My hypothesis—yet to be tested, validated, or repudiated—is that when your respiration is fully settled in its natural rhythm, allowing the vital energies to rest with the flow of respiration, then the respiration settles into a rhythm of fifteen cycles per minute, or four seconds for every complete respiration. This is about the same frequency of respiration that people have while in deep, dreamless sleep, and it also corresponds to the number of cycles of respiration that occur in a twenty-four-hour period often given in Vajrayāna teachings—21,600—which turns out to be fifteen cycles per minute. This has recurrently been my experience—when the breath settles, it settles into shallow breathing but without the sense of needing to breathe more deeply.

In summary, the vital point of your speech is to let your vital energies flow just as they are; in this way, your respiration will flow effortlessly and unobstructedly, without constriction, regulation, or control. After all, your body knows how to breathe better than you do, as it demonstrates every night when you are in deep, dreamless sleep, receiving the deepest refreshment and revitalization.

As you proceed along the path of śamatha, engaging in these practices without regulating the breath or visualizing, then the vital energies will naturally settle and begin to be drawn away from the two subsidiary channels and be directed into the central channel down below the navel. They will gradually flow up the central channel and up to the heart cakra located in the center of your chest.

Another important element of subtle-body physiology that developed in ancient India is the winds (*vāta*). These winds are of five types, each regulating a different function within the body. One of these five is the vital energy wind (*prāṇa vāta*), comprising the vital energies that are specifically correlated with the mind. Modern neuroscience reveals a great deal of information about the brain that has never been talked about in any contemplative traditions—the various parts of the brain, the activations of synapses, the dendrites, and so forth. The working theory in neuroscience is that all manner of subjective experiences are correlated with processes taking place in the brain. Similarly—but not the same in any way—it is a principle in Vajrayāna that whatever you are experiencing, whether rage or resting in sublime pristine awareness, is correlated to processes taking place in your subtle vital energies. When you achieve śamatha, these vital energies come into the central channel, then up to the heart cakra, converging and resting there. At that point, your coarse mind—your human psyche—has gone dormant, becomes passive, and is no longer activated. All that remains is the subtle continuum of consciousness, which is also all that remains when you are in deep, dreamless sleep, when you faint, or when you go under general anesthesia. Your ordinary mind dissolves into this subtle continuum of mental consciousness—also called the *substrate consciousness* in the Dzokchen tradition—when you achieve śamatha, which closely corresponds to the *bhavaṅga*, or "ground of becoming," as it is discussed in Theravāda literature.

When your heart stops, you stop breathing, and your brain goes flat-lined, then doctors assume you are dead. But all that has happened is your human mind is no longer functioning because the physiological basis for the mind being activated—primarily, but not exclusively, the brain—has ceased. Yet just because the mind is no longer immediately detectable, doesn't mean you have been annihilated or consciousness has become nothing. Rather, the ordinary, human functioning mind has dissolved into a subtler ground—a continuum from which it arose at conception and into which it dissolves when you die.

In the early formation of the embryo, your vital energies are in the heart. These vital energies came from a preceding life, together with its subtle mindstream, which then developed and became differentiated during the formation of the embryo. The inverse takes place when you die: the complexities and multiple functions of different types of subtle energies in the body simplify and draw into one, converging at the heart. Now your mind has melted into its relative subtle ground, the substrate consciousness, and the vital energies—which are subtle and physical—are located in your heart cakra. For these reasons, "Regarding the vital point of your speech," let your vital energies flow effortlessly and unimpededly. In order to do so, it is of utmost importance to let your respiration settle in its natural rhythm.

Moving on to the vital point of your mind, in the practice of śamatha the mind starts at a coarse level of functioning, then moves to increasingly subtler levels as mastery in the practice develops. Among the vital points of body, speech, and mind, the easiest one is to be able to settle your body in its natural state, as described, whether sitting upright or in the supine position. It is a subtler practice to allow your respiration to settle in its natural rhythm and, correspondingly, to allow your vital energies to rest right where they are without disturbing or blocking them. Even subtler, and the subtlest within this triad, is the vital point of the mind.

How is settling and resting the mind in its natural state to be achieved? As Düdjom Rinpoché's commentary says,

> Regarding the vital point of your mind, without disturb-ing your mind through any activity, such as reflecting on the

past or anticipating the future, cut off conceptual elaborations concerning the three times and rest your mind in an
unstructured, undistracted state.

There is nothing superfluous in these instructions. Many people encounter
a lot of problems in their practice because they overlook the vital points of
body, speech, and mind. Again, Düdjom Rinpoché says that the practice
should be done "without disturbing your mind through any activity, such as
reflecting on the past or anticipating the future." That is, do not get caught
up in rumination by going down memory lane, anticipating the future, or
becoming absorbed in hopes and fears. All of these agitate and disrupt the
mind. It's like putting a child to bed: put the child to bed comfortably, hap-
pily, safely, and then let the child be. Likewise, in this Dzokchen approach
to śamatha, you are putting your mind to bed—so do not disturb your
mind. For example, when a memory or an image arises pertaining to the
past, the natural inclination is to follow after and go to the referent of the
image instead of simply resting in the present and observing the image of
some past event, person, or activity.

For example, if a memory of my mother arises, that particular image is
like a snapshot in the mind. The image is right there in the present, and
yet it is purely a mental event—it is not a person and is certainly not my
mother. Instead, when it comes to mind, I can choose simply to observe the
image as an image and allow it to release, resting unwaveringly in the present moment. Perhaps then there is an interval with no images arising, but
before long, another thought or image is bound to emerge. I may remain
hovering motionless in the present moment, observing whatever appears
but without going to the referent and, therefore, ruminating or telling a
story. The point here is that whatever thoughts or images appear that per-
tain to the past or future, you do not have to go with them to the past or to
the future. Rest right there in the immediacy of the present moment and
simply observe these images and thoughts *as* images and thoughts, without
being drawn away to their referent. This is a crucial instruction for developing a practice in which the activities of the mind will not disturb your
awareness. Thus, simply observe the activities of the mind without identifying with them, so that your mind is not disturbed.

The phrase "conceptual elaborations" does not mean only thoughts, but also stories. These conceptual elaborations occur when you are ensnared in a narrative, thinking the thoughts, and letting one thought trigger another continually in a binding chain of these involuntary and sometimes quite obsessive and frequently compulsive thoughts. To "cut off conceptual elaborations" does not necessarily mean that as soon as a thought arises, you should try to cut it or terminate it. Although that is a legitimate śamatha practice, it is rather high intensity and is not the best practice for many people. If a single thought, image, discursive thought, or memory arises as a momentary event, it becomes a conceptual elaboration *only* when you hitch a ride on it or are captivated and carried away by it.

All of us have had the experience of having a thought arise in the mind that then ricochets and catalyzes more thoughts. When this happens and there are many thoughts in motion, your awareness must remain unmoved—not drawn to the referent of the thought. This means, then, that you are not absorbed in conceptual elaborations concerning the past or ruminations about the future. You are fully able to observe your thoughts but have cut the cord of identifying with and being carried away by them.

When your mind is no longer engaged with or disturbed by these various activities and conceptual elaborations, then there is very little left to do other than to "rest your mind in an unstructured, undistracted state." That is, you simply rest without doing anything with your mind. When you lay your child down to sleep, you do not "structure" your child; you do not do anything more than let your child rest. It is the same with the mind. In this "practice" of simply resting, it is important to understand that although you are putting your mind to bed, so to speak, you are *not* putting your awareness to bed. Rather, you let your awareness shine brightly and vividly, the awareness remaining radiantly clear, lucidly aware, and attentive, while your mind rests in an unstructured, unconfigured way. Lucidly resting in this way doesn't require *doing* something to the mind—generating this, altering that, modifying something or other. At the same time, in meditation you are neither spacing out and falling into laxity or dullness, nor becoming distracted and falling into excitation or agitation. Śamatha is what's left when you are not doing anything else with the mind, including, for example, not letting it become structured by drowsiness, dullness, or sleep. If it does sink into these states, it becomes structured as a sleeping mind, then you identify with it, fall asleep, and lose all clarity and explicit knowing of anything.

These are the vital points of the body, speech, and mind. They are not trivial and not easy to put into practice, so I suggest taking them in sequence. First, learn how to embrace the vital point of the body so that you can relax more and more deeply without losing the clarity, vividness, and acuity of your attention. Second, attend very closely to the natural flow of your respiration, which you may be tempted to alter by guiding the breath to be longer or more rhythmic. The human tendency is to attend to something that can be controlled, regulated, or modified in a way that pleases or protects. In your attention to the breath, however, you need to relinquish all control and simply attend to it very closely with awareness that is spacious yet focused, releasing any desire or inclination for it to be one way over another. This is a practice of *identitylessness*, which is briefly discussed below. Finally, simply "rest your mind in an unstructured, undistracted state," cutting off the identification with thoughts so that conceptual elaborations do not separate you from the immediacy of the present moment. The past is gone, the future is yet to come, so rest in the reality of the here and now. This final point of the mind is sometimes called "settling the mind in its natural state," which can be sufficient for achieving śamatha.

Regarding identity, the delusion of "I am" is an error that is affirmed as a root delusion throughout all schools of Buddhism. It is the mistaken belief that insists *I* am autonomous. *I* am the controller. *I* am my body. *I* am my mind. *I* own things that are mine. *I* am in charge. *I* control and do things to expand my ego and sense of identity. When you attend very closely and continuously to the flow of your respiration while releasing any inclination to control and manage it, practically speaking you are practicing identitylessness. This letting go of the sense that "I am the controller" is a big step in the right direction toward vipaśyanā.

How many times have you been engaged in a conversation and felt a strong urge to control it, adjust it, direct it, to cut in, to get the other person to agree, be quiet, or go along with it? Participating in a conversation with someone you respect, requires *listening*—a skill that has been developed to varying degrees in different people. Are you willing to listen to the other person and let them express their full range of thought about what's on their mind? Or do you feel the impulse to cut in and take over the conversation? Having a meaningful conversation involves sharing your best with the other person when you are speaking and doing nothing else but listening when you are listening. A very dear friend and Benedictine monk Father Laurence Freeman said to me once, "The greatest gift we can give to another person is our attention." Sometimes such attention means listening without ego and attending to the other person. In this way, you should listen to the breath not only with the ears, but experience the breath and the entire system of body-mind calming down, balancing, and soothing—settling body, speech, and mind in their natural states and embracing the vital points of body, speech, and mind.

Visualization

Düdjom Rinpoché's commentary continues,

> If you can remain there, that is enough. If you cannot, imagine at your heart a red syllable *hūṃ* about an inch in height, or any size that you find appropriate. Let this image arise vividly, without forcefully grasping it with your mind, and steadily focus on this clear image by naturally letting your awareness loosely settle upon it.

As Düdjom Rinpoché says, "If you can remain there, that is enough." This is the preparation: establishing the basis of śamatha. If you can do just that, that's enough. However, many people *cannot* do that; they feel unrooted, adrift, and as if there's nothing to hold onto. The normal tendency is to grasp and hold onto things with your mind, desires, and memories: "This is my personal history." "These are my thoughts." "This is my breathing." Grasping provides a sense of security, a sense of "I am." If you can release the ego-clenching and remain in the open presence of your mind, then that is sufficient for achieving śamatha.

The process of allowing your coarse human mind to rest so that it dissolves right back into its relative ground is analogous to falling asleep.

Though, in the normal process of falling asleep, although you are tired, you may be quite awake and clear when you lie down; but as you release into sleep, the clarity of your mental awareness subsides. Over time, the five sensory modes of consciousness implode into mental consciousness, and you slip into deep, dreamless sleep. At this point, you are not explicitly aware of anything; the clarity of your awareness is veiled. The path of śamatha is comparable to that of falling sleep in the sense that the mind slowly calms down over time. Toward the culmination of the practice of śamatha, the five sensory modes of consciousness fall away and dissolve into the subtle continuum of mental consciousness. The mind internally becomes quieter and quieter. Instead of losing clarity, as happens during the falling-asleep process, the clarity of your awareness increases as the natural luminosity of your substrate consciousness is unveiled. In fact, the radiance of your substrate consciousness is normally veiled by the activities of the mind. The further you progress along the path of śamatha, the more awareness manifests as brilliantly clear and lucid, even as your human mind is shutting down.

If you cannot rest your mind in its natural state—because you are bored, distracted, restless, uncomfortable, or need something to latch your mind onto, for example—then you need a target on which to direct your attention. Therefore, "imagine at your heart a red syllable *hūṃ*." Here Düdjom Rinpoché is referring to the Tibetan syllable *hūṃ*, but you could visualize the Sanskrit syllable or the English letters. It is a seed syllable representing the mind and is radiant ruby red in color. Imagining this "at your heart" is referring to the heart cakra. You are to imagine it as being "any size that you find appropriate," which means that you do not want the *hūṃ* to be too big, like the size of a fist, nor too small to "see" mentally, like a pinhead. Rather, an appropriate size would be somewhere between the size of the nail of your pinky finger and the nail of your thumb.

When he says to "let this image arise vividly, without forcefully grasping it with your mind," this means not to furrow your brow, tense up, nor forcefully concentrate in order to visualize the red syllable *hūṃ* at your heart. Instead, let it arise vividly and "steadily focus on this clear image by naturally letting your awareness loosely settle upon it." An important note is that in visualization, when you concentrate your awareness anywhere in the body, you are merging the vital energies related to the mind into that point where you are visualizing. There, they can become compacted; and since they are physical, they influence the physical body. With this in mind, intensely trying to visualize something at your heart can harm your physical heart if you are not skillful and deeply relaxed. Use caution and care with any kind of visualization, but especially those directed at your heart. If you are going to do this at all, go very gently and softly, and remember that this is directed at your heart cakra, not the physical organ of your heart.

Further, many people have a hard time visualizing anything, let alone maintaining it with continuity. It is not easy to maintain any kind of image in a sustained fashion for more than a few seconds. The psychologist Stephen M. Kosslyn at Harvard University conducted a study in which he found that among Harvard undergraduates, the longest they could hold an image in mind before losing it is seven seconds. William James, more than a century ago, thought the maximum was three seconds. As mentioned, it is very easy when doing any kind of visualization practice, especially for śamatha, to give too much effort, to fail, get frustrated, and then push harder; this is a stressful approach.

It is here that Gyatrul Rinpoché provides helpful advice. He commented that if you cannot visualize even the English letters *h-u-m*, let alone the rather complex configuration of *hūṃ* in Tibetan, then just *imagine* that it is there. Without trying to visualize it or see it clearly with your mind's eye, gently imagine its presence.

To begin to get a sense for how this works, imagine that a dear friend is standing right behind you. It is not necessary to visualize the details, such as the person's eyelashes, chin, and what kind of clothes they are wearing. Instead, imagine only that this person is standing right behind you. This can be done without being good at visualization since you are more simply imagining their *presence* without visual detail. Similarly, imagine that there is a rich, ruby red, glowing *hūṃ*, correlated with its pronounced sound "hung," at your heart and symbolizing the mind. It is enough to imagine it being there, as your attention has a referent, a target. Steadily and naturally focus on your imagination that it is there. "Naturally" means to do so without forcing it, tensing up, or pushing too hard; but rather, to do so in a relaxed way, letting your awareness loosely settle upon it.

When Gyatrul Rinpoché introduced me to Dzokchen, he placed a strong emphasis on cultivating a relaxed awareness. It is a relief not to be pushing all the time. There is a place for effort—though, not so much effort that you hold it too firmly and become exhausted, and not so relaxed that you lose the object and are carried away by distraction or become spaced out. Düdjom Rinpoché's instruction here is one method to rest in an unstructured, undistracted state. Relax as you imagine and hold in mind the presence of the *hūṃ*. From this place, the mind begins to calm, and you experience deeper relaxation, stability, and clarity.

An Alternative Meditative Object

For some people, however, this visualization method does not work either. There is no such thing as the one right śamatha method, and the Buddha prescribed different methods for people of different dispositions. Settling the mind in its natural state works for some, while imagining the red *hūṃ* at the heart works for others. When you find a method that works, you know it is effective if you become more relaxed and your mind becomes clearer and more composed as you practice.

If neither of these two methods work, Düdjom Rinpoché advises,

> If you also find it difficult to rest there, place a small or large object—such as a seed syllable, a stick, or a pebble—in front of you. Then direct your visual gaze upon it, without moving your eyes or fluttering your eyelashes. Without bringing anything to mind—such as judgments about good and bad mental states—and without thinking about or meditating on anything, release your awareness into utter ease.

For your small or large object, you can use, for example, a drawing, a painting, a stick, a flower, a pebble, or an image of a seed syllable, such as *oṃ*, *āḥ*, or *hūṃ*. Whatever object you use, place it in front of you at about a forty-five-degree angle downward (approximately following the line of your nose), and about two or three feet away on a platform so that it is easily seen. From here, "direct your visual gaze upon it, without moving your eyes or fluttering your eyelashes." Again, do not contract or strain your eyes. With the object in front of you, breathe normally and ensure that your mental practice does not inhibit the flow of breathing. Let your breath flow naturally, and then gaze down very gently and softly. In directing your visual gaze, you do not achieve samatha with your *visual* awareness; you achieve samatha with your *mental* awareness. Your visual gaze is directed and guides your mental awareness and attention. Thus, you are looking at the object, but also attending to it.

Then "without bringing anything to mind—such as judgments about good and bad mental states—and without thinking about or meditating on anything, release your awareness into utter ease." This ease is pleasant and soothing, and does not get caught up in the activities of the mind. Although this text was written fairly recently—in the twentieth century—these are the same teachings that had been given for centuries in nomadic and rural Tibet, places that have nothing like the intensity of our modern world. Even for them, he is saying to "release your awareness into utter ease."

Further, he adds,

> From within that state, whatever conceptual appearances arise, do not follow after them, but, applying yourself to the meditative support, bear it in mind nonconceptually, vividly, and undistractedly.

In other words, it is necessary and important to be aware that thoughts have arisen, but to do so without taking interest in them, having judgments, preferences, aversions, or following after the referent of these various conceptual images, thoughts, and so forth. Instead, he instructs not to follow after whatever arises, but to apply yourself to the meditative support, and to "bear it in mind nonconceptually." You are not thinking about, labeling, or judging it, but are simply attending to it with mindfulness. This mindful attention is nonconceptual, vivid (free from laxity or dullness), and undistracted (free from excitation or agitation). Do this without letting your eyes be diverted or your mind stray off, so that both your visual gaze and mental gaze are focused.

Regarding all three methods, we see that Düdjom Rinpoché starts with something very simple, yet subtle: sitting and letting your mind rest in an unstructured, undistracted state. If that practice is too subtle for you, he goes on to describe the practice of visualizing a mental object. For those who find that still too subtle, he recommends directing one's gaze onto a physical object. This is a very gentle approach. There are other variations as well, such as mindfulness of breathing, although he does not mention it here. However, for some people, mindfulness of breathing will be preferable to gazing at an image, stick, or stone.

Imbalances of Attention

Once you are fully engaged in the practice of śamatha, imbalances of attention will inevitably arise. Regarding these imbalances, Düdjom Rinpoché says,

> If laxity arises, lift your gaze, firm up your posture, arouse your consciousness, invigorate your awareness, and focus single-pointedly. If scattering and agitation occur, lower your gaze, relax your posture, relax deeply, and rest in your natural state.

If your mind starts to become lax, dull, or spaced out, then elevate your gaze. Raise the object you are attending to so that you are focusing on it higher up. Elevating your gaze is a very practical technique that may help elevate the clarity of your attention. If your body becomes lax or dull, then "firm up your posture." While meditating, it is common to sit in an appropriate posture for the first few minutes, then begin to slump. In the supine position, you cannot slump, but you could start to space out into dullness and laxity. However, if you are sitting upright—whether on a chair or cross-legged—firm up your posture and sit at attention. From here, "arouse your consciousness, invigorate your awareness, and focus single-pointedly." To "invigorate your awareness" means to inspire, enliven, refresh, and focus your consciousness. For example, if you are getting bored, pay closer attention.

This raises a point that I have found to be experientially true: based on my experience, there is nothing that is intrinsically and objectively boring. By saying that people, things, situations, places, or books are boring, what is really happening is that the quality of my awareness is dull, and therefore, whatever I am attending to seems boring. "Boring" is a quality of subjective awareness; not a quality of objective entities or people. Mindfulness of breathing was the first Buddhist meditation I practiced more than fifty years ago. Breathing in, breathing out . . . Isn't that kind of boring, such that if you have seen one breath, you have seen them all? However, it is the quality of awareness that is brought to the flow of respiration that is dull.

If you are training in full-time retreat to achieve śamatha, sometimes you might get bored. You may have been doing it so long that the novelty of meditating has worn off and you are pining for something new, fresh, and interesting. This means that whatever object you are attending to, you are simply not finding it interesting, whether you are resting in awareness, observing thoughts, focusing on the red *hūṃ*, a stick, or a pebble. It is understandable to find yourself bored, but in the practice of śamatha, the three qualities of relaxation, stability, and vividness are necessary. The quality of vividness and interest that you have may wane because you may believe the object itself is not intrinsically interesting. Typically, objects that are really interesting are ones that either provide a lot of pleasure or a lot of pain—in other words, pleasant and unpleasant things. Objects that are neither objectively catalyzing pleasure, discomfort, or unhappiness can be bland, easily sinking us into boredom. Although we may have begun the session with a relatively high degree of clarity, vividness, and acuity, that subsides exactly when the object and practice become boring. If you become bored, and there is nothing on the outside to peak your interest, you will go into rumination because you find it more interesting than your breath. In that case, the breath did not arouse clarity of attention, because it was not objectively enticing and attention-catching in the way that pleasure and pain are. Pain is not boring; nobody being tortured has ever said, "Oh, please stop. I'm so bored." When people are experiencing extraordinary bliss or joy, there is no boredom. If you can maintain a high degree of clarity, even of the breath, you may practice twelve hours a day without ever getting bored. You can be resting in awareness and be aware of being aware, and if the clarity of your awareness of being aware is at a high level, then it is not boring. In sum, and this is a key point: anything can be boring if the quality of awareness that you are using is dull.

Continuing, Düdjom Rinpoché says to "arouse your consciousness, invigorate your awareness, and focus single-pointedly." The latter may be done by simply focusing more intensely, arousing oneself, taking a fresh interest, and looking more closely. Reboot, refresh, restore. In so doing, if you find you become habitually or repeatedly bored, dull, or spaced out, then go back to your motivation. Why are you doing this? Is this merely a hobby or a curiosity? Do you have only a casual interest in this practice? When you review the four revolutions in outlook that Gyatrul Rinpoché emphasizes, they will give you incentive, motivation, strong drive, and determination that will subjectively arouse and restore greater clarity and vividness to your attention. In this way, a simple object like a stick or a stone will not be boring if you bring a high degree of attentional clarity to it. Arouse the interest at a deeper level so that, although the breath may not be interesting, the *practice* is interesting. It is interesting because you believe there can be enormous benefit here.

Consider the analogy of a person going to medical school with the aspiration to become a psychiatrist. Perhaps they are motivated by compassion and a desire to be of service and to live a meaningful life. In the meantime, this medical student has to spend weeks studying the functions of the liver, kidneys, bowels, and so forth. Even though much of that study may eventually have no relevance whatsoever for them as a practicing psychiatrist, if they do not study those subjects and pass the exams in the first four years, they will not get their medical degree and, therefore, will not become a psychiatrist.

Again, going back to the foundations that Gyatrul Rinpoché highlighted, if you reflect upon your precious human life, and so forth, then you are developing conative momentum, resolve, and determination, like students just beginning their medical training. Although becoming a psychiatrist may be years ahead, still they remain focused. Perhaps they want to join a specific hospital or medical group, and this keeps them going on the days they are really tired, exhausted, or bored. They overcome it because of their deeper level of motivation that allows them to maintain their interest and engagement, which, therefore, allows them to sustain a level of mental clarity.

If you find yourself simply becoming bored with śamatha, then go back to your root motivation or aspiration for practicing. Why are you doing this in the first place? Is it because you just want to have a bit of stress reduction and a little peace of mind? If so, then fifteen minutes in the morning and fifteen minutes in the evening may do it. If your practice is directed toward such mundane and easily reachable goals, then that is okay. A lot of people are quite happy doing a bit of meditation to make saṃsāra a little more pleasant. If that's all they want, that's all they get. That level of aspirational motivation is about the same as that of a person who flits around from hobby to hobby, never going deep into any one activity.

People have been getting bored in meditation for as long as people have been meditating. There are some who get bored and give up, and others who overcome it; the latter are often those who become the great contemplatives, capable of benefiting many beings. If you can bear in mind the potential long-term benefits of śamatha and keep your eyes on the prize, this focus on the bigger picture will help boost your resolve, especially if you fall into laxity or dullness.

The other main type of mental pitfall that can pose an obstacle to meditation is falling into attention deficit, which may manifest cognitively as difficulty focusing, problems paying attention, or a short attention span. Düdjom Rinpoché describes this issue and its remedy, saying, "If scattering and agitation occur, lower your gaze, relax your posture, relax deeply, and rest in your natural state." While some children and adults are officially diagnosed with attention deficit disorder, most of us suffer from some form of attention deficit, to one degree or another, as a condition of living in modernity. Although some people take medication for this disorder, at best, that can help only with symptom relief. Attention deficit is a problem that stems from imbalances in the mind, so, at some point, these mental imbalances must be addressed and not just their neurological correlates.

Then there is attention hyperactivity, to use a modern term; in the Buddhist terminology, the English translation is "scattered," "agitated," or "falling into excitation." If you become *scattered*, your attention is going out, sparking this way, spurting that way, or being drawn to distraction. However, *agitation* is not necessarily something that is drawn outward; it might be coming from within as a result of your mind becoming tight, constricted, and unstable. For example, while focusing on the red seed syllable *hūṃ*, you may be agitated by something from within—in terms of subjective impulses of the mind. Maybe an aversion to or dissatisfaction with the practice is developing. Desire and aversion may be stirring and disabling relaxation. If your mind becomes scattered and agitated, and your attention is dispersed, the antidote is to "lower your gaze, relax your posture, relax deeply, and rest in your natural state."

I learned this firsthand while doing my first intensive śamatha retreat in 1980 under the direct guidance of His Holiness the Dalai Lama. He gave me a seed syllable to focus on within a broader context of practice, and on many occasions, my mind wandered into excited and scattered states. My initial antidote to that was like having a dog on a leash who is pulling hard, wanting to sniff this, or run after that; every time the dog tries to run off, the natural tendency might be to yank the leash and bring the dog back; the stronger the dog tries to pull away, the harder you pull. Every time my attention wandered, I repeatedly yanked it back—force meeting force; power meeting power. At this time, I was relatively new to meditation, and the tendency for mind-wandering and dispersed attention had been ingrained from the first thirty years of my life. In this way, my little seedling of samādhi cultivation was not stronger than the mind's profound tendency to disperse and scatter. The more I yanked, the more frustrated, tired, and stressed I became. I was losing the war: I could win a lot of little battles, but each time, it would be at the cost of tightening up. Contracting just created more tension and constriction. Like increases like.

His Holiness never instructed me to do that, but as an American, I kept trying harder and harder, which did not work out very well. Düdjom Rinpoché's response here is not to tighten up; that is, do not yank the leash by grabbing your attention and forcefully bringing it back. The easiest thing is to "lower your gaze" and then "relax your posture." When the mind gets scattered and tight, there is often going to be some correlated tightening of the body, especially in the muscles of the face, mouth, jaw, eyes, shoulders, and neck. When this happens, "relax your posture, relax deeply, and rest in your natural state."

The important lesson here is to let go of the grasping, because every time you are carried away by a thought, it means that you have contracted around and identified with it. You become immersed, like in a miniature nonlucid dream, and often do not even know you are thinking. This is because the mind has become tight and condensed, becoming absorbed into the wandering thought.

When this gripping and yanking occur, the correct response is to "relax deeply." This means to come back to the culmination of settling your awareness in its natural state—relaxed, still, and clear. Within the looseness that is unfettered by grasping, you are free of hope and fear, and aware of the thoughts, images, memories, emotions, and desires that arise in the space of the mind. You will be so relaxed that you will not grab these mental constructs nor get caught in their grip. You simply witness the movements of the mind, not identifying with them. From this relaxed place, you rest in the stillness of awareness clearly illuminating the space of the mind and are not drawn away, scattered, or agitated. It is possible even to observe thoughts and images appearing in an agitated way without letting your awareness become agitated. The only way to do that is to relax more and more deeply. This is a skill that is to be cultivated, and is of urgent necessity in these modern times.

In 1975, I had just finished one hundred thousand recitations of the Vajrasattva mantra, and an enormous amount of unexpected energy was brimming and bubbling out of my body. I spoke with Geshé Rabten and told him, "There's just so much energy coming up; it's bubbling, bubbling! It's really agitating! What should I do?" He looked at me and said simply, "Relax." When I asked him *how*, he responded, "Well, just relax." It wasn't until I encountered Gyatrul Rinpoché that I began learning how to relax and was able to follow the instructions "lower your gaze, relax your posture, relax deeply, and rest in your natural state."

This "natural state" is one in which you are simply not doing anything to your mind—not structuring, modifying, or improving it. The Mahāmudrā tradition gives the following classic image of what it is like to rest in your natural state: visualize a bundle of hay that is tightly bound with a strong rope. Then, somebody comes along with a very sharp knife, cuts the cord, and whoosh! The hay is now freed; it flies into the air and gently settles in its natural state. That is what you do to your mind.

The tendencies of excitation, agitation, mind-wandering, and rumination are very deeply ingrained. Some people are more prone to such rumination or compulsive ideation than others. This was true in rural India, nomadic Tibet, and even at the time of the Buddha, where the cultures were certainly much slower—no internet or any of the massive stimulation in the modern world. The Buddha identified some people as being of a temperament such that they are especially prone to obsessive-compulsive, discursive thinking. This is a mind that has a blabbermouth, cannot stop thinking, and is compulsively carried away by thoughts that arise. With all of the overstimulation in modern culture, it is obvious why attention deficit hyperactivity disorder is so prevalent. This is a symptom of our era, and it seems to be increasing—faster, faster, faster!

This idolization of speed began to arise at the very beginning of the twentieth century, with the rise of the internal-combustion engine, which gave us cars, motorcycles, and such. Now there is the obsession with obtaining and consuming the latest model of laptop, cell phone, vehicle, and more. All of this agitates the mind. We are in a petri dish sitting in a centrifuge of modern civilization that is designed to throw everything about chaotically. Unfortunately, this is where a lot of people's minds are going—into chaotic agitation and scattering.

However, if it is just a little episode of slipping attention, then, as the problem is quite superficial and temporary, you can apply the similarly easy antidote of lowering your gaze. If you are focusing on a visual object, seed syllable, stick, or pebble, then bring your eyes down a bit so that your gaze follows downward. Then, generally speaking, ground your awareness so that it is less vulnerable to excitation. This is why in the beginning of the practice of settling body, speech, and mind, your attention and awareness are brought down to the tactile sensations of the contact of your body with the chair, cushion, or floor.

❖Meditation: Settling Body, Speech, and Mind in Their Natural States

https://wisdomexperience.org/alan-wallace-dzokchen-meditation-2/

Find a comfortable position with regard to the vital points of your body, speech, and mind.

In line with the Mahāyāna underpinnings of Buddhist Vajrayāna practice, begin by arousing the most meaningful motivation you can. I suggest that you approximate, to the best of your ability, the aspiration and resolve to achieve perfect enlightenment for the sake of all sentient beings. That is your aspiring bodhicitta. Then, activate this aspiration by applying engaged bodhicitta to the practice for this session.

Normally, there may be a sense that *you* are located up in your head—it has certainly been claimed many times by people who mistakenly equate the mind with the brain. However, there is no person inside your brain. With a sense of release, let your awareness descend from your head down into your torso. Experience the tactile sensations throughout your torso. Be mindfully present and let your awareness continue to descend down to your buttocks and thighs. Whether you are sitting on a chair or cross-legged, let your awareness descend to the tactile sensations of your body and its contact with the ground. Allow your awareness to become grounded in these tactile sensations where the body is in touch with the chair, cushion, or floor. This attentional descent is quiet and nonconceptual. Simply be present with these sensations of being physically grounded.

Then, like a fragrance filling a room, let your awareness fill the entire space of your body. From the soles of your feet up to the crown of your head, be mindfully present throughout this entire somatic space. Without imagining or visualizing your body, let your awareness simply and nonconceptually experience the tactile sensations throughout this field.

With a mindful presence throughout the space of the body, begin to note areas of the body that feel tight or constricted—the shoulders, mouth, forehead, cheeks, jaw, chest, abdomen, and so on. Wherever you feel such constriction, as you breathe out allow the tightness to release. Soften your eyes and the muscles around the eyes so that your face rests in an expression of repose, as if you were sound asleep.

In terms of the vital point of the body, settle your body in a state that is relaxed, comfortable, and at ease. Let your body be still during the course of this session. If you are fidgeting or moving about, this will destabilize the flow of your attention, so allow your body to be composed and still.

Let your spine be straight. If you are sitting upright—either cross-legged or in a chair—slightly elevate your sternum and relax the muscles of your belly so that your belly expands without impediment when you breathe in and naturally contracts as you breathe out. This way of breathing is comparable to filling a vase with water: the water flows down to the base and then fills up from there. Likewise, in terms of your experience of the breath, although the air is going down just to the lungs, the sensations of breathing flow down to the belly and expand as you inhale. Breathing in this way, let the sensations of the in-breath first expand the belly, then the diaphragm, and finally, perhaps the chest. Let your breath flow naturally and effortlessly, with your body striking the vital points of being relaxed, still, and with a posture of vigilance or sitting at attention. Psychologically, you can cultivate and maintain vigilance even in the supine position. The body is totally relaxed, but mentally, you can be utterly vigilant, lying down at attention.

Having thus settled the body in its natural state, moving from coarse to subtle to subtlest, the vital point for the speech is settling your respiration in its natural rhythm. Attend primarily to the flow and rhythm of the respiration with each inhalation and exhalation—whether it is long or short, relax deeply with every exhalation. Especially as you come to the end of the out-breath, let your mind be very quiet, conceptually still, and attentive. Continue to relax and release as the breath comes to the end of the exhalation, though not to the extent of pushing the breath out, but rather letting it flow out effortlessly and fully. Then, without needing to exert any effort at all, the breath will flow in easily. Simply let the breath flow in. Whether the breath is long or short, deep or shallow, let the body breathe without interference; do not try to do anything to the breath.

The beginning of the inhalation is subtle. You may feel the need to pull it in, but do not. You don't suffocate when you fall deep asleep; the body doesn't forget to breathe; it breathes at its best when you are out of the way. Now, let your body breathe at its best, without you getting in the way; but unlike in deep sleep, be mindfully attentive to the respiration and its flow. By so doing, the nervous system and the subtle body of the vital energies settle. You are no longer disturbing the flow of your respiration with thoughts, hopes, fears, anxieties, or emotions. Now that you are out of the way, the breathing settles into its natural rhythm, so that with each breath, the body gets what it needs and gives back what it does not need in terms of the nourishment from air. From this place, you may experience your whole body quieting while the breath is soothing and calming the body.

As the respiration settles in its natural rhythm, unforced and unimpeded, now you have the subtle physiological base for the vital point of the mind. You strike this vital point by allowing your awareness to rest right where it is in the present moment, explicitly aware of being aware, but without directing it here or there. Even if all appearances, activities of the mind, thinking, and remembering suddenly vanished, you would still be aware—aware of the simple, immediate reality of being aware. Rest in that nonconceptual and undistracted simplicity by maintaining the lucidity and clarity of awareness and the flow of clear cognizance without any specific referent. For some people this is the best and most effective method; for others, it is not.

Gyatrul Rinpoché comments on this, saying, "In order to engage in the formal practice, first of all you should sit in the correct meditation posture."[14] He kindly advises that if you cannot sit comfortably, then lie down or sit in a chair. Then he advises, "Allow the speech to remain silent and breathe naturally. Do not force the mind to be too tense or too slack; just remain relaxed in your own pure awareness nature." Gyatrul Rinpoché continues, saying, "Sometimes as you sit, it may occur to you that there are two processes occurring: that of apprehending the mind and that of apprehending the apprehender."

Continuing from the instructions in Düdjom Rinpoché's commentary, now try imagining that there is a glowing, ruby red *hūṃ* syllable right in the center of the heart cakra, in the center of your chest, but do not worry if you cannot clearly visualize it. The Tibetan letter is quite elegant and beautiful, and symbolizes the power of the mind and of awareness itself. Whatever image comes to mind of this syllable, let it come vividly, and then rest there. The more relaxed you are, the easier it will be to sustain that image, allowing it to continue to glow. It becomes a placeholder for awareness, so that your awareness is stable relative to this image. For some this may be the optimal and most effective method; for others, it is not.

For a minute or two, let your eyes be open and your gaze very soft. Let your gaze come to settle on a physical object right in front of you and focus the flow of your mental awareness right where your eyes are directed. Soften the eyes, relax the forehead, and let the flow of your mental awareness remain right there without moving your eyes or fluttering your eyelashes, and without being drawn away by distracting thoughts or other sensory stimuli. Focusing on a sensory image can help to quiet the conceptual mind as your awareness rests there.

Blink whenever you need to, but let the flow of your visual gaze remain steady so that your eyes do not wander and, therefore, your mind does not wander. In this way, very gently relax the flow of your mind and attention, compose it with the continuity necessary to maintain the clarity of attention. Now you have stepped out onto the road of śamatha. There's an entryway for everyone, and this is an easy entry.

Bring the meditation to a close by dedicating the merit of this session so that you may achieve perfect awakening for the benefit of all beings . ❖

❖ Abbreviated Meditation on Settling Body, Speech, and Mind in Their Natural States

https://wisdomexperience.org/alan-wallace-dzokchen-meditation-3/

This is a brief meditation that can be done daily in order to highlight the vital points of body, speech, and mind.

Find a comfortable position. Let your awareness descend into the body right down to the ground where your body is in contact with the chair, cushion, or floor. Ground your awareness in these tactile sensations, cognizant that they have no labels and are devoid of thoughts. Likewise, let your awareness of these bare tactile sensations be nonconceptual. Allow the field of your mental awareness to expand and permeate the entire field of somatic sensations so that you are mindfully present. Settle your body in a state that is relaxed, comfortable, at ease, still, and vigilant. If you are sitting, sit at attention with a straight spine, slightly lifted sternum, and loosely relaxed abdominal muscles, without impediment or constraint to the breath.

Then, in terms of the vital point of the speech, which is subtler than the body, attend closely to the rhythm of the respiration, but without intentionally regulating it at all. With every out-breath, relax deeply and utterly release thoughts, imagery, and activities of the mind into inner silence. Settle the inner speech of the mind in its natural state of effortless silence.

Relax completely and perhaps even pause once you have exhaled, if it feels natural. On the sweet spot at the very beginning of the inhalation, see that your mind is very quiet, attentive, nonconceptual, and relinquishing all control and effort. Renounce yourself as an agent and simply witness the breath flowing in as effortlessly as if you were deep asleep.

Next is the vital point of the mind. As your mind relaxes, set it at ease, releasing all concerns, hopes, and fears about the future and recapitulations of the past. Simply allow your awareness to settle and rest right where it is—directing it neither outward nor inward, but allowing it to rest in its natural state, which is utterly relaxed, still, at ease, and effortless.

Bear in mind that your awareness of being aware has been there all along. Before I mentioned it, you were already implicitly aware of being aware, and you were not giving any effort to it. Throughout the course of the day, you are implicitly aware of being aware; you never think you've become unconscious or fainted until you have. This awareness of awareness is effortless and ongoing. Rest in that awareness of awareness, letting your awareness again be relaxed and at ease. Awareness is, by nature, luminous and clear, illuminating all experiences, appearances, thoughts, and objective states of mind—although, on many occasions, its natural luminosity is veiled by dullness and distraction. Allow your awareness to rest at ease, in stillness, and in its own natural clarity. In this way, you allow the mind to settle in its natural state. Bring this initial settling to a close by dedicating the merit of this session to the achievement of your perfect awakening for the benefit of all beings. ❖

This settling of body, speech, and mind is something that could be very helpful to do many times a day. It's only a matter of minutes, or sometimes seconds—once the body is relaxed, still, and vigilant, the flow of the breath is effortless and unimpeded, and your awareness is relaxed, still, and clear— to come to this grounded state.

This is a dynamic equilibrium of body, speech, and mind in a state of balance. You are not doing anything, yet you are also not dopey, dull, spaced-out, or agitated. It is dynamic in that you are ready to go—whether to listen or engage fully in any type of activity.

If your posture is cramped, tight, crooked, or slouched, then it will be difficult for the respiration to flow in a natural, effortless way. If your speech— which is closely correlated with the flow of respiration and inner speech of the mind—is not resting in silence, then there will be no sustainable balance in the mind. From coarse to subtle, from body to speech to mind, balance is being restored through this practice of settling.

This is a way to refresh the sanity, wholeness, coherence, and composure of your mind, creating more conative, attentional, and emotional balance. The term "conation" is well known to psychologists but has yet to make its way into our common vocabulary. So it's high time to begin now. Just as there is attentional balance, free of laxity and excitation, and emotional balance, free of extremes, "conative balance" refers to having the right degree and kinds of desires that are truly conducive to a state of balance and well-being. Cognitive balance, which is cultivated through the practice of vipaśyanā, similarly trains the mind to be free of cognitive biases that cause us to apprehend what isn't there and not to see what is there. What would happen if everybody calmed down and spent two or three minutes restoring these different modes of balance? For instance, how would students perform academically and behaviorally? It would be a great investment to devote the first five minutes of every class to a practice that allows everyone, including the teacher, to calm down, get grounded, and find balance. Following the practice, the teacher can then teach in an environment where the students are ready to hear and listen. The pioneering American psychologist William James so insightfully declared, "The faculty of voluntarily bringing back a wandering attention, over and over again, is the very root of judgment, character, and will. . . . An education which should improve this faculty would be *the* education *par excellence*."[15]

This approach is not religious or philosophical; it is a way of restoring the balance of the body, speech, and mind, with an emphasis on the mind. What is more important than learning how to purify your mind so that you are no longer suffering from your inner afflictions? What is more meaningful than cultivating your mind so that the inner wellsprings of virtue, well-being, and peace of mind are unveiled? The meaning of life is the cultivation of genuine well-being. William James further comments that a person "who has daily inured himself to habits of concentrated attention, energetic volition, and self-denial in unnecessary things . . . will stand like a tower when everything rocks around him, and his softer fellow-mortals are winnowed like chaff in the blast."[16]

Düdjom Rinpoché's instructions go on to say,

> Similarly, without thinking about anything apart from simply directing your consciousness to a distinct sound, a pungent smell, and so on, or else the natural exhalation, inhalation, and pauses of your respiration, you may place your attention on one of these in a relaxed way.

As a reminder, in the last chapter we discussed Düdjom Rinpoché's instruction on the vital point of the mind, in which he said, "without disturbing your mind through any activity, such as reflecting on the past or anticipating the future, cut off conceptual elaborations concerning the three times and rest your mind in an unstructured, undistracted state." This is a complete and sufficient instruction for achieving śamatha. He simply states, "If you can remain there, that is enough."

If you cannot remain there, however, he then provides a visualization practice in which you focus your attention and your vital energies on the red *hūṃ* at your heart. Whichever practice you are engaging in, you should simply note the presence of other appearances that could be distractions. These include distinct sounds, pungent smells, the sensations of breathing, tactile sensations, thoughts, images, memories, and so on. The key here is simply to note these things arising without identifying with or being carried away by them.

Consider the analogy of being alone in a house with glass doors, and a burglar comes skulking around, checking to see if any doors are open—but he's timid, cowardly, and unarmed. As soon as the diffident burglar shows up outside your door, if you note him immediately, and he sees you noting him, he will probably slip away, and that will be the end of it. You do not need to pull out a gun, chase him down, tackle him, or call the police. All you need to do is let him know that you noted his presence, and that is suffi-cient for him to disappear.

Similarly, when distractions arise in your practice, if you do not grasp at them, then there will be no need to release anything. Sitting quietly, no effort is required to be peripherally aware that the breath is flowing in or the breath is flowing out. These sensations will not distract you if you do not identify with them and do not allow yourself to be carried away by them. It is sufficient simply to note them, and any thoughts will release themselves.

This point—"without thinking about anything"—is crucial. There are many people who think that you cannot observe thoughts. I once met a distinguished philosopher of mind at a major university where I was giv-ing a lecture. Referring to the Buddhist practice of resting in the stillness of awareness and observing thoughts arise—like overhearing the conver-sation of some people in an adjacent room—I commented that it can be very useful to observe thoughts, imagery, and anything else that may arise in the space of the mind. When my lecture was over, this man came over to me, seemingly quite upset and agitated. Speaking in a loud, authoritarian voice, he glared down at me and thundered, "You can't observe thoughts; you can only think them!" I was baffled, as that was a debate in which I was not willing to engage. It felt like I was coming in fresh from the ocean having had a swim, and a person shouted at me, "You can't swim! It's not possible to swim! Human bodies are heavier than water; they sink!" When someone so blatantly denies your own experience, you are speechless. He was not aware that I had spent thousands of hours over the past thirty years observing my mind—something, apparently, he had never experienced and could not imagine. Roughly 90 percent of contemporary philosophers of mind place their faith in reductionism—believing the mind is nothing more than a function of the brain. This raises the age-old question, Which comes first, the dead chicken of the mind sciences that rejects the value of introspection for observing the mind firsthand, or the rotten egg of materialistic reductionism?

Here, we could say that you are *thinking* a thought if you have identified with it and attended to the referent of the thought. The practice that we are discussing here of observing and noting thoughts and sensations as they appear does not involve suppressing or constricting thoughts, getting the sounds of your environment to pipe down, or shutting out the fragrance of incense in your room—it is not a matter of controlling the environment or even the mind. Instead, simply let thoughts and external stimuli arise freely and uninhibitedly, noting them just enough so that they do not carry you away.

A Comparative Glance at Mindfulness, Open Presence, and Śamatha

The quality of relaxed attention that merely notes the presence of thoughts and sensations is what Düdjom Rinpoché is talking about when he says, "place your attention on one of these in a relaxed way." Whether the object is a stick, stone, flower, or a red *hūṃ* at your heart, if you place your attention on it in a relaxed way, then there will not be any constricting or tightening.

This is not the same as what is commonly known as "open presence"— where you are resting openly and being aware of and simply noting nonjudgmentally whatever arises—or the similar idea of mindfulness practice as moment-to-moment nonjudgmental awareness that is currently popular. Düdjom Rinpoché's comment is in the śamatha section of the text—before even venturing into Dzokchen. Open presence cannot abide within pristine awareness without this pristine awareness first having been excavated. This is done by cutting through both the coarse mind of a human being and the subtle mind of the substrate consciousness—possessed by all sentient beings—to the very subtle mind, the primordial consciousness; that is pristine awareness.

Even though you may be resting in awareness, you are not resting in *pristine* awareness (*rikpa*) if you have not realized emptiness and embraced the Dzokchen view. Resting single-pointedly in the awareness of awareness can be a very effective way to achieve śamatha, as it involves withdrawing your attention from the five sensory fields of experience. However, if you are simply resting in awareness and are open and attentive to everything that arises—sounds, smells, sights, tactile sensations, thoughts—that is neither a śamatha practice, nor open presence. One could say that it is mindfulness in the modern psychological sense of the term, but it is not mindfulness[17] in the Buddhist sense of the term—they are not even similar.

Unfortunately, misinformation about the modern term "mindfulness" is widespread. There may be benefits to being open to each moment nonjudgmentally, but this is not the Buddhist definition of mindfulness, and it is certainly not the essence of Buddhist meditation. Such modern mindfulness techniques are also not śamatha, because in śamatha, if you are equally open to, attentive to, and interested in any appearances arising within the five sensory domains and the mental domain, then there is no reason to expect that your five physical modes of consciousness would then withdraw into mental consciousness and that those sense doors would close. In śamatha, you withdraw your attention from the five sensory domains into the mental domain, and within that space, the activities of your mind subside, and the coarse mind dissolves into the subtle mind. In what is being called "open presence," it would not do that, because you are focusing outward as much as inward; you are open to everything.

With the achievement of śamatha, you have gained access to the first *dhyāna*, a technical term for a deep state of samādhi. When this occurs, your mind shifts from the desire realm to the form realm. The desire realm is the world you experience with the six doors of perception, augmented by science and the tools of technology. As long as your mind is operating in this realm, although you may have developed excellent samādhi, you have not achieved śamatha, since your mind is still in the desire realm. Achieving śamatha means that you cross the threshold into the first dhyāna, which is in the form realm. When your mind crosses the threshold or is absorbed into the form realm by means of access concentration, then your senses must be fully withdrawn from all five physical domains.

The late Dzokchen master Domang Yangthang Rinpoché was widely acknowledged as a highly realized *vidyādhara*, as he had clearly achieved śamatha and vipaśyanā and had identified rikpa. These attainments were recognized by his peers, including Düdjom Rinpoché, Dilgo Khyentsé Rinpoché, Chatral Rinpoché, and others. In his pith instructions entitled *A Summary of the View, Meditation, and Conduct,*[18] Yangthang Rinpoché states, "If you wish to look into the mirror of the actual nature of your mind, do not look outward. Rather, look inward. Looking outward involves the delusion of reification. By looking inward, you observe your own mind."[19]

Similarly, in the practice of śamatha as described by Düdjom Rinpoché, although you may start by meditating on an external object (such as a stick or pebble), as you advance in the practice, you withdraw your five external senses and draw your awareness inward, so that you are equally not interested in or attentive to appearances in the five sensory domains. You withdraw from the five sensory domains into the domain of the mind. This is the core, fundamental essence of practice. Within the domain of the mind, you rest in the ongoing flow of simple awareness of awareness. You are aware of the sheer luminosity and cognizance of awareness, and your interest in anything else falls away. Interest in any other appearances is present only insofar as you note them, but they do not carry you away. As you go deeper and deeper into samādhi, your senses will withdraw from the five physical domains, and your mind will calm—this will take you right into śamatha.

At a superficial glance, this could look like the Dzokchen practice of open presence, but it is not—for the simple reason that in these practices of śamatha, there is no *view* (Skt. *darśana*, Tib. *lta ba*); it is simply a technique, method, or a variety of methods that anybody can practice. You could be a devout Christian, Muslim, Jew, or atheist, and you can do this practice. It is a contemplative technology used to refine your attention, mindfulness, introspection, and samādhi. Your mind is refined and purified of the five obscurations—hedonism, malevolence, laxity and dullness, excitation and anxiety, and afflictive uncertainty—and then the coarse mind dissolves into the subtle mind. It is crucial to note that this technology distills the flow of your attention, so that when you turn to vipaśyanā, you can fully gain the insights for which that practice is designed.

Düdjom Rinpoché concludes his instructions for transforming obstacles and distractions in śamatha by saying,

> Alternatively, you may place your attention by resting vacantly without any basis. It is permissible to settle your attention in any of these ways.

"Alternatively" means apart from the previous methods he has given. You may settle "your attention by resting vacantly without any basis"; that is, without fixing your awareness on any object, placeholder, anchor, referent, or anything else. You can even leave your attention "resting vacantly" in the space in front of you. In principle, you could leave it anywhere, but then, in so doing, rest it "vacantly without any basis." Be careful to note that he is not referring to cultivating laxity, dullness, or getting spaced out. What he is talking about is actually where he began—to place your attention anywhere you like and then rest vacantly without fixing your attention to any referent, sign, target, or vector. Rest and relax more and more deeply, but without losing the natural clarity, luminosity, and acuity of your own awareness—without shrouding it with dullness or becoming spaced out.

An image that may be useful is to imagine a hypothetical sensory deprivation tank. It is hypothetical because, having experienced a sensory deprivation tank myself, I would more accurately describe it as a tactile sensory accentuation tank. In this hypothetical sensory deprivation tank, imagine that you become oblivious even to the tactile sensations throughout your body, as well as the other four sensory fields. Your mind also utterly calms and goes silent—all thoughts, images, and activities of the mind subside without losing clarity. When the mind has gone dormant, as if you were deep asleep, and the five physical senses now have no content, of what are you aware? You are aware of being aware. No effort is required at all, because you were already implicitly aware of being aware before you got into the tank. This is similar to going deep into śamatha in that you withdraw from all five physical senses and immerse your awareness in the mental domain, like lucidly falling asleep. This approach to śamatha is called "śamatha without a sign," without a target, without any effort being applied to directing your attention to any vector. When you are simply resting, having released all activities of the mind and merely noting whatever arises, what remains is what you already had: awareness of awareness—the awareness of being aware. If you can sustain that awareness and maintain clarity of awareness illuminating itself, clearly aware of being aware, then it does not become boring. It is not that the awareness of which you are aware becomes more and more interesting, but rather, as you go deeper and deeper into samādhi, the clarity with which you are aware of being aware increases, and there is nothing boring about this luminous clarity.

From Chaos to Calm

Düdjom Rinpoché's commentary sums this up by saying,

> By meditating in this way, at the beginning you may think there are many appearances of conceptualization. Nonetheless, you should continue to meditate without regarding these appearances as either faulty or favorable; by so doing, they will gradually subside.

This is the classic wisdom and experience of thousands of yogis over hundreds of years. Samādhi was developed in India centuries before the Buddha came along, and it was a refined art. You may know this experience of feeling overwhelmed by a multitude of thoughts and images arising in your mind. Coming freshly into the practice before having engaged in it, you might think your mind is relatively calm, not particularly excited, or agitated. But when you start practicing seriously and not as a casual hobby, you may be astonished or even appalled at the sheer proliferation of discursive thoughts, rumination, images, and memories cascading forth like a waterfall. You may then conclude that meditation is stirring up your mind. I've read in the popular press that meditation may even be unhealthy for your mind! But it does not make sense how a simple practice could agitate your mind suddenly to start spewing a myriad of mental content. This shows that your mind was already agitated, but you didn't notice it.

When looking at other people and the outer conditions—traffic, noise, work, news, media—it is apparent that the external world is unbalanced, agitated, and chaotic. Amid this turmoil, you may say that other people are not okay, although *you* are. Then awareness gets drawn inward to your own mind, and you might feel, "I thought it was the environment that was chaotic, but my own mind is at least as turbulent!" You could be in solitary confinement with virtually no stimuli coming from the environment at all, and when the outward noise dies down, you start to hear the cacophony and tumultuousness of your own thoughts, desires, memories, and fantasies. It can be deafening and quite upsetting to see that you have been carrying this around all along.

When I was first taught śamatha in 1972, Geshé Ngawang Dhargyey said that noticing how chaotic, unruly, and wild your mind really is, is the first sign of progress. The term I translate as excitation is *göpa* (*rgod pa*) in Tibetan. *Göpa* is an adjective, and literally means "wild"—for example, a *tagö* is a wild horse who is untamed, kicking, running, and jolting. Like an untamed horse, the mind bolts, jumps, skitters, and jerks all over the place. The first sign of progress is recognizing how chaotic, untamed, and unsubdued the mind is. People can be unaware of their own mental tendencies and think they are fine until their attention is drawn to how angry and violent their minds can be. Everybody else around them may have noticed, and when confronted with this they may sincerely respond, "I am not angry!"

We can be quite oblivious to that which is most intimate: our own minds. We will continue to be oblivious if we keep focusing outward and finding fault in other people and situations. When we turn inward, we recognize that the chaos we experience around us is not the fault of everybody or everything around us, but rather, our own mind is the root of our problems.

Düdjom Rinpoché says, "you may think there are many appearances of conceptualization." Indeed, you may be flabbergasted at the sheer volume and intensity of these thoughts, but do not then be dismayed or think you do not have what it takes. Although you may feel mentally defective, it is only in the normal way. But as the musician Bruce Cockburn wrote, "The trouble with normal is it always gets worse." Know that you are not *irreparably* mentally defective though. So, observe conceptualization and "continue to meditate without regarding these appearances as either faulty or favorable"; simply attend to everything without judgment. Plainly note whatever arises, but do not psychoanalyze or try to fix anything. By so doing in a way that is discerning and nonjudgmental, all conceptualization "will gradually subside."

Düdjom Rinpoché further states,

> Then, well-being will arise in your body and mind, and your mind will be unable to rise from this nonconceptual state. By proceeding gently, as if you have no desire to move, you will remain single-pointed. These are the signs of familiarization with śamatha.

Then, as conceptualization is calmed, joy or a sense of "well-being will arise in your body and mind." It is not necessarily bliss or ecstasy that arise as your mind becomes calmed, settling in its natural state; rather, it is a sense of well-being in your body and mind that arises. This is because, with the mind and vital energies being so closely intertwined, as you calm the mind through the practice of śamatha, the whole nervous system and the flow of the vital energies throughout the channels, cakras, and so forth, will all be refined and come to a state of balance. Energetically, your nervous system will be refreshed and revitalized, and your ground state of being will be increasingly saturated by a sense of well-being, which will also arise in the mind.

This arising of a sense of well-being is not stimulus-driven; that is, it does not happen because you are thinking happy thoughts or focusing on something pleasant. Rather, this well-being is surfacing because your mind is becoming calm, settling into equilibrium, and resting in its natural state. The hallmark of that state is a sense of mental well-being. Since the mind and body are so closely related—especially on this subtle, energetic level—as the system of vital energies is refined, tuned, and balanced, and these vital energies rest just as they are, you will then increasingly experience your body within a mode of well-being, as opposed to ill-being or fundamental discomfort. When the mind is in a state of imbalance, you mentally experience genuine ill-being—which is not aroused by any unpleasant stimuli—for this is a symptom of the mind that is still caught up and ensnared by mental afflictions.

When he says that "your mind will be unable to rise from this nonconceptual state," does this mean you have fallen into a trance, cannot move, and are captured in samādhi? No, this is not describing a loss of free will. He is saying instead that when you rest in this nonconceptual stillness permeated by a sense of well-being, the mind is not going to become distracted or carried away, and there will be no desire to come out of that state. You can emerge from that place, but you will need to exert some effort, as it is not going to slip away on its own. This is because you are utterly content floating in a field of well-being, both somatic as well as mental or psychological. Further, the phrase, "By proceeding gently, as if you have no desire to move, you will remain single-pointed," emphasizes that this practice should be done in a way that is resting and relaxing—not done by pushing, being ambitious, or proceeding with grasping. As such, this composure and unification of your awareness will be sustained; and this relaxed composure and single-pointedness of mind "are the signs of familiarization with śamatha."

The Tibetan term for meditation is *gom* (*sgom*), and is closely related to the term *ghom* (*goms*), which means "to familiarize, become acquainted with, accustomed to." Thus, etymologically, the Tibetan word for "meditation" has a very strong connotation of just becoming increasingly familiar with something. In terms of the corresponding Sanskrit term *bhāvanā*, this word literally means "to cultivate"—and what you are cultivating is your mind, awareness, and stability, as well as refining and developing other wholesome qualities. This is done gently—not with ambition, tightening, or ego.

In my experience of listening to many reports of meditation experiences, the majority of problems people encounter in practicing meditation come from too much tension, tightness, pushing, expectation, desire, and ambition. All of this causes one to get frustrated or uptight, which triggers other symptoms of stress, such as irritability, disappointment, and low self-esteem, among many other afflictions.

When His Holiness the Dalai Lama began training me in the practice of śamatha in the spring of 1980, he made an unforgettable pithy statement, saying, "Expectation is the foundation of failure." When he and I speak together, we go back and forth between English and Tibetan, but he said this in English to make sure I understood. Here, he did *not* say that *aspiration* is a foundation of failure; if you do not aspire, you will never succeed. *Expectation*, however, implies an aspiration with strings attached: "I expect to achieve śamatha in six months. I expect this person to behave this way. I expect the economy will improve," and so forth. Expectation is a kind of desire with attachment. If you expect other people to behave in accordance with your desires, then you have set yourself up for disappointment, because the world is not at your command. Your *meditation* is also not at your command. When practicing śamatha, how many thoughts arise? That is not under your control.

When you enter into practice, it is done with a strong conative momentum; that is, with a profound aspiration, determination, and resolve to practice, achieve śamatha, and reach the culmination of the path in this lifetime. Why not aspire to achieve rainbow body in this lifetime? Why should you put any limits on your aspirations when the bodhisattva ideal is to achieve enlightenment in order to liberate all sentient beings from suffering and bring them to a state of perfect joy? That is a grand aspiration, but there is no expectation that after a certain number of years or lifetimes all sentient beings will be free, and then your work will be done. You can have tremendous desires and aspirations; the more intense they are, the more powerful they could become, but not if there are strings attached—the strings of attachment. Learn how to practice with great aspiration, but without hope, fear, or expectation that your meditation will turn out a certain way.

❧ Meditation: A Dzokchen Approach to Mindfulness of Breathing

https://wisdomexperience.org/alan-wallace-dzokchen-meditation-4/

Rest your body in a posture that is relaxed, still, and vigilant. Let your awareness descend into the body right down to the ground.

Passively allow your respiration to settle in its natural rhythm. By so doing, your vital energies will be allowed to flow unimpededly and harmoniously.

Releasing all grasping onto hopes, fears, desires, and aversions, simply rest your awareness right where it is, utterly relaxed, still, and effortless. Ceasing to identify it with the dullness or excitation of the mind, the natural luminosity of your awareness will be unveiled, unobscured. Relax there with these three vital points of body, speech, and mind.

With this foundation, venture into the preparatory practice for śamatha and vipaśyanā: Let your eyes be at least partially open and soft—relaxing and softening all the muscles around the eyes—and allow your gaze to rest vacantly in the space in front of you without focusing on any visual object. While so doing, continue to let your awareness rest effortlessly right where it is without directing it anywhere. Sustain the flow of your awareness in a relaxed way that is still, unwavering, and naturally clear.

Do not suppress thoughts, mental images, or activities of the mind; let them be, as you rest in the stillness of awareness. Simply note with no conceptual elaboration the motions of the mind, any noises that suddenly arise in the auditory field, movements within the visual field, or tactile sensations, without being drawn away by them. It is enough to continue in this way insofar as you can do so without becoming bored, spaced out, or distracted by internal or external stimuli, while also maintaining your level of interest in the practice.

If you start to become spaced out, disoriented, or uncertain about what you are doing—because you are not doing much of anything—and if you would like to ground your awareness in something happening in the present moment in order to stabilize your awareness, then you may practice mindfulness of breathing, which the Buddha taught specifically to people who were prone to a lot of rumination and mind-wandering. For such people, the Buddha encouraged mindfulness of breathing as a very soothing, gentle way to calm the dispersion, agitation, and conceptual proliferations of the mind.

The following practice follows a particular approach that is in tune with Dzokchen. Continue to rest your awareness right where it is—relaxed, still, and clear. Attend primarily to the effortless awareness of being aware. Peripherally, without any striving at all, deliberately note the rhythm of your respiration. You do not need to focus on the body or on tactile sensations; rather, rest right where you are. Rest in awareness resting in its own place.

Being aware of the body, still without any effort, you will be aware of the rhythm of the respiration. Note the flow of the in-breath and the out-breath, and perhaps a natural pause, brief or long, after the out-breath. Observe when the breathing is flowing inward and when it is flowing outward—be aware simply of the rhythm. Without looking for, or specifically focusing on, the body—tactile sensations, the belly, or anything else—and without effortfully directing your attention anywhere, rest your awareness right where it is so that you can effortlessly be aware of the respiration, its flow and its rhythm. Let your awareness continue to be spacious; it is not inside your head or inside a small container. Awareness is co-extensive with the space of awareness, which has no boundaries, center, or periphery. Primarily be aware of being aware. Let this be your main focus, but then simply note peripherally the relative duration of each in-breath and out-breath; that is, the rhythm of the breath with its in-breath, out-breath, and the pauses that occur.

Again, you may find yourself getting spaced out, disoriented, or feeling a bit at a loss. Because you are doing so little, you may feel the urge to do a bit more to keep yourself grounded in the present moment and not drift off into dullness or be easily drawn away by thoughts and memories. If you would like something more to do to help stabilize and maintain the continuity of attention, then you may practice the following: While resting in the stillness of awareness, when you peripherally note that the breath is flowing in, simply arouse, refresh, and intensify the flow of your attention.

Vividly be aware of being aware and draw your awareness right into that. Direct the spear of your vital energies and mind right into the very nature of awareness itself; penetrate it as you breathe in. And as you note the breath is flowing out, deeply relax, releasing all effort and striving as you exhale; let go of your awareness into space with no object—the space empty of thoughts and images—while still sustaining the flow of awareness of awareness.

When the breath flows in again, do not contract or withdraw your awareness into some tiny space inside your head. Rather, accentuate, heighten, and intensify your awareness of awareness, withdrawing from all appearances, but not drawing your awareness inside some imaginary space in your head. Focus and turn inward upon awareness, transcending the very sense of there being a subject in here. In focusing inward, there is no hard target—it is just awareness. As you breathe out, release your awareness into space with no object, not even focusing on space itself as an object. Release into objectless space—empty of appearances, empty of thoughts, and nonconceptual.

When the experience of concentrating in upon the experience of awareness itself during the inhalation is the same as releasing into space with no object, and when there is a continuous, unbroken flow of awareness of awareness as you turn inward and release, you are ready for your next step: As you continue to breathe in and breathe out, suspend this oscillation of attention, like a pendulum coming to rest in the center. Simply rest your awareness right where it is with no fluctuation. Sustain that flow of mindfulness, without distraction and without grasping.

Bring this meditation to a close by dedicating the merit and virtue of this practice to the perfect awakening for yourself and all sentient beings. ❖

❖ Meditation: Deepening Your Approach to Mindfulness of Breathing

https://wisdomexperience.org/alan-wallace-dzokchen-meditation-5/

Having aroused bodhicitta as your motivation, call upon your true spiritual mentor, your spiritual guide—your lama, ultimately the buddha within, which is your own pristine awareness—call for blessings to inspire and nurture you on this path.

Strike the three vital points of body, speech, and mind as you settle your body in a posture that is relaxed, still, and vigilant. Begin by relaxing the body so deeply from within that the inner speech and commentary of the mind release into silence. As you relax deeply into the respiration, the breath begins to flow effortlessly.

Then, with even deeper relaxation and a sense of letting go, release all hopes and fears, all desires and aversions, and lightly settle your awareness in the present moment—right where it is, loose, at ease, and so utterly relaxed that you cannot be aroused to identify with thoughts or any activities of the mind; you allow them to come and go but are not perturbed or driven by them. Remain still, dispassionately aware of whatever arises in the mind without being moved by it. Resting in that uncloaked awareness, the natural luminosity of your own awareness is unveiled. Be there in that state of ease, stillness, and clarity.

Relax primarily in this most intimate knowing, the intimacy of your awareness of being aware. That is one thing you have in common with the buddhas—they, too, are aware of being aware. Rest effortlessly in that awareness, just as the buddhas themselves rest effortlessly in their own awareness.

Without exerting any effort, you will naturally be aware of the ebb and flow of your breath, the rhythm of the respiration. There is no need to try to make this happen; rather, it rises up to meet you, as if you are on the seashore with wave after wave rising upon the shore and withdrawing back into the ocean. Without your awareness moving or being directed anywhere, let the waves of the rhythm of respiration rise up to meet you. As the breath flows in, arouse, focus, and intensify your awareness right in upon itself. There is no contraction or convergence inside the head; it is simply a withdrawal from all appearances, mental and physical. Naked, unmediated awareness of awareness is the way to discover the nature of consciousness. With every out-breath, relax and release your awareness into an object-less, open expanse of space, which clearly reveals that your awareness is not inside any container. Awareness itself is as vast as the space of awareness, so release into that space with every out-breath, while ever so gently sustaining the flow of awareness of awareness.

As you turn your awareness inward with each in-breath, you come into the luminosity of your own awareness. It is this silence, this nonconceptual, unmediated experience of the knowing of knowing that transcends cognition, all the activities of the dualistic mind.

Then, as the breath flows out and you release awareness, release, too, any thought or image that may have come to mind. It is as if your out-breath were a gentle gust of breeze blowing away dry leaves, which disappear into the sky, returning you to silence.

With each in-breath, arouse the vividness and clarity of your awareness, thereby dispelling any trace of laxity and dullness. With each out-breath, as you relax and release deeply, release the energy behind excitation and rumination. Letting go of this energy, you thereby trim the sails of your mind and balance the flow of your attention.

Then, let go of even the effort of oscillating the flow of your attention. Let the pendulum come to settle in the center, as your awareness rests right where it is. There is no need to do anything with it at all, as it is already self-aware effortlessly. Without taking interest in any appearances, sensory or mental, rest right there in the knowing of knowing—vividly aware of the sheer luminosity and cognizance of your own awareness. Note the movements of the mind just enough that if thoughts pertaining to the past arise, they do not lure you away from the stillness and draw your awareness to a past which is no longer. Likewise, when thoughts pertaining to the future arise, they do not pull you away and entice you into thinking about a future which is yet to come. Even when thoughts about the present moment arise, they are simply conceptual veils that will not illuminate but will, instead, obscure the simplicity of distilled awareness that is otherwise without additives and is sheer luminosity and cognizance. This is the nature of ordinary consciousness, here and now. You are viewing it and knowing it, and now the meditation is nothing more than sustaining that view of your own awareness without any elaboration. Continue from this place for the remainder of the session.

Bring this meditation to a close by dedicating the merit of this session to the perfect realization of your own pristine awareness in order to be of the greatest benefit to all others. ❖

Four Types of Mindfulness

REGARDING THE CULTIVATION of śamatha within the Dzokchen context, and drawing explicitly from the teachings revealed to Düdjom Lingpa by the Lake-Born Vajra, when you are committed to achieving śamatha, there are four types of mindfulness that arise one after the other. Before the first type can emerge and become your vehicle—your method for following the path of śamatha—you must clearly distinguish between the stillness of your awareness and the movements of the mind. You must know experientially that thoughts can be observed without becoming entangled in them. Mental images can be observed without going straight to the referents of the images. Desires and impulses can be observed without having your attention hijacked by the object of the desire. Memories, hopes, and fears can be observed in the present moment without your attention being drawn to reflections of the past or projections into the future. Likewise, through disciplined training, emotions can be observed without awareness fusing with them and, therefore, being caught in their grip.

In all such cases of the untrained mind, when the mind is in motion, awareness is in motion. By practicing śamatha—especially within the Dzokchen tradition—you are cultivating the ability to rest in the awareness of awareness and, within that stillness, to recognize clearly that *here* is the stillness of awareness, and *there* are the movements of the mind, the thoughts, images, desires, memories, emotions, and so on.

Once you not only think of awareness and the movements of mind as distinct from each other, but truly *know* this distinction within your own experience, then you are ready to achieve the first of the four types of mindfulness: *single-pointed mindfulness*. When resting in single-pointed mindfulness, you are simultaneously aware of the stillness of awareness and the movements of the mind existing in the same instant, like resting in the calm eye of a storm and observing the winds and movement around you without getting sucked into them. In other words, there is no oscillation between experiencing the stillness of awareness and the movements of the mind; even though they are different, both exist in a single field of awareness wherein you are aware that awareness is unfluctuating and unmoving, while simultaneously noting the movements of the mind. When you are regularly able to do those concurrently, and can do so most of the time during meditation sessions, then you have achieved single-pointed mindfulness.

One of the clear indicators that you have achieved single-pointed mindfulness is that you can rest with a sense of ease and freedom from grasping in the stillness of awareness and, at the same time, be aware of what arises in the space of the mind. An example of this is the ability to notice a thought as soon as it arises, as opposed to only noticing thoughts at some point after they have already arisen. When awareness becomes very subtle, you might actually be aware of a thought that is *about to* emerge. It is like you are there in the birthing room and can see a perturbation, a kind of movement, and out emerges the thought. The same is true for images, desires, memories, emotions, impulses, and so on—your awareness remains still and aware of each change moment by moment.

If you cultivate and sustain this single-pointed mindfulness, then after some time your mindfulness will segue into the second type: *manifest mindfulness*. This is a quality of mindfulness that manifests in a sustainable way through familiarization. It is not a technique, but rather, it occurs while you are in the flow of sustaining stillness and are aware of the movements of the mind without becoming disturbed, moved, or drawn away by them. As you become increasingly familiar with both the stillness and the movement within the mind, you enter into what is referred to in modern psychology as a state of *flow*. From this place, your meditation becomes easier and less effortful, enabling you to rest in progressively deeper states of relaxation, continuity, and clarity. How long you stay in that state of mindfulness will depend upon how conducive the environment is, how well prepared you are, how much momentum you bring from past lives, and any number of other variables.

The third type of mindfulness—*mindfulness devoid of mindfulness*—is an absence of mindfulness in the sense that it involves not bearing anything in mind. You could cruise along for weeks or even months with increasing familiarization. Then, your awareness becomes totally immersed in the pure, unelaborated, simple, unmediated experience of the sheer luminosity and cognizance of awareness. While immersed there, the awareness that would otherwise flow out to the visual, auditory, olfactory, gustatory, and somatic domains is drawn inward, and no sensory input is experienced. Your eyes could be open, but you do not see anything; your ears are open, but you do not hear anything; your body is present, but you do not have a sense of being embodied. Everything is withdrawing into the mental domain as if you were falling asleep, but without losing the intensifying clarity, luminosity, and brightness of awareness. Resting in the stillness of awareness and attending to the space of the mind, the kinetic energy of the mind gradually subsides. Your senses have imploded, and within the cinema of the mind, the screen goes blank. When you come to that point, you have then arrived at the mindfulness devoid of mindfulness.

It is *devoid* of mindfulness because although you are sustaining an ongoing flow of clear, stable attention, you are no longer bearing in mind the contents of the mind, the thoughts, movements, and so forth, because they are gone. You are gazing into a vacuity, a space empty of appearances and free of thoughts. This is the point at which your awareness has been absorbed into the substrate; it corresponds closely to the Theravāda experience of the bhavaṅga, or ground of becoming. Here, you have not yet fully achieved śamatha, but the flow of your awareness is now absorbed in this sheer vacuity, this space of the mind devoid of content, appearances, and thoughts. When you have fully achieved śamatha, you are resting in the substrate consciousness, which is luminous by nature, and it illuminates that empty space of awareness.

Gyatrul Rinpoché comments on this mindfulness devoid of mindfulness saying,

Here in your meditation experience, you may no longer experience the sense fields of form, sound, sight, taste, and touch. It is
somewhat like entering into a deep sleep. You do not really know
what's going on around you; you cannot hear things; you cannot see things; you cannot feel things, smell, taste, etc. When
you arise from meditation, it is similar to awakening from a very
deep sleep. You do not know what happened or where the time
went.[20]

When your awareness is absorbed in the pure vacuity of the substrate—not
to be confused with emptiness—then the mind has become nonconceptual, free of concepts, and, therefore, free of any notion of time. There are
stories of yogis in Tibet who deeply practiced śamatha and only ended up
not knowing what happened or where the time went.

About this, Gyatrul Rinpoché remarks,

This is the experience of impure [śamatha], because you are
unable to recall what happens during the experience. It is almost
as though the mind goes into a blank state. This is not liberation, nor is it the ultimate result. This is, however, a stage in the
experience.[21]

In other words, if you have such an experience, you have not erred and you
should not be worried. This is simply the experience of the mindfulness that
is devoid of mindfulness, within which you are not explicitly aware of anything and are simply immersed in the substrate. You have not passed out
or fallen asleep but have almost achieved śamatha and are gazing into that
vacuity.

The fourth type of mindfulness is *self-illuminating mindfulness*. Having
achieved the transitional state of mindfulness devoid of mindfulness, where
your awareness is absorbed in this empty field, you then turn your awareness
in upon itself; you draw it away from that sheer vacuity right into itself, like
a heat-seeking missile that goes out and then boomerangs back upon its origin. Awareness is directed right into the substrate consciousness, and then
you dwell in the self-illuminating substrate consciousness, which is lumi-

nous, blissful, and nonconceptual. Now, you have achieved śamatha with the experience of self-illuminating mindfulness. At this point, the mind has been temporarily purified of the five obscurations—hedonic craving, ill-will, laxity and dullness, excitation and anxiety, and afflictive uncertainty—and you cross the threshold from the desire realm to the form realm. This transformation is not irreversible, but these five obscurations will be subdued for as long as you don't let your achievement of śamatha deteriorate. You have now reached the stage of *pure śamatha*, in which one has "the experience of remaining in a state of single-pointed concentration for an indefinite period of time."[22]

Pure Śamatha

Those who have achieved śamatha can effortlessly remain in samādhi for at least four hours. Having taken a break, you can easily slip back into samādhi with utterly pure, unfluctuating, relaxed, stable, vivid, and intensely clear śamatha, imbued with the three qualities of bliss, luminosity, and non-conceptuality. When you come out of meditation and enter into the post-meditative state, you are now fully aware of your environment and other people and are able to bring with you that inner calm, stillness, intense luminosity, acuity, and high resolution of awareness that you experienced when simply resting in the substrate consciousness. This is what Gyatrul Rinpoché calls "pure śamatha," during which, and even between formal meditation sessions, the five obscurations are largely dormant.

Describing the qualities of this pure śamatha, Gyatrul Rinpoché says,

> Here there is tremendous clarity. Although the mind is still, it is lucid and clear. There is total recollection of the experience throughout the meditation and in the post-meditative experience.[23]

When you come out of meditation, you have a very clear sense of what occurred while you were in meditative equipoise. You are not spaced out or immersed in the substrate but are dwelling self-luminously in the substrate consciousness.

The great Tibetan scholar Jé Tsultrim Zangpo (1884–1957) comments on this as well. He was a principal disciple of Tertön Sögyal Lerab Lingpa, the Thirteenth Dalai Lama's Dzokchen guru. In his brilliant essay *An Ornament of the Enlightened View of Samantabhadra*,[24] he discusses the importance of maintaining a śamatha practice, saying,

> Thus, if you do not have a practice for releasing all such effort and then settling your body, speech, and mind in their natural states, it will be difficult to practice the effortless path.[25]

In this way, you must have a practice, first of all, that is effortful through the cultivation of the four immeasurables, developing the spirit of definite emergence, bodhicitta, and so on. Then, develop the motivation and release the effort as you go into the Dzokchen approach to śamatha.

Jé Tsultrim Zangpo continues,

> So in order to pacify all the karmic energies and conceptual fabrications, you must apply yourself to the practice of settling your physical, verbal, and mental behavior in their natural states. If you do that for a very long time, that is an effective method for achieving stillness, but it may prevent you from being able to cut off thoughts of reification when appearances arise as illusions.[26]

In other words, if you refine the initial settling of the mind or the vital point of the mind, described earlier by Düdjom Rinpoché, that is enough to achieve stillness and śamatha. Remaining there, however, may prevent you from awakening, because you might wish to rest there complacently and indefinitely. The disinclination to rise from that stillness that is imbued with bliss and luminosity will prevent you from being able to cut off thoughts of reification when appearances arise as illusions. Eventually, you will need to get up for food and drink.

In this state, when coming out of meditative equipoise in śamatha, all manner of appearances will arise to you. Although you have calmed the mind and achieved inner stillness, you have neither begun to realize the actual nature of reality, nor have you moved the slightest bit along the path to awakening. You are yet to cut through the delusion of reification—the reification of your mind, yourself, and awareness itself—and the grasping to a belief in the true and inherent existence of phenomena around you. If you have only achieved śamatha, then you have only come to the freeway on-ramp leading to enlightenment. You have not yet entered the irreversible path; you have simply done the preparation.

This is what Siddhārtha Gautama discovered as a young prince at the age of twenty-nine when he swiftly trained as a prodigy in samādhi. He trained under Ālāra Kālāma and then Uddaka Rāmaputta, who both achieved high levels of samādhi in the formless realm. Each of them thought that they had achieved *mokṣa*, or liberation, but when Gautama emerged from states of samādhi, he recognized they had not. He realized that when you come out of those rarefied states of the formless realm back into the desire realm, with people and all the hubbub in the world, your mental afflictions have not been severed. The five obscurations can return, and fundamentally, you have not even begun to address the connate delusion of reifying yourself, your mind, your body, and everybody else in the entire environment. In other words, the fertile ground for all the mental afflictions is still as fertile as ever, which means you have not taken one step along the path of liberation. This is what Gautama recognized. Even though his two teachers invited him to sit on a throne and teach Dharma with them, he refused, for he saw that liberation had not been gained. His discovery has remained a core insight within the Buddhist tradition ever since: Śamatha alone does not liberate; it does not necessarily even diminish the tendency of reifying everything around you, which is what perpetuates saṃsāra.

Jé Tsultrim Zangpo goes on to address the imperative of moving beyond śamatha into the realm of inquiry, insight, vipaśyanā, saying,

> So you must again strive in various activities of the body, speech, and mind, as you did before, and try to cause appearances to arise as illusions.[27]

Through your training in vipaśyanā to ascertain the nature of apprehended objective phenomena and the subjective apprehender of phenomena, you can see appearances arise as illusions, appearing to be *out there* and existing anywhere. He continues,

> Thus settling your body, speech, and mind in their natural states is a superb method for developing stillness of the mind, and applying yourself to the practice of letting be is essential for developing the wisdom that realizes the emptiness of true existence. For a disciple who is imbued with such stillness of the mind—not disturbed by compulsive thoughts—and with the exceptional wisdom that ascertains the absence of true existence of whatever appears, it is easy for the guru to point out the dharmakāya, the primordial consciousness that is present in the ground of being.[28]

Such a disciple who has fully achieved śamatha and gained realization of vipaśyanā, penetrates the veils of appearances and sees how all appearances seem to exist from their own side, but that nothing—not the sun, moon, Earth, galaxies, atoms, people, or anything else—actually exists from its own side.

That is the essence of this text by Düdjom Rinpoché, which describes a progression from śamatha, to vipaśyanā, and then to identifying the Dzokchen view by which dharmakāya—pristine awareness, primordial consciousness—is pointed out. In this way, the conditioned mind is cut through to the unconditioned, the unborn, the unceasing; it is cut through to the primordial consciousness that transcends space and time. This is easy to have pointed out to you if you have such preparation in śamatha and vipaśyanā. However, many individuals without śamatha and without much training in vipaśyanā have had the great fortune of coming into the presence of a truly accomplished and realized Dzokchen master, and even though they received pointing-out instructions designed to enable them to identify their own pristine awareness, they were unable to sustain such an awareness. Even those who have received the blessings of the guru and have had experiences of cutting-through may gain some genuine glimpse of pristine awareness, but it does not last nor irreversibly transform and purify the mind.

Without śamatha as a foundation, followed by the inquiry and insight of vipaśyanā, the connate tendency to reify everything is going to come creeping back—like black mold onto the walls of your mind—unless you eradicate it entirely through the union of these two. Without having vipaśyanā, whatever glimpse you have of pristine awareness—of rikpa—will not be sustainable, because as soon as you reify yourself, your mind, and other phenomena, this pristine awareness becomes obscured by the delusion of reification. In sum, the identification of rikpa is not sustainable without a deeply developed foundation of vipaśyanā, and a realization of emptiness by way of vipaśyanā is not sustainable without śamatha.

By dwelling in that manifest mindfulness and seeing appearances as appearances, rather than reifying the referent of appearances, you will experience episodes of bliss, luminosity, and nonconceptuality, which will all be fused into one experience when you fully achieve śamatha. Along the way, when you come off the cushion and look around, you will see these appearances of empty forms, including those forms that feel solid to the touch. Even before you have gained any genuine realization of the emptiness of inherent nature of all phenomena, you will sense that there is nothing inherently existent behind even those things that appear solid.

It is important, however, not to lose your common sense. For example, when crossing a street and seeing the appearance of an eighteen-wheeler truck approaching without a stoplight, you may consider the possibility of stepping in front of the truck, but do not think, "Well, after all, tactile sensations are empty, so I'm sure I'll be fine." You will very quickly find out that trucks *do* exist—just not by their own inherent nature—and you will be crushed if you step in front of it.

As you fathom the nature of external, apprehended objects, you will see them as dreamlike. In a dream, however, you could be crossing a street, and if you are not lucid and step in front of a truck, it can crush you in the dream. In reality, there is no physical truck there; there is nothing there. But nevertheless, within the context of the dream, cause and effect are still operative. This point is crucial: The fact that phenomena in the surrounding world display cause and effect in every single moment does *not* mean they inherently and objectively exist. Conversely, the fact that no phenomena truly exist by their own nature does *not* mean they have no causal efficacy. This point will be expounded upon later in this text.

With śamatha, when things appear—memories, thoughts, past trauma, fantasies, emotions, and so on—you rest in awareness lucidly and free of grasping, attending to whatever comes up in the mind. From this place, you recognize that nothing that arises in your mind—not the image of a truck, or an image of a despot, a tyrant, or an abuser—can actually harm you. You will know this directly, whether or not thoughts have ceased.

As Lerab Lingpa writes,

> By settling the mind in its natural state, sensations of bliss may arise, such as pleasant physical and mental sensations; experiences of luminosity, such as the clarity of consciousness; and experiences of nonconceptuality, such as the appearance of empty forms, as well as a nonconceptual sense that nothing can harm your mind, regardless of whether or not thoughts have ceased.[29]

This sounds strikingly similar to being in a dream and becoming fully lucid. In a dream, when you are fully lucid—which means nothing is being reified in the dream—you know it is a dream and that nothing or nobody is really there. You are not this person, and this is not a body—even though it appears to be. Your body in the dream is not made of molecules and is not physical. The laws of physics do not hold in dreams. If you are thoroughly lucid within the dream, everything objectively and subjectively appears and has causal efficacy, but nothing is really there. There is nothing more to it than appearances. When deeply lucid, you can view a dream from the perspective of the substrate consciousness, which illuminates the dream and functions as the source from which the entire dreamscape arises and into which it eventually dissolves back. Viewing the dream from this thoroughly lucid perspective means that you could step right in front of an eighteen-wheeler truck, knowing assuredly it is just an appearance, and it could drive right through you without any pain or harm. Whereas if you are not lucid, you will probably be run over and become roadkill.

A friend of mine who is adept in lucid dreaming commented to me that once in a lucid dream she was approached by a mugger, a man with a knife who was holding her up and threatening to stab her. She told me that she reached out and grabbed his hands with the knife in them, and then thrust the knife into her guts. I asked her, "Well, did that hurt?" She replied, "No, it was a dream knife, dream body, and dream guts, so how could a dream knife harm dream guts? I just disarmed him. I sheathed his knife by putting it into my abdomen." Insofar as you are lucid, you can be fearless of anything that arises. If you are lucid in a dream where a nuclear warhead is coming across the sky and lands right on top of your head, no problem—flick it away! Likewise, as you progress along the path to achieving śamatha, you know that whatever arises in your mind cannot hurt you. As you are lucid in a lucid dream with respect to the space of the mind while dreaming, now you are lucid with respect to the mind while in meditation. It is the same space of the mind and the same appearances.

This is a miniature liberation, though people can still harm your body as that possibility has not yet been transcended. You are not free of suffering and its causes, but you see that nothing that arises in your mind can harm you. In other words, you are mentally healthy, because you are not confusing mental events with objective, physical events. A person who is recalling an earlier trauma and is repeatedly traumatized by those memories suffers again and again. In this case, the person is in all likelihood not simply remembering the images or emotions in the present but is suffering and reliving the past trauma while in the present. But if you have achieved the degree of composure and inner calm that flows like a great river on and off the cushion, then whatever memories come up in the space of your mind, you know that they cannot hurt you, and they certainly cannot retraumatize you.

All too often, we conflate thoughts with the referents of the thoughts, and then suffering ensues. This conflation is a kind of delusion and, in a more extreme form, is what people with schizophrenia do; they experience thoughts and images arising, and they think they are reality—they do not see mental events as mental events. They suffer because they are often not able to tell the difference between what is real and what is not, mistaking the nature of the reality they are experiencing. It is similar with the mind that takes its contents to be objectively, inherently existent.

Going Deeper into Śamatha

Gyatrul Rinpoché states,

> People who have achieved [śamatha] naturally experience com-
> passion as they view the predicament in which other living
> beings are ensnared. Pure compassion arises as they begin to
> clearly perceive the nature of emptiness in all aspects of reality.[30]

This first point is critical—that once you have achieved śamatha, your natural orientation will become one of great compassion, which is rooted in
your own newfound sense of well-being. This claim requires a bit of explanation. As mentioned above, once you have achieved śamatha, your ground
state or default mode within saṃsāra is one of genuine physical and mental well-being. You are composed, calm, and rest in an ongoing flow of a
sense of well-being both on and off the cushion. The stability and clarity of
your awareness are sustained in between sessions, so that whatever activity
you are engaged in or wherever you go, you bring that inner calm, stability,
coherence, clarity of attention with its unprecedented vividness, and sense
of well-being. You are not enlightened, have not even entered the path yet,
but are bringing this well-being *to* the world—it is not something you get
from the world. When you experience this—not just as a little sip now and
then, but when it is the pool in which you dwell and the air you breathe—
then you have found a sense of well-being that is not yet irreversible but is
sustainable. It does not fade as soon as you come off the cushion and engage
with the world of social activities, for example.

If you have prepared well, it could merely be a matter of months of full-
time practice in retreat before you achieve śamatha. This could happen with
the optimal circumstances, conducive environment, spiritual friends, good
instruction, and good inner cultivation. With the well-being, serviceability
of the mind, clarity, vividness, calm, and emotional composure you derive
from the practice of śamatha, the misguided ways in which others try to
find happiness become apparent. Everybody wants to be sustainably happy
and free of suffering. Nobody wants to have a few good times and then feel
miserable. Look around and see how people pursue happiness but instead

find fleeting glimpses of happiness in mundane pleasures, one problem after another, and no emotional stability. As Śāntideva says in *A Guide to the Bodhisattva Way of Life*,

> While they seek to be free of suffering, out of delusion, they hasten after the causes of suffering, and while wishing to find happiness, again, out of delusion, they destroy the causes of their happiness as if they were their foes, as if they were their enemies.[31]

Such hastening of the causes of one's own suffering is rampant among people at all levels of society. It is heartbreaking to see so many people seeking in vain to find a sustainable sense of genuine well-being while looking for happiness in all the wrong places. If you ask them why they are unhappy, dissatisfied, angry, or upset, they will point their fingers in all directions except to their own minds. They may even point their fingers at their own brains, as if this mindless organ is the true cause of their dissatisfaction. What a poor scapegoat the brain has become! Out of delusion, compounding problems are created, individually and collectively. All of this is unnecessary; if you can be free—if you can attain this sense of physical and mental well-being by achieving śamatha—then you know all others could also be free. Anybody can do it. You do not have to be Buddhist or adhere to any religion, but you do need a very strong, pure resolve and motivation, and know why it is valuable. If you weren't taught śamatha, you could complete a three-year Vajrayāna retreat and still be no closer to śamatha at the end than you were at the beginning. Śamatha doesn't happen by accident; it takes dedicated, intentional practice over time.

If you are leading an unethical way of life, then you must withdraw from that, engage in purifying practices, and then lead an ethical way of life, in order to form a sound foundation for truly transformative meditation. Once you experience the transformative effects of these practices, you will begin to experience compassion for everyone around you. You wish them to know about these practices, to find a conducive environment that would really nourish and support them in the cultivation of the mind, to have good spiritual friends, and to find a guide. This pursuit is so immeasurably worth the small sacrifices made in order to achieve this ultimately sustainable quality of well-being.

Great Compassion

In this way, achieving śamatha gives rise to spontaneous compassion. Compassion is not simply sadness, sympathy, or feeling sorry for the world. Rather, it is seeing that every individual, however misguided, delusional, or evil their actions may sometimes be, does not have to suffer. You see that they could be free of suffering and its causes, and then compassion arises— May it be so! Thoughts of bodhicitta may arise, and with it an immeasurable, unconditional, all-encompassing compassion for everyone around you. As you attend to others, *great compassion* (*mahākaruṇā*) may arise. Great compassion is not merely the aspiration that all beings may be free of suffering and its causes; it is the firm resolve to *bring* all beings to that state of liberation. In order to fulfill this promise, one arouses bodhicitta: *I* shall achieve perfect awakening in order to completely deliver every sentient being from all suffering and its causes.

Rest assured that this will happen if, prior to your intensive practice of śamatha, the mind has been refined by cultivating the four immeasurables—loving-kindness, compassion, empathetic joy, and impartiality— like a farmer preparing a field by plowing, cultivating, sowing, watering, and fertilizing it in preparation for growth and bountiful harvests. When those aspirations of the four immeasurables filter into your motivation for śamatha practice, you will experience a sense of well-being that turns into bliss, luminosity, and nonconceptuality. Then, upon achieving śamatha, because of that great momentum of attending to all those around you by way of the four immeasurables, you will find an enormous satisfaction. The strong feeling will arise that you could remain there without needing to come out for food, water, or the bathroom. However, even though you would be content to stay in your separate peace of śamatha, you won't, because you will feel too connected to the world. You will also know that, even for your own sake, it is not enough simply to achieve śamatha, because nothing irreversible has taken place; you have not yet entered the path, and not one mental affliction has been totally severed. You know there is still more to be done for yourself, and immeasurably more to be done for others. That wisdom is expressed in the first sentence of Gyatrul Rinpoché's quote: "People who have achieved [śamatha] naturally experience compassion as they view the predicament in which other living beings are ensnared."

Gyatrul Rinpoché then says, "Pure compassion arises as they [those who have achieved śamatha] begin to clearly perceive the nature of emptiness in all aspects of reality." To realize emptiness is to realize nirvāṇa and obtain freedom from suffering and its causes. Realizing emptiness is not merely a subduing of obscurations or mental afflictions, which is what you achieve with śamatha. Even so, through practicing śamatha, you may get a glimpse of emptiness when coming out of meditation, when you see all appearances arising as insubstantial. You may sense the emptiness of appearances, but you are not investigating the nature of those appearances, because you are not yet practicing vipaśyanā. Having dwelled in the mind of seeing appearances as mere appearances, when you come off the cushion and are attending to other people, the environment, and so on, you may see everything as simply appearances arising in your own substrate, insubstantial, not located in physical space, and intangible. Before you fully venture into the practice of vipaśyanā, you may see them as dreamlike. This may give you an inkling of nirvāṇa, which will more profoundly arouse your compassion. Not only could everybody around you experience the genuine well-being of having achieved śamatha, but they could realize the empty nature of their minds, which is nirvāṇa. Realizing that everybody around you could have not only this temporary peace of śamatha but also utter freedom, your compassion expands and deepens. From that place, *great* compassion can easily arise.

Gyatrul Rinpoché continues,

> These are only a few of many qualities as taught by the Buddha which are the direct result of accomplishing quiescence [śamatha]. Quiescence is the preparation and basis for the main practice which is the cultivation of the primordial wisdom of insight [vipaśyanā]. These two meditations are complementary. The success that one has in developing insight is dependent on the success that one has with developing quiescence.[32]

If you want to have more than a fleeting glimpse of emptiness, you will need both śamatha and vipaśyanā, with the practice of vipaśyanā rooted firmly in the serviceability of the mind that is achieved by śamatha. In this way, vipaśyanā filters in, saturates your mind, and begins utterly to purify mental afflictions. To the extent that you would like to reap the full harvest, the full benefits of vipaśyanā, you must fully achieve śamatha—not just dabble in it.

The Clear Light of Death

I once asked His Holiness the Dalai Lama about the likelihood of losing śamatha after fully achieving it. He replied that it is very unlikely. If you have achieved it in this lifetime, you can probably keep it for your whole lifetime, and that would then be the mind with which you pass through the stages of dying. Gyatrul Rinpoché commented that once you have achieved śamatha, if death occurs gradually, mindfully, and without great pain, then there is a great chance of dying lucidly. When you come to the culmination of the dying process and, because the brain is now flatlined, your coarse mind is no longer supported by the brain, then all that remains is the substrate consciousness.

If you have achieved śamatha and have directly experienced the substrate consciousness, then the dying process changes. Instead of simply becoming unconscious when your brain flatlines, you slip into the substrate, like lucidly falling into deep, dreamless sleep. You experience the dissolution of your senses withdrawing into mental consciousness, mental consciousness dissolving into the mind, and the mind dissolving into the substrate consciousness. Since you have already lucidly ascertained and dwelled in the substrate in a self-illuminating fashion, you know it immediately. Then, for as long as you are there, you can remain lucid—even after you are clinically dead. Being able to remain lucid after death, rather than just mindlessly slipping into unconsciousness, is extraordinarily useful. As long as you are resting in the substrate consciousness, your body will not decompose, because the vital energy is still in the heart cakra. This is not the same thing as resting in the *clear light of death*, but it occurs immediately prior to that.

In *The Vajra Essence*, the Lake-Born Vajra says,

Depending on their faculties, some remain unconscious in that state for six hours, twelve hours, one full day, or two or three days. However long you stay there, that is the phase at which you dissolve into the actual substrate to which you descend."[33]

That is all there is to "resting in peace" before you need to move on—three days at most, or maybe just as long as it takes to drink a cup of tea.

What a shock this will be for those who were counting on their death being eternal rest or oblivion. How utterly unprepared they will be for what comes next—the daunting reality that consciousness never ceases. All the fundamental elements of the natural world—matter, energy, and consciousness—are conserved; they never arise from nothing or from something fundamentally different from them, nor do they ever turn into nothing. Matter-energy transforms into other configurations of matter-energy, but never turns into something nonphysical, such as consciousness. Consciousness transforms into other configurations of consciousness, but it neither emerges from nor dissolves into anything physical.

The karmic energies will arouse you beyond the silence and vacuity of the substrate, and the next thing that comes will be a breaking apart, a dissolution, a fading away of your conditioned mind. You will cut through it naturally, and what remains then is the clear light of death, which is when rikpa manifests to you spontaneously and effortlessly. If you have realized only śamatha, then you will probably pass through and miss that opportunity. However, if you have not only achieved śamatha, but also gained profound realization by way of the practice of vipaśyanā, identified the Dzokchen view, and ascertained and dwelled in rikpa, then this will allow you to immediately recognize the clear light of death. Having arrived and rested there lucidly, you are primed for the next phase when the clear light of death manifests. Your earlier realization of rikpa, called "the child" rikpa, will recognize "the mother" clear light. Like a child crawling onto their mother's lap, your earlier realization of rikpa will merge with the rikpa that is now manifesting spontaneously as the clear light of death, and then you will be able to rest in rikpa.

This is called *tukdam* in Tibetan, and there are many reported and confirmed cases of its occurrence. Many yogis, including some quite recently, have manifested this tukdam after death, their bodies remaining in this state longer than three days—sometimes a week, two weeks, three weeks, or even longer—with no decomposition, a warmth at the heart, and their complexion remaining as clear as if they were in good health. People have even reported a pleasant fragrance emanating from such bodies, making it clear that they are not corpses in the usual sense. A yogi in tukdam is not dead, because dead bodies decompose, but also not alive, because living bodies breathe; and yet these yogis show no brain activity or heartbeat. The practices that we are discussing in this book are a preparation for radically transforming the dying process, so that when the clear light of death arises, you ascertain it, you dwell in it, and thus receive its enormous purificatory power. One can even achieve right there the enlightenment of a buddha by way of manifesting the dharmakāya.

Now Is the Time

For those of you who see full-time retreat in your future, the foundation that Gyatrul Rinpoché has described above is like an extremely fertile, well-tilled, well-mulched, well-watered, and sunlit field. When you sow the seeds of śamatha in such a field, all of these preliminaries prepare you to enter a deeper phase of practice where you are truly equipped, fully prepared, and are a suitable vessel to devote yourself full-time to the practice of śamatha and to achieve it expeditiously. In a full-time retreat focused on śamatha, whatever other practices you are doing—guru yoga, the four immeasurables, bodhicitta, and so on—are included within this finite retreat time as supports for your śamatha practice and aim to achieve śamatha.

Once achieved, the śamatha practice that has been served by all other practices becomes the servant to these practices. With this powerful, elegant, refined, and spectacularly serviceable mind that has been honed through śamatha practice, you then turn to the practice of the four immeasurables and to bodhicitta, enabling you fully to achieve bodhicitta and become a bodhisattva. When applied to your guru yoga practice, you may then have the sense that you have never truly practiced guru yoga before, or perhaps previously you were just splashing around in the kiddie pool. Now *this* is guru yoga! Achieving śamatha will immensely benefit your practice of vipaśyanā, bodhicitta, and any other practices such as *lojong*.

I have been guided to emphasize the ideal "total retreat" situation, where the primary focus is on the practice of śamatha. In total retreat, there arises a deep sense of contentment with what you have, and there are very few desires for what you do not have. But there are those who love practicing śamatha and have pure aspirations, but for now must work for a living, support families, and care for children, elders, or companion animals. Most people live a life full of day-to-day responsibilities. What about those who, for the time being at least, cannot rearrange their lives to commit to full-time retreat? Does this mean they have to postpone the practice of śamatha?

Let me offer a heartening perspective that speaks to this dilemma. I once received an email from a grandmother who lives in a large city and is not in strict retreat. She is sincere, has a sound understanding of Dharma, very deep faith, pure guru yoga, and relatively few concerns and activities. Although practicing Dharma is her highest priority, she has demands on her time and cannot spend eight or ten hours a day in meditation. She wrote to me that her sessions are anywhere from one to three hours at a stretch, and she is experiencing continuity and finding bliss. She asked me, "Do you think I've turned a corner?" Among the four types of mindfulness in the series, she achieved the single-pointed mindfulness some time ago, and now it looks like she is rolling right into manifest mindfulness and has so much confidence, joy, enthusiasm, and gratitude. This shows that simply having gratitude for the teachings and for the opportunity to practice is a suitable basis for successful practice. She is doing so well that achieving śamatha in this lifetime is a real possibility.

As this practitioner revealed to me, she is flourishing in Dharma and making progress in śamatha, even though she is not in an ideal situation for such practice—having grandchildren, needing to shop and run errands, and so forth. However, her faith is deep, her guru yoga is pure, her motivation is strong, and so she is truly thriving in Dharma. As an elder, she does not have many mundane desires, such as making money, becoming famous, or acquiring material possessions. She is now a person who has given up all attachment to this life, is making her mind Dharma, and is not wasting a moment.

If you have faith in the buddhas, in Guru Rinpoché, in Buddha Śākyamuni, then it is wise to recognize the importance of sincerely praying, "May the circumstances come so that I can achieve śamatha." As I have been told by my lamas, we have achieved śamatha many times in the past but did not back it up with vipaśyanā or bodhicitta. We blissed out in śamatha, but then lost it in the *bardo*, and in our next lifetime, we strayed off to something else.

If you have faith in the path and have a pure motivation, you can then trust that blessings will flow and are already present in your circumstance right now—this will enable you to take the next step on your path. There is a story about a person whose house flooded, and he stood on the rooftop calling to God, "God, help me! Help me! Rescue me!" Then a helicopter hovered over and the crew said, "Grab the rope!" whereby he responded, "No, I'm waiting for God!" Then a person came over in a canoe and said, "Hop into the canoe!" but the guy retorted, "No, I'm waiting for God!" Blessings are manifesting right now, and this moment presents the optimal circumstances to engage in the practice that is the most beneficial for you *now*—not at some other time. You simply need to recognize the opportunities present.

Taking Gyatrul Rinpoché seriously, you are in the perfect circumstances for the kind of practice that is most beneficial for you, whether you are in strict retreat or not. Right now, you are in the most favorable circumstances for engaging in practices to transform and purify the mind. Now is the perfect time to practice lojong, transforming everything in this moment—both felicity and adversity—into beneficial practice. Lojong, or mind training, is absolutely indispensable as a prelude to entering into an effective śamatha practice. I will discuss some of the more influential iterations of this profound practice in more detail in the chapters that follow.

❖ Meditation: Resting the Mind in Its Natural State

https://wisdomexperience.org/alan-wallace-dzokchen-meditation-6/

Let your awareness descend into the space of the body right down to the ground. Settle your body with the qualities of ease, stillness, and vigilance.

As if you were having an out-of-body experience, simply witness the body breathing without identifying with it or with the breathing. Passively but alertly observe the flow of the respiration, letting this flow settle in its natural rhythm, effortlessly and without constraint.

Relax your awareness so that it settles right where it is; where it already was before you directed it here and there. Now, do not direct it anywhere. Release all grasping and observe your awareness as it settles into stillness. Surrender your identification with the mind, mental states, and activities, and unveil the natural luminosity of your awareness. Rest right there with your awareness relaxed, still, and clear.

Having brought about this state of dynamic equilibrium, let your eyes be at least partially open, let all the muscles around the eyes soften, and vacantly rest your awareness and visual gaze in the space in front of you. By so doing, you will sense that there is a greater experience of spaciousness. There is not the sense of being inside your head, as can happen when meditating with closed eyes. Space is everywhere, and the experience of your head consists simply of tactile sensations arising in the space of awareness. Let your awareness continue to rest right where it is—relaxed, still, and clear. Then, without deliberately paying attention or giving any special interest to any of the five sensory domains of experience, and while resting in the stillness of awareness, peripherally and deliberately be aware of the movements of the mind, as if viewing them from afar. Düdjom Lingpa gives the analogy of a cowherd watching his cattle move, stand up, sit down, and play around, without controlling or identifying with them. Likewise, observe the movements of the mind come and go. Simply note appearances and movements arise in the space of the mind; note them just enough not to be moved by them, drawn into them, and then carried away to their referents.

Distinguish between the stillness of your awareness and the movements of the mind.

Let anything that comes to mind simply be. Release any impulse to modify, terminate, perpetuate, identify, or appropriate any activities of the mind. View them as if from afar, like watching clouds form and then dissolve back into the sky.

Discerningly observe, but without judgment—without deeming anything as good or bad. Observe these appearances without preference, as none of them can harm or help you in any way. Do not identify with them as "mine," appropriate them, or reify them as if they exist by their own nature from their own side. They are merely appearances, and they do not exist in and of themselves—they are like the appearances in a dream. View them for what they are; observe mental events as mental events. They are empty, so view them as such.

Sustain this flow of mindfulness, of bearing in mind the sheer luminosity and cognizance of your own awareness, this self-knowing awareness. Bear this in mind as continuously as possible. Secondarily, bear in mind the movements that arise within the mind. Continue this unbroken flow of mindfulness.

Also, monitor the flow of mindfulness with introspection, by which you are able to observe whether the flow of mindfulness has been diverted and you have become distracted or your attention has been carried away by excitation. As soon as you introspectively note that scattering and agitation have occurred and awareness has been set in motion, let your first response be to loosen up and relax in body and mind—and, as Düdjom Rinpoché said, "lower your gaze, relax your posture, relax deeply, and rest in your natural state." If you still find your awareness being tugged or drawn away, then release the grasping and identification with whatever captured it. Once you are a free agent again, return to the present moment, to the awareness of awareness, and note the movements of the mind once again.

Monitoring the flow of mindfulness with introspection, recognize as quickly as you can the occurrence of laxity and dullness, when the clarity of your awareness is dimmed. When you note that you have descended into laxity and dullness and lost clarity, then "arouse your consciousness, invigorate your awareness, and focus single-pointedly." Restore the flow of mindfulness and do so with the intention to remain in that flow.

In these two ways, you will balance the sails of the mind by remedying the two extremes of excitation and laxity, and will thus make your mind serviceable.

Bringing this meditation session to a close, conclude on the note of conation, recognizing that through offering and receiving such teachings and engaging in such practice, there is virtue and merit. Goodness is stored and restored. Direct this merit to the fulfillment of your deepest and most meaningful aspirations. Dedicate the merit from this practice to your own enlightenment for the sake of all sentient beings—the bodhisattva's dedication—and to whatever else you find most meaningful. ❖

II. The Main Practice: Generating the Primordial Wisdom of Vipaśyanā

HAVING DISCUSSED the preparation of śamatha, we now turn to the second of the two main sections, the main practice: generating the primordial wisdom of vipaśyanā. Śamatha subdues the mental afflictions, and vipaśyanā severs these afflictions from the root and brings liberation, as long as it is unified with śamatha.

As you may recall, the original Tibetan name of this text, *The Illumination of Primordial Wisdom*, is *Yeshé Nangwa* (*Ye shes snang ba*). I chose "primordial wisdom" as the translation for *yeshé* because in this practice a kind of primordial wisdom is generated. Why is it primordial? The primordial wisdom of vipaśyanā has always been there in rikpa, or pristine awareness. Rikpa does not go through any bad days or phases where it loses its direct insight into the actual nature of reality. Rikpa has always and will always know reality as it is. Rikpa is buddha-mind, and that is a wisdom that has always been present.

From the perspective of ordinary beings, when we practice vipaśyanā, we are generating and developing fresh, new wisdom—the wisdom generated through the cultivation of hearing, thinking, and meditating. Then, when we cut through delusion, we actually achieve such primordial wisdom through the practice. When the light of wisdom that knows reality dawns, we are then able to identify the view of the nature of existence from the perspective of pristine awareness. When this happens, we will see that this wisdom has been here all along. From an ordinary being's perspective, we are cultivating this wisdom; however, from the perspective of pristine awareness, it has always been here. Such awareness was always our birthright and our inheritance, but we needed to apply the effort necessary to sweep off the dust—first with śamatha, then with vipaśyanā—in order to have the sense of cultivating wisdom, and finally recognizing it was already there in the first place. Therefore, in this sense, we can say that we are generating the primordial wisdom of vipaśyanā.

> This section has four parts: (A) coming to conviction by means of the view, (B) practicing by means of meditation, (C) sustaining continuity by means of one's conduct, and (D) realizing the fruition.

The first topic, coming to conviction by means of the view, deals with gaining certainty and cutting through all doubts until you have fully fathomed the Dzokchen view. Secondly, once you have achieved this, there is practicing by means of meditation, which involves sustaining and deepening the continuity of the view. This is done by sequentially gaining understanding, experience, and then realization through meditation. Thirdly, in postmeditation there is sustaining continuity by means of one's conduct, which means that your conduct should sustain and deepen the realization gained while in meditation. This is achieved by way of the view, and then, more experientially and nonconceptually, by way of meditation. Thereby, the insight, the authentic way of viewing reality by means of your conduct, will be sustained in your whole lifestyle. The final topic, realizing the fruition, is the integration of the triad of view, meditation, and conduct, which is the achievement of buddhahood, manifesting by way of rainbow body.

Tibetan syllable *HŪṂ*
Painting by Brendon Palmer-Angell
https://www.brendonart.com/

PADMASAMBHAVA, DORJÉ DROLÖ (EIGHT FORMS)
Eastern Tibet, Karma Gardri Painting School, nineteenth century
Ground mineral pigment on cotton
Rubin Museum of Art | Gift of Shelley and Donald Rubin
C2006.66.214 (HAR 261)

DÜDJOM RINPOCHÉ
© Urgyen Sangharakshita Trust

GYATRUL RINPOCHÉ
Drawing by Brendon Palmer-Angell
https://www.brendonart.com/

A. Coming to Conviction by Means of the View

C OMING TO CONVICTION by means of the view does not involve some kind of indoctrination, nor does it mean taking a leap of blind faith. That kind of "conviction" would not lead to liberation. Simply believing something to be true does not liberate; you need to *know* with certainty that it is true. This kind of conviction can be achieved by investigation, by completely and competently using your intelligence. The wisdom, or *prajñā*, needed for this is the highest use of intelligence.

In our modern world, what do the most brilliant people—those with the highest IQs, the greatest ingenuity, and novelty—usually do? Commonly, they start businesses, develop technology and science, compose music, create art, construct buildings, plan military campaigns, and so on. So much intelligence, especially of exceptionally smart people, is often devoted to mundane goals: hedonic pleasure, wealth, power, prestige, or novelty. However, in a profoundly contemplative culture like classical India or Tibet, the contemplative way of life was widely viewed as the highest way of life, and contemplative inquiry was considered the highest type of inquiry. Many brilliant people in these societies chose to pursue a spiritual or religious vocation—even if that meant renouncing their worldly position and familial obligations. Many of these individuals subsequently became great scholars, bodhisattvas, and *siddhas*.

The subsections of section A, "Coming to Conviction by Means of the View," are given as follows:

(1) determining external apprehended objects, (2) determining the internal apprehending mind, and (3) identifying the view of the nature of existence.

First, in regard to determining external apprehended objects, you ask, How do they actually exist? Second, in determining the internal apprehending mind, you ask, How does the mind exist? Third, there is identifying the view of the nature of existence.

Interestingly, this set of practices starts with directing your attention outward to the world that appears to be real and objectively "out there." Having achieved śamatha, the highly serviceable, refined, and purified mind is applied to the contemplative investigation of the nature of "external apprehended objects"—space, time, matter, energy, earth, water, fire, air, and space—asking, How do they exist? Next, using that external investigation as a basis, you turn inward to the nature of the "internal apprehending mind," in order to realize its actual nature. Once the nature of external phenomena and internal phenomena are determined, you then investigate how you view the nature of existence from the perspective of rikpa. To do this, you must first identify rikpa. This is done by cutting through conditioned mental states, including the coarse mind, or human psyche, and the subtle mind of the substrate consciousness. This allows you to fathom the nature of unborn, pristine awareness and to view the nature of existence from that perspective, which is the culmination of the practice.

1. Determining External Apprehended Objects

T HE NEXT verse in Düdjom Rinpoché's root text states,

All such things as māras, obstructive beings,
samaya-breaking demons, reifying demons,
and hatred-generated demons
are just appearing aspects of the mind.

Düdjom Rinpoché, a man of vast erudition, could say many things about the array of obstacles that can arise for a practitioner on the path, but he chooses to offer what some might think is an odd summary. With his encyclopedic knowledge of Buddhism as a whole, and Dzokchen in particular, he discusses demons associated with impulses and obstructive forces of the mind—craving, ego, anger, and breaking one's samayas, vows, and precepts. All of these things are sometimes seen as manifesting outward, but are, in fact, "**just appearing aspects of the mind.**" They are neither separate from the mind, nor inherently existent.

In traditional Tibetan culture for at least twelve hundred years, Tibetans would likely view each of Düdjom Rinpoché's Tibetan terms for various kinds of demons in a similar way that a modern person might regard terms like electrons, protons, atoms, cells, viruses, and bacteria. Not many people have seen those things, yet their existence is widely accepted. Why focus on demons, māras, and obstructive forces? In the traditional culture of Tibet, there was widespread belief in demons, spirits, and incorporeal beings who inhabit the world. According to the Madhyamaka view, none of these beings have any inherent objective existence. He emphasizes how they seem to be external, to exist by their own inherent nature, yet are not really "out there." Because they seem to be external, the temptation is to point outward and blame them for causing you to break your samayas or to reify things, for obstructing your practice, and for increasing your mental afflictions.

Düdjom Rinpoché challenges us to see that if we blame other things as being responsible for our failings—identifying them as external obstructions, demons, hindrances, hassles, nuisances—then we are fooling ourselves. These are all just appearing aspects of our own minds. However, **"appearing aspects of the mind"** does not mean that they are mere figments of the imagination. In this text, demons appear in the section on *external* apprehended objects. They seem to be outside of us, yet are neither out there, nor in here. This goes not just for these specific types of demons cited here, but for everything that appears, as Düdjom Rinpoché will soon discuss. This includes you, me, the next-door neighbors, your spouse, family, children, and so forth. They seem to be truly existent but are also not really out there. Of course, other people are certainly not mere figments of your imagination either. They are empty of inherent nature and yet exist independently of us. That is, when one person dies, everybody else does not die.

When we view other people, places, and situations as obstacles, we tend to reify them. When we point blame at others—saying that they are the cause of our suffering, they obstruct our practice, they create hassles for us, they cause us to break our samayas, they are a bad influence, they are irritating, and so forth—this creates mental afflictions, all rooted in the fertile cesspool of reification. These are the **"obstructive beings, samaya-breaking demons, reifying demons"** about which Düdjom Rinpoché speaks.

Then there are the **"hatred-generated demons."** They occur when you regard people, places, situations, and activities as your enemy because they have catalyzed hatred in you and led you to break your commitments and ethical principles. They are then viewed, designated, and referred to in these negative ways, thereby reifying them as such. Insofar as you are viewing them in that way, then that is how they arise to you, as you are in the center of your own maṇḍala. There is no doubt that the person in question exists independently of you, but how they manifest to you and how they are viewed in the aforementioned ways solidifies and freezes them in your mind as such. When you are designating and viewing people, places, and situations in this way, they do not exist independently of you—they exist solely relative to the way you regard and label them.

This is a central, core theme of lojong, and why it is possible to transform not only adversity but felicity into the path. Adversity is not objectively real, and even if it were, there would be nothing you could do about it. Everyone individually has so little power in this world, but you can change your view by shifting it to see that both adversity and felicity were never objectively, inherently there in the first place, thereby further preparing you to eradicate the three poisons of attachment, hatred, and ignorance.

Turning to his commentary on this root verse, Düdjom Rinpoché states:

> As exemplified by obstacles that are designated as māras and obstructive beings, everything that appears as oneself and others, as physical worlds and their sentient inhabitants, seems to be truly existent, yet, apart from being the delusive appearances of one's own mind, in actuality, nothing whatsoever is determined to exist. Appearances do indeed appear, but real things are not real. Regard these simply as illusory apparitions, which, like the appearances of a dream, appear vividly and randomly, even though they do not exist.

Everything we designate and characterize as "māras and obstructive beings" are these demonic, destructive forces, and impulses in the mind that sometimes appear externally and seem "to be truly existent." Māras are not preventing you from practicing as you wish—the māras of your mental afflictions, psycho-physical aggregates, desires and aversions, and even death. Everything seems to be truly out there, existing by its own nature. They *appear* in this way and are grasped accordingly, thereby leading to delusion.

When he says, "apart from being the delusive appearances of one's own mind, in actuality, nothing whatsoever is determined to exist," this means that nothing exists from its own side. That is, when you investigate how things actually exist, you cannot determine them to be really there. On the other hand, it is incorrect to conclude that things do not exist at all. They neither really exist, nor are they really nonexistent. As he says, "Appearances do indeed appear"—appearances of yourself, physical worlds, demons, māras, and so forth—"but real things are not real." They do not exist by their own nature, but rather come into existence by the power of conceptual and verbal designations. He then counsels, "Regard these simply as illusory apparitions, which, like the appearances of a dream, appear vividly and randomly, even though they do not exist."

When in the midst of a dream, even a lucid dream, you cannot say that your experience does not exist at all, for that would imply you are not even having a dream. While nonlucidly dreaming, you not only think those appearances exist, but also that they *inherently* exist. That is why people have nightmares and can feel tortured by their dreams. Even if you are lucid and know you are dreaming, you cannot say that appearances of people, yourself, and so forth, do not exist at all. They exist enough to appear, interact, and have causal efficacy. Then, when you awake and reflect on the dream, you can ask yourself, Does that environment exist someplace? No, it does not. Does that person who I was in the dream exist? No. Do the people I encountered or what happened in the dream exist? No. From the perspective of a dream, yes, they exist, whereas, once you wake up, you see they never existed at all. Yet, they still appear, "vividly and randomly," catalyzing appearances and experiences of joy, pain, frustration, and so on.

The parallel here is that, from the perspective of your omnipresent and omniscient pristine awareness, all aspects of your thoughts, behaviors, appearances, and existence in this moment are known. Pristine awareness is primordially awake. It may be something in which you have confidence and intuitively affirm, but it does not believe in you. Pristine awareness does not regard you as truly existent at all. There was never a point in time when you actually *became* a sentient being. There is no place in space where right now you actually are a sentient being. Since you have no past and no present, you also have no future as a sentient being. You are nowhere to be found.

What is it that makes you a sentient being? You are a "mind-haver," which is the literal translation of the Tibetan term *semchen* (*sems can*), translated as "sentient being." It is this sentient being's mind that so afflicts and torments you every single day and on many occasions. Exactly when did this sentient being's mind first come into existence? Was it at conception? When the baby was born? When life first appeared on the planet? Look for the origins of this mind that torments you and is the reason why you take yourself seriously as a sentient being, merely believing in the idea of buddha nature. It may seem ridiculous and far-fetched to consider that something that does not actually exist (you as a sentient being) believes that you have something that is primordially beyond the very boundaries of existence and nonexistence (pristine awareness). There is humor in feeling that you have this or that, as if it's something outside of yourself that you own. It is like climbing to the top of Mt. Everest and declaring that the mountain is yours and the view is yours.

Düdjom Rinpoché concludes his commentary on this first subsection with the following paragraph:

> Moreover, apart from being mere designations, their nature is beyond being an object of the conceptual elaborations of existence and nonexistence. Thus, in actuality, by not even regarding them as objects to be apprehended as illusions, you will come to a conviction in the primordial wisdom that uniformly views all phenomena, all of which are one's own appearances, as being like an illusion.

When he says, "Moreover, apart from being mere designations," this refers to the way that language superimposes labels, words, and categories onto all external apprehended objects in the surrounding environment. Regarding these appearances, he continues, "their nature is beyond being an object of the conceptual elaborations of existence and nonexistence." This is actually a Dzokchen approach for understanding Madhyamaka: In Dzokchen, because rikpa is primordially nonconceptual, the conceptual categories of "existence" and "nonexistence" are nowhere to be found in the reality that is viewed from the perspective of rikpa. You have causal efficacy, and there is a perspective from which it is true that you are a sentient being. But you cannot fit the ultimate nature of reality into conceptual constructs that are fabricated by a fundamentally delusional mind. It is like a psychotic person trying to persuade his psychiatrist to believe things from his perspective. The doctor knows that the psychotic patient's stories are not actually true, and has no interest in becoming delusional also by believing in these delusions.

From a Buddhist perspective, you are delusional until you fully awaken to your pristine awareness. Freud said that every time you fall into a non-lucid dream you are temporarily psychotic, for you believe the subjective contents of the dream to be objectively real. You go through this temporary insanity five to seven times every night whenever you dream, then you wake up and think that you are awake—but pristine awareness begs to differ.

When Düdjom Rinpoché says, "Thus, in actuality, by not even regarding them as objects to be apprehended as illusions, you will come to a conviction in the primordial wisdom that uniformly views all phenomena, all of which are one's own appearances, as being like an illusion," this points to the importance of not locking onto, or fixating on, appearances as illusions. To do so would be to put illusions into one of your familiar conceptual boxes, which would only serve to reify them further, digging you deeper into delusion. The tendency to reify is connate, so you must be careful here.

Moreover, he explicitly states that not only are all these appearances empty of inherent nature, but they are also all your "own appearances," or *rang nang*. Everything that manifests to you—distant galaxies, elementary particles, other people, and so on—are your own appearances; that is, they are appearing to your own mind. By sheer logic, this implies that if all appearances you are seeing are appearing aspects of your own mind, then you are at the center of the entire universe that you experience. In this view, there is a universe for every sentient being, who resides in the center of that world. It is not only poetic to say that you are in the center of your own maṇḍala. From this place, it is necessary to stop reifying and start taking responsibility for your universe as it appears to you.

It would be useful to pause here and consider this question of how the apprehending mind tends to perceive external objects and the way to obtain clarity about the actual nature of external phenomena. In his commentary on this section of Düdjom Rinpoché's text, Gyatrul Rinpoché gives a panoramic view of this process of obtaining such clarity. He begins by saying,

> The first stage of establishing the nature of objects that are apprehended as external involves awareness of how the mind grasps onto external objects as truly existing. This refers to all objective appearances that are perceived outside of the self.[34]

Here, Gyatrul Rinpoché begins by emphasizing how it is the mind that imputes the quality of being external onto appearing objects. The mind grasps onto everything you are seeing—people, situations, the surrounding world, and so forth—because everything around you appears to be "out there," as in a dream. Whether you are dreaming lucidly or nonlucidly, everything that appears to you appears to be truly existent. However, the difference between the lucid and the nonlucid dreamer is that the nonlucid dreamer is completely deluded, believing everything out there to be objectively real. For lucid dreamers, things still appear to be out there, but the dreamer is not fooled into believing that things in the dream are inherently existent and, as such, they do not suffer due to the events in the dream.

Gyatrul Rinpoché continues,

> All such appearances are grasped onto by the subjective mind as truly existing. Due to this, many scholars will dissect objective appearances into atomic particles and then into nothingness, thus coming to understand that their nature is void of true existence.[35]

The subjective mind objectifies all appearances as being objects in and of themselves. The nuclear physicist Ernest Rutherford upset many people in and outside of physics in the early twentieth century by making a groundbreaking discovery: when he closely investigated the structure of atoms, he saw with clear, compelling, empirical evidence that atoms were actually constructed of a tiny dense nucleus at the center of the atom around which electrons orbited. This meant that atoms consist almost entirely of empty space. This discovery was unsettling to people because they thought the world was made up of dense material, like tiny grains of sand, and that things were solid down to the atomic level. Rutherford showed that everything is almost entirely space—99.99 percent space—giving the illusory appearance of solidity.

Then quantum mechanics came along and concluded that even elementary particles do not exist prior to and independent of the act of measuring them. There is only a field of possibilities, empty of any discrete, solid matter; and even that probability field is not objectively real.

When going into the deep teachings of Madhyamaka and Dzokchen, the more you analyze, the more you find that everything dissolves into space, and that nothing exists from its own side. This discovery was not first made by Düdjom Rinpoché, nor by Gyatrul Rinpoché, nor by Guru Rinpoché, nor even by Nāgārjuna. This is the primordial wisdom of all the buddhas.

In the monastic training of multiple schools of Tibetan Buddhism over the past several centuries, great scholars have studied Madhyamaka at length and mastered the Middle Way view. For example, some of my own teachers—His Holiness the Dalai Lama, Geshé Ngawang Dhargyey, Geshé Rabten, Geshé Ogyen Tseten, and so on—have studied the great Madhyamaka treatises, commentaries, and sub-commentaries. They have investigated every aspect of reality as it appears in tremendous detail—all categories of reality as presented in the Abhidharma. They have analyzed every aspect of objective reality and, upon careful, exhaustive ontological analysis, have determined that nothing exists from its own side. Geshé Rabten, one of my teachers in the Gelukpa tradition, completely devoted four of his twenty-four years of training to understanding, memorizing, receiving teachings on, and debating Madhyamaka, followed by meditating—all to understand what Düdjom Rinpoché points to in the first two brief sections of this root text.

Gyatrul Rinpoché continues his analysis on how the minds of sentient beings confuse the actual nature of both the objects they perceive and the perceiving mind, saying,

> According to this system, objective phenomena arise from the mind and exist in the mind of the apprehender. Although you

think that objective appearances truly exist, the inanimate and animate world would not exist if it were not for the mind. Failing to recognize the mind's nature and allowing the mind to remain in the experience of confused perception, you actually believe that objective appearances are true just as they are perceived. It then becomes very difficult to accept that objective appearances do not have true, inherent existence and are created by the mind.[36]

Dzokchen is the "system" to which he is referring. When he says, "objective phenomena arise from the mind and exist in the mind of the apprehender," this means that they exist in the same way they appear—as in a nonlucid dream where you believe appearances to be truly existent. As long as you are stuck there, he continues, "It then becomes very difficult to accept that objective appearances do not have true, inherent existence and are created by the mind."

INTERLUDE:
Two Approaches to Understanding
the Nature of Emptiness

THERE ARE TWO complementary approaches to more fully understanding the actual nature of appearances, which Düdjom Rinpoché
summarized in these two sentences: "Moreover, apart from being mere designations, [appearances'] nature is beyond being an object of the conceptual
elaborations of existence and nonexistence. Thus, in actuality, by not even
regarding them as objects to be apprehended as illusions, you will come to a
conviction in the primordial wisdom that uniformly views all phenomena,
all of which are one's own appearances, as being like an illusion."

The first and more elaborate approach is of gaining vast knowledge, giving a detailed ontological analysis, debating, and investigating the nature of
existence—from elementary particles up to buddhahood, dharmakāya, and
everything in between—and thoroughly finding that everything is equally
empty of inherent nature, and thus, realizing great emptiness. Then, when
you have that conviction, you turn to meditation—optimally with the basis
of śamatha, so that the full benefits, complete integration, and wisdom of
vipaśyanā can be attained.

The second approach is one of realizing that all appearances arise as
aspects of the mind. This is the approach taken by Karma Chakmé Rinpoché. These were the next Mahāmudrā and Dzokchen teachings I received
from Gyatrul Rinpoché after he taught this text by Düdjom Rinpoché, and
they are published in the book *A Spacious Path to Freedom*. At the conclusion of the chapter on vipaśyanā in that book, Karma Chakmé Rinpoché
writes,

Geshés dwell in monastic colleges for many years and study both Madhyamaka and the Prajñāpāramitā. They memorize many volumes and, devoting their lives to explanations and discussions, they cut through conceptual elaboration from the outside. That way is difficult to learn, difficult to understand, difficult to know, and difficult to realize; among those who study and acquire knowledge in that way, there are many who fail to realize the meaning.[37]

Those who failed to realize the meaning failed because they did not go beyond the conceptual understanding of debating and memorizing the texts. They did the hearing and thinking, but not the meditating. Vipaśyanā without śamatha is like a rocket without liftoff. There is not enough thrust to go into the orbit of the union of śamatha and vipaśyanā and thereby escape from saṃsāra, so then the gravitational pull of delusion takes one right back to an ordinary perception of reality where one's mental afflictions persist.

Many fail to realize the meaning because they did not get around to meditating, which is very common nowadays. Very few modern-day monks and nuns who complete their academic training have their "hair on fire" to go off into retreat, put the teachings into practice, and achieve śamatha, vipaśyanā, the stages of generation and completion, tekchö and tögal, Mahāmudrā, the Six Yogas of Nāropa, and such. Instead, they start teaching other people, without having first achieved śamatha, which is the indispensable foundation for vipaśyanā and all Vajrayāna meditations.

Karma Chakmé Rinpoché states, "The entire meaning of all that education is included in this examination of the mind,"[38] where you are seeking to understand the nature of external reality by way of understanding the nature of internal reality. It is reasonable to surmise that he is referring to demolishing delusions of the outer world completely by demolishing delusions of the inner world, which is exactly the opposite of what modern education does. Even the study of the mind in the Western tradition entails studying other people's minds, brains, and behaviors; there is hardly a major university or college in the world that encourages people, especially those interested in the mind, to refine their abilities of attention and introspection so that they can rigorously explore the mind firsthand.

Regarding this internal approach to vipaśyanā, Karma Chakmé Rinpoché says, "This cuts through conceptual elaboration from within, so it is easy to learn, easy to understand, easy to know, and easy to realize."[39] "Easy" is the correct translation, but perhaps a more experientially accurate translation of the same term is "simple," as it may be simple to grasp the concepts, but not so easy to put it all into practice. The first approach is complex, which might be the right medicine for some. However, the approach to understanding the nature of emptiness from within is not complex; it is also not easy, but it is simple in the sense of the opposite of complex. It is not easy for people who have not achieved śamatha, but the practice of vipaśyanā is direct and straight to the point for those who have.

If you have achieved śamatha and fathomed the obscurative nature of the mind and consciousness, then you know, relatively speaking, where your human mind came from, what its nature is, how it interfaces with the body, and what happens at death, and you will have some intimation of the mind's potentials, especially of the substrate consciousness. There have been Mahāmudrā and Dzokchen adepts who have achieved śamatha, then turned to vipaśyanā and gained realization of emptiness within a matter of weeks, rather than spending years of studying and debating—and still failing to gain an experiential realization of emptiness.

Karma Chakmé Rinpoché gives an analogy for how these two approaches differ, saying,

> Cutting through conceptual elaboration from the outside is like wanting dried pine wood and drying it by cutting off the pine needles and branches one by one. So that is difficult. In contrast, cutting through conceptual elaboration from within is easy, for it is like cutting the root of the pine tree so that the branches dry up naturally.[40]

"Cutting through conceptual elaboration" is quintessentially referring to cutting through reification. Trying to do so "from the outside is like wanting dried pine wood and drying it by cutting off the pine needles and branches one by one." In other words, it is a slow and inefficient process. Instead, "cutting through conceptual elaboration from within is easy, for it is like cutting the root of the pine tree so that the branches dry up naturally." This second method goes directly to the source of the mind that creates the conceptual elaborations, cutting the roots so that the solidity of reification dries and burns up quickly.

Further elaboration is made by Jé Tsultrim Zangpo in his essay *An Ornament of the Enlightened View of Samantabhadra*, stating,

> Moreover, a person with sharp faculties who can determine that this mind, which plays such a dominant role, cannot be established as truly existing from its own side as something really, substantially existent, is someone who can determine the absence of true existence even with subtle reasoning, simply by having been shown partial reasons for establishing that absence.[41]

In other words, such a person with sharp faculties—one who has achieved śamatha and fathomed the nature of the obscurative mind—readily determines that this mind cannot be established as truly, substantially existing from its own side. This person has ascertained that this mind plays such a dominant role, and is primary among the triad of body, speech, and mind.

It is possible to determine the absence of true existence even without subtle reasoning—simply by having been shown partial reasonings for establishing that absence. What are these partial reasonings? By logically determining that the mind is devoid of any true origin, location, and destination, and that it has no physical qualities, such as color or shape, you see that it is immaterial, insubstantial, and has no physical attributes. On this basis, you can know that the mind is not inherently real, because it never really came into existence, is not located anywhere, and does not go anywhere.

For people who have not determined, ascertained, or fathomed the obscurative nature of the mind, it is more difficult to recognize how the mind, with its power of conceptual designation, could possibly bring the whole of reality into existence. You are in the center of your maṇḍala, surrounded by an entire universe consisting only of appearances (which are aspects of your own mind), arising to you as existent because of the conceptually designating mind. If you have fathomed the mind, then these partial reasonings are quite sufficient for assuring you of the absence of true existence. However, again, in order to engage effectively in the main practice of vipaśyanā, it is imperative that you have the basis of śamatha.

Jé Tsultrim Zangpo continues,

> For, such a person—just by force of a revelation as to whether or not the mind has any color or shape, and just by force of being taught the reasons why the mind is devoid of any [true] origin, location, or destination—will proceed to establish the fact that the mind lacks true existence by way of subtle reasoning that refutes a subtle object of negation.[42]

Therefore, if you fathom this one thing, you will truly, deeply, and thoroughly fathom the empty nature of your own mind, thus easily fathoming the empty nature of all other phenomena.

Here, we are getting down to the level of connate ignorance, which is not something you learn by studying physics or refuting materialism; this is an inborn level of ignorance from all past lives. You are born with it, and it is still here because of its subtlety, which makes it difficult to access and identify. This is why there are powerful reasonings by brilliant scholar-contemplatives like Nāgārjuna, Candrakīrti, Sakya Paṇḍita, and Jé Tsongkhapa that help guide us through these nuances along the way. His Holiness the Dalai Lama continues to draw from the deep well of these brilliant minds who have expounded Madhyamaka above all. This is the way to pierce through to the subtle object of refutation and negation from within, which is easy if you have achieved śamatha.

Jé Tsultrim Zangpo concludes by saying, "Thus, by the extraordinary power of relying on such reasoning, people with superior faculties are able to realize the emptiness of all phenomena."[43] "Superior faculties" refers to those who have ascertained the obscurative nature of the mind, then found ease in fathoming the ultimate nature of the mind, and therefore, realized the ultimate nature of all phenomena. But he cautions, "However, it is very important for people like us to hear and reflect upon the Madhyamaka treatises, to comprehend all the reasons that establish the absence of true existence, and to establish the nature of emptiness as it is taught in the Madhyamaka."[44]

Further support of the second approach comes from Gyatrul Rinpoché, who refers to how all objective appearances are created by the mind and are not inherently existent, saying, "Similarly, all objective appearances are nothing more than mental labels."[45] This does not mean to make it up as you go, or that whatever you think or imagine is and will be true. Instead, the appearances by way of the six senses are all appearances to your mind; they are not appearances to somebody else's mind. Also, all appearances of things that seem to be objects out there are empty of existence from their own side, and are dependent on conceptual designation. Gyatrul Rinpoché refers to classic Prāsaṅgika Madhyamaka, saying that they "are nothing more than mental labels."

Gyatrul Rinpoché continues,

> You can say, "This is a table. This is a house." Each one of these objects has its name because it appears to you to be that object. Therefore, you have a label for it. In truth, its nature is illusory and it doesn't really exist any more than the illusory appearance that a magician creates. Therefore, you must have confidence in the primordial wisdom awareness of the illusory nature of all appearances. Through this you are able to establish the nature of objects which are apprehended as external.[46]

You can test this for yourself by finding a table or house nearby. Each one of these objects has its name because it appears to be that object. It appears already to be a house, a casa, a *kangba*, or "house" in any other language. A house is a house and a table is a table. Call it whatever you think, but it appears to have its own identity prior to being called anything in English, Spanish, Tibetan, or any other language. Everything appears to be out there, and to have its own defining characteristics, waiting for whatever you happen to call it. Call it "schmuff" or "schmoodle," but it is what it is, and you merely think that you are giving a name to something that already exists from its own side.

Does everything appear to you as if it is discrete, has its own characteristics, is from its own side, and has its own borders? It is not too soon to practice vipaśyanā and investigate how each one of these objects has its name only because it appears to be that particular object and is therefore labeled as such. How many labels does Buddhism have for elementary particles? Not many. According to specific cultures, there are labels for things that are valued and important, and no labels for things that are not deemed as important. Informed by the culture you live in and what is considered to be important within that culture, you create the reality you inhabit by labeling appearances around you and interacting with them as if they actually exist in that way. These teachings are a way to cut through the reification of those verbal and conceptual designations in order to begin to fathom the actual nature of your mind and of reality, and therefore, begin to heal your mind and heal the world.

❖Meditation: Recognizing the Illusory Nature of All Appearances

https://wisdomexperience.org/alan-wallace-dzokchen-meditation-7/

Find a comfortable position and arouse the motivation of bodhicitta that is in accordance with these teachings. Awaken your best approximation of not merely an aspiration, but a resolve and a promise to all sentient beings, with all the buddhas as your witness: "I shall achieve perfect enlightenment for the sake of all sentient beings, and I shall remain as long as there is even one sentient being still subject to suffering and its causes, until all are free." With this motivation, strike the vital point of the body by relaxing. Be mindfully aware as the body settles into a state that is relaxed, still, and vigilant.

Then, strike the vital point of the speech by allowing this inner voice of the mind to settle in its natural state of effortless silence. While so doing, let your vital energies be just as they are, flowing naturally as your respiration effortlessly and unimpededly settles in its natural rhythm.

Moving along this trajectory from coarse to subtle, arrive at the subtlest: the vital point of the mind. As if breathing out with a sigh of relief, let go of all grasping—the grasping of hope and fear, desire and aversion, of identifying with thoughts and emotions—then release and utterly relax. Free of grasping to and identifying with the obscurations of the mind, unveil the natural luminosity of your awareness and, thus, effortlessly allow awareness to settle right where it is, resting in a state of ease, stillness, and clarity. Sustain this flow of mindful presence rooted in the immediacy of the present moment, without distraction and without identifying with or appropriating anything. Appearances are just appearances; they do not belong to you or anyone else.

Let your eyes be at least partially open. Open all six doors of perception: all of the five physical senses plus mental perception. From the stillness of awareness, experience panoramically—not excluding any appearances, and without editing or censorship—all manner of appearances arising to your awareness. As if in the center of an auditorium, view six cinemas playing simultaneously around you, without the five sensory screens overlapping; that is, you do not validly see smells, hear colors, or taste sounds. There is a sixth screen that is also unique—that which appears only to mental perception. With your mental awareness, you are able to see appearances arising in any of these six fields of experience. It is only with mental perception that you experience all the appearances in a dream. As in waking experience, in a nonlucid dream, you think all those appearances are "out there," independent of your own mind. As the Buddha in his pith instructions to Bāhiya counseled, "In the seen, let there be only the seen; in the heard, let there be only the heard; in the tactilely sensed, let there be only the tactilely sensed; and in the mentally perceived, let there be only the mentally perceived." Do not superimpose or project anything upon any of the sense fields. Whatever appears within the visual domain, see it for what it is and nothing more. Likewise for the other sense fields, including thoughts, images, and mental appearances—they are only appearances.

Directly focus on the five portals to the world, including your body, the portal to the phenomena arising in the external world, which are appre-hended by the mind. Do these appearances exist out there? Are they in the very nature of the atoms, fields, particles, waves, neurons, dendrites, synapses, or glial cells? If the answer is not already obvious to you, observe them. Know directly, unequivocally, and without any trace of a doubt, the actual nature of these appearances that seem to be out there, but in reality do not exist in physical space.

I am smelling the aromas from the kitchen, tasting the food on my plate, feeling my feet on the ground, seeing the colors in the room, hearing the sounds from outside. These sensations and appearances seem to be coming from over there and out there, but they are delusive appearances. None of these qualia—appearances by which we apprehend the world—are "out there."

The very nature of your consciousness is luminous and cognizant, and all appearances of the world around you—as they arise in dependence upon physical stimulation of the five physical sense organs—are simply expres-sions of the luminosity of your consciousness; they have no existence apart from that. They would not exist at all if they were not being illuminated by your consciousness. No consciousness, no appearances. Without con-sciousness, the entire universe would not look, smell, feel, taste, or sound like anything. It would be a universe that is in every way invisible, and that is no universe at all, because no one would know anything about it.

Right now, view appearances as manifestations to your awareness, with no objective existence apart from that. When you close your eyes, visual appearances are not waiting for you, because they were never "out there" in the first place; they do not exist anywhere when you close your eyes. Then, when you open your eyes, that is the first moment of existence of those appearances. The same is true for every other appearance of the physical senses. Every one of these appearances is a creative display of the luminosity of your own awareness.

You know a lot more about the external world and all of its inhabitants than what you can see, hear, taste, touch, and smell. Think of people you know either directly or indirectly. By way of sight, sound, and maybe touch, you know how they appear. You also know a lot more about them than their physical appearance. Thinking of someone in particular, what more do you know about this person? Does this person have a personality, feelings, desires, emotions? Does this person have a past, hopes for the future, mental afflictions, virtues? What is most important to you about this person? Most likely, it is not how they look or sound, but who they are as a person with a mind.

Since you cannot see people's inner qualities or measure them with instruments of science, reflect on how they appear to your mind's eye. By so doing, you are looking into a mirror. This is not to say that each person, who exists independently of you, does not have those qualities, but rather, that you do not know what qualities that person has from their own perspective. Unless you are clairvoyant, all you know is what *you* know—your own appearances of that person. When you perceive other people, what you see are your own qualities projected out onto others. It is like taking the colors from the palette of your own experience, disposition, and memories, and painting others from your own color palette. The more people you come to know, the more you will know yourself, because as you are painting all of them, you come to understand all of them as expressions of your own personality. If you know despicable people, you then know about despicable aspects of your own mind. All those people who are indifferent to you are expressions of your own indifference. The same is true for compassionate, greedy, patient, generous, foolish, and intelligent people. As you meet each one, you are learning more and more about yourself because all the appearances you witness are manifestations of your own mind. They do not come from anywhere outside of you.

Those situations as you know, regard, and designate them, are what they are because of the way you view them. They are all your own appearances. All appearances of your environment, friends, and enemies are internal. Everything and everyone you know in the surrounding world are not inherently "out there." These appearances seem to be out there, but they are not, which is why they are called "delusive appearances." They would not appear, be designated, or labeled to you unless they came from you.

Rest in this emptiness of inherent nature, the emptiness of everything around you that appears in the external environment. Recognize that every person, object, and situation you identify and label in your world comes into existence solely by the power of your own conceptual designation, which means they never really came into existence at all. This is also true of every other sentient being: each of us reside in the center of the world we conceptually designate. Other sentient beings and the inanimate world do, of course, exist independently of us, but they are brought into existence by the power of our own and others' conceptual designations. Independent of verbal and conceptual designations, nothing exists inherently by its own intrinsic nature. Rest in the knowing that all phenomena are empty of inherent nature, and all appearances are made manifest by your own mind.

Conclude by bringing to mind your most noble aspirations and dedicate the virtue from this meditation session to the fulfillment and realization of your eternal longing for your own and everyone else's benefit. ❖

An Evolution and a Revolution in Viewing the Actual Nature of Reality

Viewing Phenomena as Dreamlike

IT IS SHOCKING that we have been wrong all our lives, thinking that there are things outside of us that are existing and real. This view is so different from what most scientists still believe. Stephen Hawking declared, as if it were an established scientific truth, "The human race is just a chemical scum on a moderate-sized planet, orbiting around a very average star in the outer suburb of one among a hundred billion galaxies."[47] This characterization of human existence is an unverified scientific hypothesis rooted in materialistic belief. Materialists think that we are an utterly miniscule afterthought in the evolution of the universe and that it does not matter whether or not we exist. While scientists widely acknowledge that consciousness is a mystery, they assume it is an insignificant mystery in terms of the cosmos as a whole. This mere assumption is antithetical to the Dzokchen view.

The view presented in this text is a frontal attack on the view of the universe that materialists are saying is true. There is no middle ground between the materialistic vision of existence as a whole and the Dzokchen view. They are utterly incompatible to the core.

When Düdjom Rinpoché wrote this text, he presumably wrote it for Tibetans who had probably never encountered the materialist view that the mind is simply an insignificant epiphenomenon of energy and matter. In fact, in the root text, Düdjom Rinpoché dispensed with the outer universe in two short sentences: "yet, apart from being the delusive appearances of one's own mind, in actuality, nothing whatsoever is determined to exist," and "Moreover, apart from being mere designations, their nature is beyond being an object of the conceptual elaborations of existence and nonexistence."

For people living in the twenty-first century, a bit more analysis could be helpful in order not only to understand, meditate, and gain realization, but to see that the Dzokchen view fundamentally challenges our view of everything. Modern science says that human beings are primates who evolved from more primitive ancestors, who, in turn, evolved from inorganic chemical compounds. Quantum physics tells us that elementary particles are not objectively real, independent of measurement, but there is debate as to whether or not measurement must entail conscious observation. There is no consensus in this regard about the nature of reality among physicists who specialize in quantum mechanics. The insights of quantum mechanics have led to a plethora of advances in technology, though they have been of no benefit in terms of alleviating mental afflictions, nor has science or technology enhanced our overall sense of genuine well-being.

How can we practice, start to understand, gain experience, and then actually realize the emptiness of the actual nature of the surrounding world? How can we see for ourselves the validity of the statement that everything is our own appearances, and each universe is unique to the person who is perceiving and conceiving it? In Atiśa's renowned lojong text, *The Seven-Point Mind Training*, he writes in the Sūtrayāna context, "Regard phenomena as if they were dreams."[48] By seeing phenomena as dreamlike, they lose their sense of any real substance. Like a dream, we see that everything arises as appearances from the mind, and everything is not as concrete as we once thought.

Practically speaking, in order to come to see the actual nature of external and internal phenomena, then follow Atiśa's teachings step-by-step, and take your time to fully understand, internalize, and assimilate the four revolutions in outlook so that you are viewing reality from this perspective. Additionally, if you refine your mind by way of śamatha, your whole life fundamentally changes. It is not that mental afflictions will never arise— they will still be there, trying to harass and pester you—but rather, once you have achieved and are sustaining śamatha, it is very hard for them to get a foothold in your mind. When your demons barge in—craving, selfishness, hostility, impatience, low self-esteem, and so on—stare them down (in Tibetan, *ché ré dé*). Then watch them tuck their tails and scurry away! If you have achieved śamatha, especially by the means that are highlighted in the Mahāmudrā and Dzokchen traditions, then you become quite impervious to harm from the appearances and activities of your mind. You know intuitively that anything that arises in your mind, whether thoughts or no thoughts, cannot hurt you. This is revolutionary! How often are you tormented in your mind? If you achieve śamatha, then you will not be.

William James wrote, "For the moment, what we attend to is reality."[49] If you have been spending many hours a day in meditation focusing on awareness of awareness and peripherally taking note of whatever arises in the space of the mind, then you will come to know completely that everything you are seeing consists of mere appearances arising in the mind. These appearances do not belong to anyone, are empty, intangible, and occur only in the space of the mind. By recognizing this, you no longer appropriate, identify with, or reify them. Even before achieving śamatha, when you learn to view all phenomena as dreamlike and then come off the cushion into the post-meditative state, you see that these appearances of thoughts, memories, fantasies, and mental images can no longer harm you. Though if you attend to them as if they are real, then that will be your reality, and thus, you are no longer under the safety and protection of wisdom.

What about things that arise in dependence upon causes and conditions when you are not there? I did not see this house being built or the people who participated in making my cell phone. I was not there to conceptually designate them. These things certainly arise in dependence upon causes and conditions, and they have causal efficacy. Whether it is in the construction of a house or the making of a cell phone, when did they come into existence? Objectively, there was no moment when these things came into existence entirely from their own side, and that includes everything else "out there." The moment they came into existence was the moment they were designated as being how you identify them.

From the perspective of a sentient being, Atiśa said to view all phenomena—a house, cell phone, Mt. Everest, the Milky Way galaxy, and everything in between—as if they were dreams; they are appearing but not really there. Similarly, Düdjom Rinpoché says, "Regard these simply as illusory apparitions, which, like the appearances of a dream, appear vividly and randomly, even though they do not exist." Like Atiśa, he says that these are *like* dreams, which takes us a step closer to being able to view them *as* dreams.

However, from the perspective of pristine awareness—which is the perspective from who you really are and not who you are dreaming yourself to be—this is not *like* a dream, it *is* a dream. According to the Dzokchen view, the appearance of yourself as a human being is only a dreamed character, and all the impure appearances you see around you are just a dream. It is one more revolution to view the whole, external world—which you have assumed to be so robust, made of particles, waves, fields, and so forth—as a dream. From the relative Madhyamaka perspective, this world is indeed dreamlike, but from the Dzokchen perspective it *is* a dream. These two views are not incompatible but complementary. Düdjom Rinpoché, Atiśa, Gyatrul Rinpoché, and many other Dzokchen masters are helping you take the steps necessary to view appearances and reality *like* a dream, which, as mentioned, brings you closer viewing them *as* a dream. In this way, the habitual tendencies to appropriate and reify phenomena crumble; and, along with it, ignorance, attachment, and hatred transform into the path of awakening, for the benefit of all.

A Further Evolution in the Sciences

You may well be thinking that it is absurd to say that everything is like a dream, an apparition, an illusion—including the coronavirus and radiation from dropping an atomic weapon—and declaring that everything exists in dependence upon conceptual designation. Getting radiation by living near high-powered electricity wires is an illusion? Are elementary particles, like the Higgs boson, not really out there? Was 4.5 billion dollars spent on the Large Hadron Collider to discover a particle that is not objectively real but exists only by the power of conceptual designation?

One of the great pioneers of quantum theory, Niels Bohr, said, "In our description of nature the purpose is not to disclose the real essence of the phenomena but only to track down, as far as possible, relations between the manifold aspects of our experience."[50] Our experience consists entirely of appearances, and Bohr said that physics is simply about tracking down, to the extent possible, and understanding the relations among aspects of these appearances that comprise our experience. From the next generation of physicists, Erwin Schrödinger wrote, "One can only help oneself through something like the following emergency decree: Quantum mechanics forbids statements about what really exists—statements about the object. Its statements deal only with object-subject relation."[51] He is writing to his friend Arnold Sommerfeld, another eminent physicist, asking, how do we help ourselves? We are trying to deal with the implications of quantum mechanics, and we can only help ourselves through something like that emergency decree.

Further elucidating how even science is coming to see the illusory nature of reality, Robbert Dijkgraaf, the former director of the Institute for Advanced Study, commented, "What we are learning these days is that we might have to give up that what Einstein holds sacred, namely, space and time." If we give up space and time, then what do we have left? He then cites the theory of "the holographic universe," saying, "What's happening in space in some sense is all described in terms of a screen out here. The ultimate description of reality resides on this screen. And this is like a movie projector that creates an illusion of the three-dimensional reality that I'm now experiencing."[52] This relates to the notion of quantum entanglement, which he claims is the interdependence among elementary particles that fundamentally forms the true fabric of the universe. Dijkgraaf continues, "The most puzzling element of entanglement—that somehow two particles in space can communicate; they can be entangled—becomes less of a problem because space itself has disappeared. There is no space anymore."[53] Dijkgraaf is not alone in this thinking that space-time is gone. Space-time is a way of talking—a mode of verbal designation—but it is not in the very fabric of reality itself. In other words, space and time are not ultimately real.

There is no space-time out there, which means everything you thought you were putting into that box—atoms, particles, waves, viruses, molecules, and so forth—does not inherently exist in some objective world. The relationships within human experience do not exist independently of human minds, and appearances of any kind do not exist independently of consciousness. Physicists have been looking outward to what they believe exists independent of the human experience, only to find that this presumably objective world does not exist independently of their way of talking about it. Yet, in order to be truly prepared to study relations within human experience, you must know the nature of consciousness itself.

Then came physicist Christopher Fuchs who formulated the quantum Bayesianism, or QBism, interpretation of quantum theory, which solves many of the dilemmas of quantum theory. He writes, "QBism goes against the grain by saying that quantum mechanics is not about how the world is without us. Instead, it's precisely about *us in the world*."[54] This is what anthropology, sociology, and psychology have always been about. He continues, saying, "The subject matter of [quantum] theory is not the world or us, but [it is] us within the world, the interface between the two."[55] Swiss physicist Hans Christian von Baeyer writes in a similar vein, "While the experimenter, the observer, and the theorist are investigating something external to themselves, what they are dealing with directly is not nature itself, but nature reflected in human experiences."[56] They are saying that experience is crucial, and that observation, consciousness, and mind have a fundamental role in bringing about the only reality there is; a reality that does not exist in an objective space-time that exists independently of conceptual designation.

The German philosopher Martin Heidegger questioned whether we know anything about the things-in-themselves, as they exist independently of all observation and conceptualization. Phenomenologists are leery of that, though, wanting to come back to the certainties of the world of experience. Buddhist epistemologists argue that one should not attribute existence to that which is unknowable in principle, which is the external world. Yet, the common view of the external world—with its space-time, matter, and energy—is largely assumed to exist in and of itself, independent of observation and conceptualization, even though it is unknowable in principle. The more quantum mechanics has developed, the more we see that the world out there is not only dubious but has lost all credibility. The inherently existent, objective world is gone, which means that it was never there in the first place and has not actually gone anywhere.

Further, Stephen LaBerge, a world expert in lucid dreaming, has commented that the difference between the dreaming and waking states is that waking experience is a dream with physical constraints, whereas a dream is waking experience without physical constraints. There is nothing objectively in the dream that prevents you from seeing a snowy mountain as red, seeing a giraffe that is one inch tall, or walking through walls. It is easy to conclude that all appearances are taking place in the substrate, which is a nonphysical space. Yet, what is harder to realize is that the physical world, with all its constraints on experience, is not located anywhere in absolutely objective physical space.

In a dream you can touch things, smell them, taste them, and so forth. Still, they are generated without any objective referent since the dreams themselves are nonphysical and immaterial. Even though dreams certainly arise in dependence upon both brain activity and the flow of consciousness, nothing in the brain turns into something nonphysical, such as a dream. To do so would completely violate the principles of conservation of mass-energy. Neurons never transform into thoughts; neurons are physical and thoughts are nonphysical. It would be crazy to think that neurons turn into thoughts and memories, for if they did, by the time you get old, most of your neurons might be gone because you used them all up in order for them to transform into memories and thoughts. Nobody believes that, and similarly, it is absurd to believe that nonphysical phenomena—qualia, dreams, and consciousness—emerge from the physical when there is no compelling evidence to support that hypothesis either.

What is the nature of the mind that enables human experience to occur? What is the nature of consciousness without which there are no experiences at all? The notion that experience emerges from atoms, molecules, or cells in your brain has already been discredited. Physicists do not know anything about what is inherently out there because there needs to be absolute space and time for there to be an "out there." Nor do neuroscientists or psychologists know what is really "in here," for they do not know the nature of consciousness, the nature of the mind, or how the mind interacts with the body. They cannot physically measure the mind because the only way it can be measured is with introspection, which has been marginalized ever since materialistic beliefs came to dominate the mind sciences. Consciousness remains a mystery for cognitive scientists, just as the nature of space, time, matter, and energy remain a mystery for physicists. Science has taught us a great deal about the universe, except for the nature of the apprehended world "out there" and the nature of the apprehending mind "in here."

Dzokchen has been taught, studied, and practiced for centuries, but it is timely that it has come to the attention of the modern world right when science has matured to the point that we might be able to assimilate Dzokchen and not be confused by it. This is a time when we are harming our environment to such an enormous extent, undermining human civilization, and throwing the ecosphere out of balance. How are we going to save ourselves? In order to heal the world, we must fathom the minds that created these many catastrophes that have come about due to the toxic triad of materialism, hedonism, and consumerism.

2. Determining the Internal Apprehending Mind

Turning back to Düdjom Rinpoché's text, in the subsection "Coming to Conviction by Means of the View," the next heading is "Determining the Internal Apprehending Mind." On this topic, the root text simply states,

> **Apprehend the mind, free of characteristics.**

In the first turning of the wheel of Dharma, performed by the Buddha in the deer park at Sarnath following his enlightenment, the Buddha disclosed his fundamental teachings on the four noble truths and the noble eightfold path. In this first turning, the topic of the actual nature of external phenomena—whether or not they inherently exist—is hardly raised because, here, the Buddha was emphasizing the emptiness of inherent nature of *self* as an autonomous agent and how grasping to this autonomous self is the root of a wide array of mental afflictions. This grasping is the disease, myriad kinds of suffering are its symptoms, and the medication is the noble eightfold path, which includes the four applications of mindfulness of the body, feelings, the mind, and phenomena.

The three turnings of the wheel, or the three revolutions, are done by first carefully examining phenomena in order to identify the roots of suffering and then abandoning those causes. As a result, you uproot the clinging to the body and mind as something immutable, unchanging, static, and enduring through time. Then, in the second turning of the wheel of Dharma, you observe the body, feelings, mind, and a multitude of phenomena as being saturated by a dissatisfaction that will never be transcended by any kind of hedonic stimulation. That is a revolution because virtually everyone on the planet is running around looking for stimulation in the pursuit of happiness. The third turning of the wheel of Dharma, and final revolution, occurs as you carefully scrutinize every aspect of your embodied existence, seeing that there is nothing here whatsoever that is actually "you" or "yours." In this assault on the edifice of appearances and delusion, the first cannonball strikes the seemingly permanent wall of your closed-in belief in an inherently existent self, and the wall starts to crumble. Then, the second cannonball crashes into the walls that represent your belief that enduring satisfaction and contentment can be gained by encountering pleasant stimuli. Finally, the third assault of the realization of identitylessness hits the walls of your own inborn sense of identity, which is torn to the ground with the dissolution of the reification of an inherently existent self.

This final realization reveals that appearances consist solely of the pure aspects of expressions of the luminosity of your mind, and that yourself as subject and all the objects you apprehend in the outside world have only a conventional, not ultimate, nature. As the bhikkhunī Vajirā said with respect to her own identity, "This is a heap of sheer constructions; here, no being is found. Just as, with an assemblage of parts, the word 'chariot' is used, so, when the aggregates are present, there's the convention 'a being.'" A chariot, as such, ceases to exist when everybody agrees no longer to call it a chariot—then it is only a bunch of wood, bolts, and nails. The same is true of you.

Düdjom Rinpoché's commentary on this pithy line—"apprehend the mind, free of characteristics"—provides the method for realizing such a mind free of characteristics. He begins by turning again to settling body, speech, and mind in their natural states in preparation for meditation:

> Regarding the vital point of the body, adopt the seven qualities. Regarding the vital point of the speech, let your vital energies settle naturally. Regarding the vital point of the mind, let it be neither tight nor slack. Without bringing anything to mind, rest

your awareness in an unmodified, relaxed way. With your consciousness directed inward, gaze steadily upon the mind's own nature. By so doing, there will arise a natural luminosity that is without any object, free of the extremes of conceptual elaboration, and free of any sense of apprehender and apprehended, whether as an observer and observed, an experiencer and experienced, or a subject and object. Freshly rest right there in meditative equipoise, without modification, contamination, or transformation.

You have been looking outward—where there happens to be no space or time except in a manner of speaking—so now, direct your consciousness inward. As a result, "there will arise a natural luminosity," which is an innate quality of consciousness. It is "without any object" because it has no target or referent. This is the phase of completion of practice in which you direct your awareness right in upon itself, "free of any sense of apprehender and apprehended, whether as an observer and observed, an experiencer and experienced, or a subject and object." Cutting through all the barriers and demarcations, and crossing all the borders, "Freshly rest right there in meditative equipoise, without modification, contamination, or transformation." This is Düdjom Rinpoché's pith instruction on how to fathom the actual nature of the mind. In order to do this correctly, the momentum of the preliminary practices prior to śamatha, and then śamatha as the basis, is necessary.

Through your investigation of the external world, you will see that nothing out there ever really existed from its own side. Having done that, you come right into the nucleus of that which creates your maṇḍala, your universe, and the whole of existence—the mind. Once you have transcended that nucleus, along with all of its familiar frameworks and categories, then you venture to leave all concepts behind. What is left is awareness—unelaborated, nonconceptual, radiantly clear, and steady. You then direct that sharp spear right into the very nature of the mind, surpassing the entanglement of all conceptual elaborations, like flies once caught in a spider's web. With every moment being fresh, without any repeat performances, "Freshly rest right there in meditative equipoise." In this state of equilibrium, rest "without modification, contamination, or transformation." That is, simply do not do anything at all.

Düdjom Rinpoché continues,

> This is a way of meditating for those of superior faculties, who are anointed by total immersion in pristine awareness. Most people find such awareness difficult to identify due to their minds being disturbed by conceptualization. So in that case, search for the mind by relying upon the practice of chasing solely after awareness.

The Tibetan term used in the last sentence for "chasing after" is a term that literally refers to a hunter chasing down a wild animal. In śamatha without a sign, you are experiencing awareness, but what is the very nature of the mind that is experiencing it? It is elusive, so keep chasing after it. If your mind becomes "disturbed by conceptualization" and awareness escapes you, relax deeply, release, and look again. Do not be satisfied with simply not finding it; do not give up or be lazy. Search for the mind and chase after it.

We chase after awareness by seeking out whence it originates, who is it who is aware, and what is it that is aware. We are aware because we have minds; we are semchen, "mind-havers." There is no such thing as an unconscious mind that has *zero* consciousness; even in deep sleep, there is not zero consciousness. As such, we seek after that which is aware.

Jé Tsultrim Zangpo's teachings, explored earlier, in which he speaks of how it is possible to fathom the emptiness of all phenomena simply by looking at your own awareness in the present moment, also express the power of bringing your awareness to awareness itself. You are already aware of being aware, even if you do not yet explicitly know it. The problem is that you are aware of a myriad of other things as well—sights, sounds, sensations, thoughts, and so forth—and all of these cloud the pure water of distilled, unadulterated, unelaborated consciousness, which is the sheer event of being aware.

As Jé Tsultrim Zangpo said, when you are venturing into the practice of Dzokchen, the awareness of which you are aware right now, with no preparation—i.e., without having to do something you have never done before—*is* that pristine awareness. However, by simply being aware of being aware, you have not yet become a buddha or a vidyādhara. That awareness of which you can be aware right now—also called *tamalpai shepa* (*tha mal pa'i shes pa*), or ordinary consciousness—is nothing other than pristine awareness, or primordial consciousness. This awareness can be likened to the tip of a ray of light emitted from the sun. You can be aware of that light as it reaches out and touches you, so to speak. It is closer than a hand's reach; it is right where you are.

What if you were to chase after the awareness that bumps into you, the sunbeam that strikes you, and ask from where does it come? The sunbeam is not the sun itself, and at the same time, the sunbeams do not exist independently of the sun. To be aware of the sunbeam as the light strikes your eye is to be aware that the sun is shining—otherwise, you would not experience sunlight. Hence, although the sunbeam is not the sun, it *is* the light of the sun. Similarly, if you follow this sunbeam of the ray of pristine awareness and trace it back to its source, then one day you will directly realize vidyā, or pristine awareness, rikpa. Then you will become a vidyādhara: a "holder of pristine awareness."

Thus, "search for the mind by relying upon the practice of chasing solely after awareness." Chase that sunbeam, that awareness, back to its source and look for the mind that is aware, the mind that generates thoughts and images, the mind that observes, and see if you can actually reach it, touch it, tag it, identify it.

❖ Meditation: Searching for the Mind

https://wisdomexperience.org/alan-wallace-dzokchen-meditation-8/

Going into these deep waters, remember to relax. Set your body, speech, and mind at ease. Let your awareness descend beyond the conceptual realm that seems to be up in the head. Drop down to the nonconceptual realm of tactile sensations and settle your body in a state that is relaxed, still, and vigilant.

Let the voice of your mind relax. Be content to be mentally silent. Then, release all control over the breath as you allow it to settle in its natural rhythm.

Do not do anything with the mind. You might think it is hopeless—that the mind of a sentient being will never become a buddha-mind. Sooner or later, simply let it go. A sentient being's mind will remain a sentient being's mind, so release it without modifying or transforming it. Rest in awareness without contaminating it with the junk of mental activities. See how simple, unelaborated, and pure it is compared to the complexities and, sometimes, the chaos of the mind. Be utterly at ease and effortless, so that you do not exert yourself to grasp onto and appropriate thoughts, images, or anything else. This stillness is your effortless state; this clarity and cognizance is your effortless nature.

Like sitting on a hillside facing east at dawn when the sun is yet to rise, what do you need to do to see the illumination of the sun? Openly gaze in the right direction and rest there without doing anything at all. Then, the sun will rise without you doing anything to make it rise. In this way, simply be here, looking in the right direction. If you want to fathom the actual nature of the mind, do not look outward; look inward, and let that be enough.

As you relax deeply, release completely all tendencies of grasping to the apprehender and apprehended, observer and observed, experiencer and experienced, subject and object. Relax so deeply and in such utter simplicity that all constructs and variations on the same old theme of reification of the dualistic mind release themselves and evaporate away. If you have come far enough along the journey and are deep enough into this completing phase of your practice, this may be enough.

As you are directing your awareness inward upon the mind itself and simply resting there, follow the instructions of Düdjom Rinpoché and look closely: Do you have a sense of the mind being "in here," of you being "in here"? Do you have a sense of there being a subject "in here," a perspective from which you are looking out? If so, then you are still grasping onto the subject and the mind as something real, something in here, which then reflects outwardly. If appearances seem to be "over there," regardless of whether there is an outer, external world, then you are still quietly stuck.

You are not talking or thinking about it, but it is there murmuring in the background. But how will you know, unless you chase it down, pin it to the ground, and look right into it? Therefore, chase down your mind, examine it closely, and direct the spear of your wisdom, your prajñā, right in upon that which is aware.

If you cannot find the mind, look harder. Pierce more deeply and cut through the veils of appearances and conceptual elaborations. Turn away from the mind, in terms of all sensory and mental appearances and activities. Turn inward into that which is aware, that which thinks, that which meditates. Can you find the mind that is beyond appearances? Can you find the referent of the phrase, "the mind, free of characteristics"?

Carefully search for the mind with the intention to find it. Follow the activities of the mind to their source. These thoughts, desires, memories, and mental activities are generated by the mind. When you follow them to their origin, what do you see? Any characteristics or appearances are not the mind but are simply qualities of or appearances to the mind. What is it that is apprehending those appearances? The mind experiences all appearances. It must exist, otherwise it could not be aware of anything or generate thoughts. What is this mind that observes and acts?

If you look carefully, thoroughly, and deeply, but do not find the mind, you may have a sense that it is not findable, because you would have found it by now. Can you then confidently conclude that the mind, as it exists in and of itself, is actually unfindable in principle, and does not therefore exist? It is with the mind that you have been engaging in this practice, the mind with which you have been aware, the mind that has drawn that conclusion. How can something that does not exist do anything at all? If the mind is deemed to exist, if it is really there and enacting, then you must be able to find the referent of the word "mind," as it must refer to something if it exists. Be persistent and determined, and see if the mind can find itself.

If you conclude with certainty that it is unfindable, and that it is neither existent nor nonexistent, then leave the questions behind and suspend the search, resting knowingly in that not-seeing—the supreme seeing.

Bring this meditation session to a close by dedicating the merit and virtue of this practice for the perfect awakening of yourself and all sentient beings. ❖

Taking the Impure Mind as the Path

As mentioned previously, especially when first practicing and making headway in śamatha, you may feel that you are inundated by a cascade of thoughts and are overwhelmed by how conceptually active and proliferating your mind is as you witness what seems to be an influx of fleeting, discursive thoughts flowing forth unimpededly. Perhaps you thought your mind was peaceful, until you actually looked deeper and saw the chaos and heard the cacophony.

Düdjom Rinpoché, continuing his commentary, writes precisely about this, saying,

> Moreover, if fleeting, discursive thoughts flow forth unimpededly, closely observe by chasing down the origin from which they first arose, where they are now, and where they finally cease.

Düdjom Rinpoché is describing a vipaśyanā practice here. If you are simply resting in awareness and taking the mind as the path, or investigating the mind as in the prior meditation, then a torrent of thoughts will pour forth. As you are resting in the stillness of awareness and simply, discerningly, and nonjudgmentally witnessing the thoughts, then a full range of mental afflictions—emotions, memories, and so forth—will arise. These mental events can be pleasant, unpleasant, or neutral. There might be a strong desire to witness pleasant thoughts and an aversion to witnessing unpleasant thoughts. You may prefer pleasant thoughts over those that are disagreeable, vulgar, or painful. In other words, you may want to conceal the shadow side of your mind. You may think, "Meditation is about feeling peaceful and becoming enlightened, so I don't want the shadowy mental afflictions. I'd like to think I have no mental afflictions!" When that happens, you are not doing the practice correctly at all. By resisting and then repressing or suppressing unpleasant mental afflictions, they become further reified. This approach also sets you up later for more challenges, because sooner or later, as you continue to scour the depths of your mind in śamatha, these unpleasant mental afflictions will surface again, sometimes with even greater strength and fury than if they were properly addressed at their onset.

Whether what is arising in the mind is the most beatific virtue or the most appallingly despicable abominations, do not identify with or appropriate them. Do not think that they are "mine" or "I"; instead, realize that they are simply what they are: transient appearances arising and then fading away. This is difficult to do, but if you are grasping onto mental events and thinking they are yours, then you are not only doing the practice incorrectly, you are not doing it at all. Ensure that whatever arises—whether you call them demons, goblins, or spirits—you are totally present with them nonjudgmentally and discerningly. Do not back away; but, also, do not go toward them. Do not let these transient mental appearances speak through your own mouth. They will tell you all sorts of things about yourself, other people, and so forth. Be aware of them, but do not say or do what they are saying. Do not *think* those thoughts; if you do, you will have lost control and become possessed—not by some outside demonic force, but by your own mental afflictions. This is crucially important. Whatever comes up in the space of the mind, be totally nonpreferential, such that nothing is suppressed.

In fact, when you are doing this śamatha practice correctly, not only are you not suppressing, repressing, cringing, or pulling away as things arise, but the deeper you go, the deeper you will dredge your psyche. The subconscious impulses with which Freud was so enamored—the death wish, the libido, and so on—will all come up. When you do this practice, that which had been unconscious and beneath the threshold of your conscious awareness will be stirred up and become conscious. It is only in this way that you can take the impure mind as the path, and through this simple, unadulterated, unelaborated practice of śamatha, the impure mind is purified.

By the time you come to the end of this first little trek of śamatha, even though your coarse mind with all of its impurities has dissolved into the substrate consciousness, you are not yet an arhat, a buddha, or bodhisattva. But as long as you are dwelling in the subtle mind of the substrate consciousness that is imbued with the five dhyāna factors, then you are relatively free of the five obscurations: hedonism, enmity and malevolence, laxity and dullness, excitation and anxiety, and afflictive uncertainty. When you turn your awareness in upon itself and have taken that impure mind and purified it through this utterly simple practice of settling the mind in its natural state, you come to rest in the blissful, luminous, and nonconceptual substrate consciousness, thereby achieving śamatha. Then, as long as you are resting in pure samādhi, you are mentally healthy.

A Deeper Search for the Mind

Plunging deeper into the search for the mind, Düdjom Rinpoché writes,

> Not only that, but who is the agent that experiences joys and sorrows? Who is the one who ascends to enlightenment? Who descends to wandering in saṃsāra?

If a neuroscientist were asked to identify "the agent that experiences joys and sorrows," he or she might point to the parts of the brain that are activated during these experiences. It may be helpful to know these things in some respects, but it is not necessary to identify what parts of the brain are activated in order to be free of suffering and its causes or to achieve enlightenment. There are many neuroscientific studies of the brains of meditators, but I do not know of a single study that has helped anybody to meditate or train their unruly minds better—and, therefore, suffer less.

Following the path of Dharma, you are moving up the five paths, the ten grounds (*bhūmis*), and ascending to enlightenment. Who is the journeyer that is moving out of the spiral of saṃsāra? You experience joys and sorrows because you have a mind; if you had no mind, then you would not experience anything at all. Why do you say "I am the agent who experiences joys and sorrows"? On what basis can you say that accurately? Since you have a mind, you then designate yourself upon the mind by saying "I" or "Alan" or "this person." Is it true to say that because your *mind* experiences joy and sorrow, that then *you* experience joy and sorrow?

If you think the mind is the agent, Düdjom Rinpoché counters,

> Does that mind have a beginning, an end, and an interim? Is the mind itself something real or unreal? If it is real, what kind of shape, color, and so on does it have?

Here, "the mind" refers to a sentient being's mind. Your mind was not here a hundred years ago and is not likely to be here a hundred years from now. Does your human mind have a beginning? Your mind was not there before your body, so there was a point at which it must have had a beginning. What were the conditions that gave rise to a mind? There is a Buddhist answer that is to be investigated and not simply believed, for simply believing something does not lead to liberation. Śamatha alone will allow you to see phenomenologically how your mind arose from the substrate consciousness, which is not human. It is the stem cell of consciousness, ready to be configured as a human mind, manifest with the various human sensory consciousnesses, and so forth.

Does that mind have a beginning? Unless you believe that human minds exist prior to and independent of the brain, then the mind must have a beginning. Does your mind have an end? There will be no human mind without a human brain, so it definitely has an end. But what is that end? Materialists would say that when the mind ends, it becomes nothing. But the scientific community has no idea what actually happens to the mind at death, whereas Buddhists have an answer that can be investigated. These questions are approached in the Buddhist tradition through vipaśyanā practice, with an open mind that is free from both prejudice and blind faith. Following this tradition, thrust the spear of your intelligence to fathom the mind's origin, location, and destiny.

Penetrating to the essential nature of the mind, Düdjom Rinpoché asks, "Is the mind itself something real or unreal?" That is, does the mind inherently exist, or does it only exist conventionally? The Buddhist tradition asserts that it does exist, but if you look for it, it will not be found; it is merely a convention that is collectively agreed upon. Is that what the mind is—only a name?

Düdjom Rinpoché continues, "If it is real, what kind of shape, color, and so on does it have?" Any sophisticated philosopher of the mind knows that if you look into the nature of thoughts and of that which is experiencing these thoughts, neither can be physically detected. There is no instrument or technology that can measure the nature of the mind, which indicates that the mind has no physical attributes—otherwise, it would have been already measured. Metaphysical realists would say that just because the mind lacks physical attributes, this does not mean that it is unreal, as there are many things that are considered real that lack shape or color. Most physicists would say that an electromagnetic field is real, despite it not having a shape or color. The mere fact that some physical phenomena do not have a color or shape does not prove that they are not real.

If one's introspective, or metacognitive, abilities are not yet well-developed, then one might be aware primarily of the surrounding external environment. Many people define what is real as being something they can see or touch. However, those who have refined their introspective abilities know directly that the mind and its properties do not have a color or shape, or any other physical qualities aside from mental replicas of physical qualities, like remembering the color of a fire engine or the shape of a ball. Yet these are only mental images, facsimiles of what we see with the eyes; they are not physical.

I once asked a philosopher of mind with whom I studied, What is the nature of the mental image of a banana when I visualize a banana? As a materialist, he told me that the image does not exist. At this point, I had been meditating for about twenty years, and had observed a lot of mental images and noted their causal efficacy in influencing thoughts, desires, and so on, yet he told me that the mental image of a banana does not exist. When I asked him why not, he responded that because mental images are not physical, the image of the banana does not actually exist. Clearly, he had simply equated the category of physical phenomena with that which exists, without necessarily even being able to define clearly the word "physical."

Contemporary philosophers of mind rely heavily on advances in brain science to draw conclusions about the mind. Neuroscientist Donald Hoffman critiques his own discipline when he writes, "Not only are [neuroscientists] ignoring the progress in fundamental physics, they are often explicit about it. They'll say openly that quantum physics is not relevant to the aspects of brain function that are causally involved in consciousness. They are certain that it's got to be classical properties of neural activity, which exist independent of any observers—spiking rates, connection strengths at synapses, perhaps dynamical properties as well. These are all very classical notions under Newtonian physics, where time is absolute and objects exist absolutely. And then [they] are mystified as to why they don't make progress. They don't avail themselves of the incredible insights and breakthroughs that physics has made. Those insights are out there for us to use, and yet my field says, 'We'll stick with Newton, thank you. We'll stay 300 years behind in our physics.'"[57]

Even a renowned physicist with whom I spoke was unable to define "physical." As soon as he tried to define it, there would be something unexplainable outside of the physical to stump him, for there are innumerable things that are said to be physical, but which are elusive and ethereal, and still many other things that exert influences on the physical world but are not themselves physical.

Düdjom Rinpoché continues his instructions, saying, ·

> If you think that it is unreal, repeatedly ask yourself, Does it not exist at all, or what? Inquire again and again, without forsaking the task at hand.

Here, he is saying that if the mind does not exist at all, then it is not even an illusion. It is false to say that thoughts and subjective experiences do not exist *and* are illusions, because illusions exist—otherwise, you would not call them "illusions"; you only call them something if they exist. Like Tibetan and Indian philosophers would say when referring to the "horns of a hare," hares do not have horns, so the "horns of a hare" are not illusions, because they do not exist at all. They do not rise to the level of being able to manifest as an illusion because they do not exist at all. When Düdjom Rinpoché encourages us to ask that question "again and again, without forsaking the task at hand," this means not to stop questioning, but to keep thrusting in the spear of samādhi and prajñā.

Düdjom Rinpoché continues,

> If you think there is a real thing such as this, you have fallen into a heavily fortified grasping to true existence. If you think it is empty in that it does not exist at all, you are simply speculating. If,

as a result of not finding the mind, you conclude that it has never existed, or if you feel that it must exist but can't decide whether you have found it, continue investigating and questioning.

When he says, "If you think there is a real thing such as this," "this" refers to that agent that experiences joys and sorrows, and to the mind that has a beginning, a middle, and an end. If you have flipped back into the old, connate syndrome of reifying everything you apprehend, know that you share this tendency with all other sentient beings—from animals to countless philosophers and many scientists. You know that you have fallen into that extreme if you think externally apprehended objects and the internal apprehending mind are real.

On the other hand, "If you think it is empty in that it does not exist at all, you are simply speculating." If you search for the mind, do not find it, and then conclude that it does not exist, that the word has no referent, that it is empty, null, and void, then that is simply speculation. What or who is it that is speculating and drew the conclusion that the mind does not exist at all? If it did not exist at all, there would be nothing to draw that conclusion. You cannot get something from a bowl full of nothing.

Therefore, "If, as a result of not finding the mind, you conclude that it has never existed, or if you feel that it must exist but can't decide whether you have found it, continue investigating and questioning." Do not give up; do not settle for an easy answer. As the great masters of this way of training say, do not be lazy and leap to the conclusion that since you cannot find the mind, then it must not exist. It only means that more investigation into the nature of the internal apprehending mind is needed.

In the final paragraph on this section, Düdjom Rinpoché addresses how to proceed in the face of not finding anything, saying,

> If you do not see anything at all, whether the observed or the observer, the seen or the seer, and so on; if by seeking and investigating you find nothing, just as you don't see anything by looking into space; and if awareness appears nakedly and serenely, free of any recognition of an essential nature of appearances and

awareness—unmediated, inexpressible, inconceivable, unobservable, empty and luminous, without an object—then you have internalized the instructions.

In your search for the mind, as you chase after awareness, apply ontological analysis, penetrate into how things actually exist, pierce into the nature of the existence of the phenomena under inquiry; if you conclude that you do not see anything and find nothing, then look closer. However, if you find that there is nothing to be found, this is more than merely "not finding," for you have actually discovered something—you have discovered that the mind is not findable. Whereas simply "not finding" the mind is inconclusive one way or another and means that you should keep searching. So if you find that there is nothing to be found, then, consequently, "awareness appears nakedly and serenely, free of any recognition of an essential nature of appearances and awareness," and you are now in a mode of knowing that transcends the framework and structuring of dualistic grasping of appearances "over there" and awareness "over here." Thus, you have sloughed off the dead skin of bifurcating reality into the objective and the subjective. You are free of any recognition of or grasping onto appearances and awareness as something separate and distinct.

The quality of awareness here appears free of grasping, "unmediated, inexpressible"—that is, there is no mediation of thoughts or appearances other than awareness, because awareness, by nature, is not conceptual. Concepts cannot capture the nature of awareness any more than they can capture tactile sensations; you can think about raw tactile sensations, but your awareness of them is nonconceptual and, therefore, unmediated by concepts and labels. Awareness is inexpressible, because that which cannot be captured by concepts or words is by nature "inexpressible, inconceivable." It is "unobservable" in terms of a subject-object relationship, since awareness transcends this very duality. It is "empty," because it is void of any substantiality or inherent nature. It is "luminous," because awareness illuminates everything that can be known or experienced. Finally, this awareness is "without an object," as it does not grasp onto anything. When awareness is known in these ways and is beyond the dichotomy of internal and external, "then you have internalized the instructions."

INTERLUDE:
A Deeper Investigation into External Apprehended Objects and the Internal Apprehending Mind

IN THIS NEXT section, there is the opportunity to investigate the obscurative nature of external apprehended objects and the internal apprehending mind in order to plunge deeper still into their actual nature. What follows are a series of discussions with a few meditations interspersed with the aim to bring wisdom into the field of experience. These discussions—although not introducing new sections of the root texts—will provide an opportunity for even greater clarity that can enrich your understanding and impart a broader framework for your practice to evolve and flourish.

Phenomenological and Ontological Approaches

Let's now look at some clear explanations of the culmination of ontologically investigating how the external apprehended objects that populate the world around you and the internal apprehending mind exist. This is Madhyamaka presented in the context of Dzokchen. A general principle in Madhyamaka that pertains to every mode of analysis of seeking the actual nature of phenomena is this: before you set out single-pointedly to fathom the actual nature of the phenomenon in question, first become familiar with and comprehend its phenomenological nature. How does it appear? The emptiness is an emptiness of inherent nature of that which is appearing and has characteristics. From here, you then probe into its ontological nature. In other words, first you want to know what you are talking about, and what are the referents of words in terms of appearances. How do you distinguish one thing from another? How do you distinguish "consciousness" from "mind" from "behavior" from "brain"? It is important to know what the distinctions are, as they are not absurd fabrications. If you would like to understand the actual nature of external apprehended objects, it is helpful first to study physics, chemistry, biology, botany, ecology, cosmology, the brain, the mind, and everything else that appears. Once you become familiar with the world in which you are living, and understand atoms, molecules, particles, waves, cells, the mind, consciousness, and know the referents of these terms, you are ready for ontology. You then know the characteristics of the phenomena that are the referents of the terms you are using as you imagine and conceive of the world.

That said, it is not necessary to study the physical sciences in this way, for this is not needed in order to progress on the path. It is sufficient for Buddhists to study the eighteen elements, the six sensory fields, the six modes of consciousness, and the six faculties in dependence upon which the six forms of consciousness arise so that they get a complete phenomenological picture of objective and subjective phenomena. The physical faculty that is the basis for vision is within the head, and according to modern science it includes the visual cortex, optic nerve, and retina. When it comes to the nonphysical faculty of mental consciousness, there is still a faculty in dependence upon which a human mind and human mental consciousness arise. Phenomenologically, the human mind originates from the substrate consciousness, not from the brain; when you die, the mind dissolves back into the substrate consciousness.

The Buddhist phenomenological investigation of the world of appearances is based primarily on the four applications of mindfulness. The first of these is the close application of mindfulness to the body, looking at it from the first-person perspective: What is it like to be embodied? How does the body manifest to you? How does it appear? If you are going to fully engage in the close application of discerning mindfulness to the body, then you are closely applying your mindfulness to the earth, water, fire, air, and space elements that constitute the body. Then when you let the close application of mindfulness to the body come into full bloom, starting with your own body, you proceed to include the bodies of other sentient beings. That is the way the Buddha taught it. Observe the body internally and externally, but do not confine yourself to the body of a sentient being.

Once you have closely applied mindfulness to the whole range of physical phenomena, you then turn to feelings. Some feelings arise in the body (such as tactile feelings), and many are in the mind (for example, joy and sorrow). Closely investigate these phenomenologically, looking at the factors of origination and dissolution for feelings in the same way as you did for physical phenomena.

Then turn to the close application of mindfulness to the mind—that is, everything else that goes on in the mind: mental afflictions, virtues, and the full array of the fifty-one mental processes. Observing them, ask, Where do they originate, where are they located, are they permanent or impermanent, satisfying or unsatisfying, self or not self, and what happens to them when they cease to exist? Further, look at how they function and interact with other phenomena.

Finally, turn to phenomena at large, which is the fourth application of mindfulness. This one is all-inclusive, as you put everything together and look for the dependent origination of all these phenomena.

These four applications of mindfulness are foundational Buddhist vipaśyanā practices and are often largely overlooked in the Tibetan tradition. They are immensely rich, transformative, and can be purifying in terms of mental afflictions.

With regard to science, it provides us with a wealth of knowledge about the phenomenal nature of the external world around us. This is a good basis to start penetrating into the *actual* nature of external existence. However, when it comes to the mind, His Holiness the Dalai Lama was asked, "What do you have to learn from the West, modern academia, and modern science about the nature of the mind?" He assertively responded, "Nothing!" For understanding the mind, he replied that he looked to the Nālandā tradition, which included a whole network of universities throughout India during the first millennium of the common era—before the first universities were established in Europe—that focused primarily on the nature of mind. In their approach, they were not looking primarily outward, but rather inward by directly observing the mind from a rigorous, first-person perspective.

On another occasion, he commented:

> In my recent conversations with scientists, [I have found that] they have conducted excellent investigations into the nature of the objective, physical world. But the Western science of psychology is at a primitive level. They are not able to distinguish between the sensory modes of consciousness and the mind, or mental consciousness. Neuroscientists, who present sophisticated explanations of the brain, say that the many kinds of conceptualization of the mind are all functions of specific parts of the brain. So contemporary psychology is not up to the task. In general, classical Indian academia's emphasis on nonviolence and compassion is related to the mind. About 2,000 years ago, single-pointed śamatha and vipaśyanā were used to develop discerning intelligence. Nowadays the physical sciences are quite good, unlike the mind sciences. These are not religious matters, but academic topics for the sake of increasing our knowledge, and Buddhist texts are an excellent resource from which scientists could greatly benefit.[58]

For us living in the modern world, educated in Eurocentric academia, we say "mind," but to what is this word actually referring? Where did the mind come from, where is it located, and what happens to it when we die? In modern science, consciousness is widely acknowledged to be a mystery. Based on Western academia, we are not well-prepared for probing ontologically into the actual nature of the internal apprehending mind because we have not yet determined what it is phenomenologically. We are continuously hoodwinked by the delusional beliefs of materialism, looking to the brain to tell us everything we need to know. The misleading belief is that we do not need to practice introspection to know the mind because focusing on the brain and behavior will tell us everything we need to know. This wild goose chase has not given much insight into the mind. Sooner or later, perhaps we will finally come to William James's paradigm presented one hundred and thirty years ago: "Introspective Observation is what we have to rely on first and foremost and always. The word introspection need hardly be defined—it means, of course, the looking into our own minds and reporting what we there discover. Every one agrees that we there discover states of consciousness."[59] If you want to understand primarily the mind, look at it with introspection. As auxiliary approaches, look at its behavioral expressions and neural correlates.

A lacuna in Indo-Tibetan Buddhism as it is practiced now is the detailed experiential phenomenological investigation of the mind, which is found in tremendous richness in the *Satipaṭṭhāna Sutta*, the Buddha's discourse on the four applications of mindfulness within the Pāli canon. There are excellent commentaries on this by outstanding contemporary Theravādin scholars such as Bhikkhu Anālayo and Bhikkhu Bodhi. The bounty found in the Theravāda tradition is lacking in the Mahāyāna literature because in Mahāyāna it is assumed this foundational work is already done. The phenomenological understanding of the mind is in the first turning of the wheel of Dharma, while the ontological understanding of the mind is in the second turning of the wheel. The first turning of the wheel is where the four applications of mindfulness are found, and it is where a phenomenological view of the eighteen elements is presented. When you look at these same four applications in the second turning of the wheel of Dharma, the *prajñāpāramitā*, it is not phenomenological, but ontological. It is looking at the body, feelings, mind, and phenomena not in terms of how they appear, but how they exist.

Only if you are well-versed in the teachings of the first turning of the wheel of Dharma will you receive the full benefits of the second turning of the wheel. There is a way in which the Tibetan tradition can be augmented in order to gain a phenomenological understanding of the mind.

Revisiting Düdjom Rinpoché's commentary on external apprehended objects, he writes, "apart from being the delusive appearances of one's own mind, in actuality, nothing whatsoever is determined to exist." These "delusive appearances" are misleading. When looking outward, colors seem to be "out there," but they are not. The physical things that seem to be rock solid are mostly space. An atom consists almost entirely of empty space. All appearances are aspects of your own mind. Further, "nothing whatsoever is determined to exist." Dzokchen is not an esoteric version of Cittamātra, but rather highlights the fact that we know nothing about the universe apart from appearances to our minds, and the apprehending mind itself is as empty of inherent existence as all apprehended objects.

Examining the Character of Unborn Awareness

Insofar as determining the actual nature of the apprehending mind—lest you think that this is something unique to Dzokchen, Vajrayāna, or the Düdjom Tersar lineage—I would like to lay a simple foundation within the Sūtrayāna in the teachings of Atiśa, who was regarded as a speech emanation of Padmasambhava. The teachings of Atiśa show clearly the unity of Dharma and how it is akin to an extraordinary jewel, a diamond with a thousand facets that are all aspects of the same jewel. Thus, a theme in Atiśa's *Seven-Point Mind Training* is his aphorism, "Regard phenomena as if they were dreams," especially emphasizing the phenomena of apprehended objects as dreamlike. Then the next aphorism states, "Examine the character of unborn awareness."[60]

At a phenomenological level, consciousness is not unborn but is arising moment by moment in dependence upon causes and conditions. This is true of the human mind and is also true of the substrate consciousness, or the bhavaṅga, the ground of becoming in Theravāda literature. If we use the lens of modern science to inquire whether our human minds are unborn or whether they arise in dependence upon causes and conditions, no answer will be found, as scientists are looking from the outside in. However, for millennia, Buddhists have known from where the human mind emerges, and seen phenomenologically that it arises from the substrate consciousness. Probing deeper, we see that that's how the mind *appears*, but how does the mind actually *exist*? What is the *actual* nature of the mind?

In this regard, having examined the character of the born, conditioned, moment-to-moment arising awareness and mind, Atiśa advises, "Examine the character of unborn awareness." Looking into the most ancient written commentary by Sechil Buwa on *The Seven-Point Mind Training*, he suggests that the very mind that negates the inherent existence of perceived, apprehended objects and sees that they are all empty of inherent nature—they are dreamlike in the sense that they appear but are not really there—is just as empty as the objects it apprehends. What is the method to know and examine this? *The Seven-Point Mind Training* states, "Once stability has been achieved, let the mystery be revealed."[61] That is, with stability in the mindstream, first the mystery of how phenomena around us actually exist is revealed, and then we are able to determine the actual nature of the mind that apprehends them. Turning inward upon the very nature of the mind and looking upon it with open-minded and rigorous scrutiny and investigation, it becomes clear that the mind of the past is already gone. Similarly, the mind of the future is yet to be, so it, too, cannot be seen. The mind of the present refers to the immediacy of the present where you are chasing awareness as you seek the mind, which can neither be found in the past nor in the future. Where it is *right now*, the instantaneous present moment of the mind or consciousness, is also of finite duration. There are moments, pulses, or staccato bursts of consciousness, each of which has a beginning, a middle, and an end. Then, looking into the mind and seeing the immediacy of the present moment, can you identify its beginning? Can you see when the first pulse of your human mind arose, how long it lasts, and when it vanishes? How long was the interim that is after the beginning but before the end?

Investigate the origins of the human mind with which you are very familiar—this is the mind that you do not imagine or wish you could someday realize, but rather is the human mind that you have right now. Then examine whether or not this human mind is real. The mind you are experiencing, appropriating, and identifying with right now, from where did it originate? Where is it right now? Where does it go?

When you are looking for the mind by going right into the immediacy of the present moment, you might find that by the time you are aware of the mind, the mind of which you *were* aware is already gone, and the mind of which you *could be* aware is yet to occur. Then what do you find experientially except for space? You find a mind that cannot be observed, identified, and that was never actually born or truly came into existence. When you look phenomenologically at the mind, as you are probing into that which knows—the mind which knows—then quickly, you can see that it is devoid of color and shape, as well as any spatial location within or outside of the body. When you really examine, inquire into, and investigate it, you see that the knowing mind is empty of all identifiable characteristics.

In Atiśa's oral transmission, he points to the fact that you can realize the character of the mind that is primordially unborn. There was never a moment—not in a past life, at conception, or now—in which your mind really and inherently came into existence. If you think it did, then you must be able to identify that moment.

The implications of this are groundbreaking: if the mind never actually came into existence from its own side and by its own nature, then there was never a point in time in which you *became* a sentient being. Perhaps this is the fundamental meaning of the statement that saṃsāra has no beginning. Saṃsāra is your existence as a sentient being who experiences the world of a sentient being. When you look into the mind that experiences this impure world of apprehended objects, you see that this mind never actually came into existence. Thus, you discover what is meant by a world that consists entirely of delusive, misleading external and internal appearances. Everything you think about yourself is based on appearances and on things that are not yours. Nevertheless, you appropriate and identify with them, like a hermit crab who takes a shell and feels, "My shell! Home at last!" This identification only leaves you stuck in this world of delusive appearances. However, seeing into the actual nature of these internal and external appearances, it is a relief to know that there was never a point at which you became a sentient being—you have always been the purity of pristine awareness and dharmakāya.

Observing the Apprehending Mind

Further investigating the apprehender and the apprehending mind, ask what is the basis of designation of "I" when you sense, "I am apprehending my mind"? You can look at somebody's face and say that you see them, therefore their face is a suitable basis of designation. Likewise, if you simply observe any aspect of the mind—a thought, mental image, desire, memory, emotion, fantasy, and so on—then you can say that you are observing the mind, for these mental events are all suitable bases of designation on which to impute the label "mind." It is not necessary to have a more comprehensive basis on which to designate "mind," for you cannot see all of the mind any more than you can see all of another person. Know that when you are apprehending the mind, you are not apprehending the mind in its entirety or as it exists in and of itself; rather, what you observe are bases of designation for the mind. Nobody ever sees the mind in itself, but you can certainly observe a thought, memory, desire, and so forth. This is what is meant by phenomenologically apprehending the mind.

On the other hand, there is another quite distinct experience of apprehending the apprehender, or at least seeking to do so. To do this, first turn awareness away from appearances, movements, and activities of the mind, and then redirect awareness inward with your spear of wisdom, piercing straight into the nature of the apprehender. If you try and cannot find the apprehender, then that doesn't mean the apprehender does not exist. There is an apprehender and the apprehender does exist, just as the apprehended exists; however, they are both not determinate or existing by their own nature. To apprehend the apprehender is not a search that ends in failure but is a search that ends in the surprising success of discovering that the mind is unfindable.

Gyatrul Rinpoché tells us, "If you notice this, then allow the apprehender to look at the apprehending mind, which is like observing one's own face directly without anything else in between."[62] In other words, if you notice the clear distinction between observing the mind and apprehending the apprehender of the mind—that is, when you succeed as you seek the mind and chase after awareness to find that which is aware—then you are able to identify the mind without any difference between that which is apprehending and that which is apprehended. In this way, you have shattered dualistic grasping because now there is no separation between the apprehender and the apprehended. Further, the apprehending mind is empty, and to realize that is to realize its essential nature has no identifying characteristics. Then, as you apprehend the apprehender, you also realize its essential empty nature. Resting there, though, you recognize that it is not a mere negation or simply a sheer vacuity, or emptiness; it is *not* nothing. That is, it's not that it does not exist, as it is luminous and illuminates everything you experience.

Looking at the apprehending mind—"which is like observing one's own face directly without anything else in between"—Gyatrul Rinpoché continues, "When you become aware in this way, you will begin to realize that the apprehender and apprehending mind are nondual."[63] This theme of nonduality is not prominent in the Theravāda tradition or the Pāli canon but is enormously important in the second and third turnings of the wheel of Dharma: the second turning emphasizes the "objective clear light" of the emptiness of inherent nature of all phenomena, and the third turning emphasizes the "subjective clear light" of buddha nature. This technique is a direct way to cut incisively with your spear through dualistic grasping by penetrating straight into that which is engaging in the dualistic grasping.

Gyatrul Rinpoché then advises, "During the experience of nonduality, allow yourself to remain in the freshness of the experience, without any contrived alterations."[64] Cutting through in that way means to cut through conceptual elaborations; this happens by the very nature of delving into a place that is too subtle and profound to clutter with the fabricated mentation of thoughts, concepts, and words. In that process, you leave behind the very notion of time. Even in modern quantum cosmology, time is set into motion only by the conceptual mind and the observer who conceptually demarcates or identifies a "now" relative to a past and a future. From there, the perceived universe is actuated. If there is no conceptual mind, then there is no time. Therefore, time is conceptually designated and does not occur from its own side. If there is nothing conceptually designating time, at least in terms of your own experience, then it vanishes. The coarse, conceptual mind of a human being goes dormant when you slip into that śamatha phase of mindfulness devoid of mindfulness. There is no profound realization there, but instead, it is as if the conceptual mind has gone comatose. From your perspective, you are unaware of time simply because you are largely unaware altogether. Whereas here, in this nondual space, you are brilliantly, discerningly, nonconceptually aware, and therefore, every moment is utterly fresh and unprecedented.

When Gyatrul Rinpoché says to "allow yourself to remain in the freshness of the experience, without any contrived alterations," he means not to do anything with it. That is, do not appropriate it, but rather surrender to it and release into it. He continues, "A practitioner with superior intelligence will be able to remain in this experience of pristine awareness indefinitely."[65] From this place, you have slipped out of time and are certainly not located anywhere.

Gyatrul Rinpoché then returns to the experience of engaging in such practice for novices, and says, "In the beginning, it is difficult to remain for very long."[66] Here he is actually encouraging us by saying that it is not too soon to start practicing, because in the beginning, it is normal not to be able to remain for very long in the place of seeing clearly in these ways. So, do not worry if you have not yet achieved śamatha or realized the emptiness of inherent nature of all external phenomena. Even though these realizations may not happen in one session or in one moment, you can still keep practicing over the course of one day—you can have some sessions devoted to śamatha, some sessions devoted to exploring the nature of the external world and to examining carefully the phenomenological nature of the mind, and some sessions devoted to probing into the very nature of the apprehending mind. If you have not yet achieved śamatha or fully realized vipaśyanā, it is not too soon to begin to practice.

To elaborate, he is suggesting that you can engage in this practice and go right into the nature of observing the apprehending mind and see what you see. When you no longer have a sense of there being an observer and the observed, but you are clear, luminous, and discerning, savor that spacious experience. Even though in the beginning this will be challenging to maintain, do not think that you are a failure because your mind wandered. Imagine kindergarteners thinking that they are a failure because they cannot do multiplication. That would be foolish! Start where you are and proceed gradually through the phases of the path.

Those with sharp, superior faculties have such by familiarizing themselves repeatedly with the practice. Those who have had a tremendous amount of familiarization from a past life come into this lifetime and move swiftly on the path. They are already riding the wave of their realization from past lives, but only because they practiced in past lives. From the perspective of the future, this is our past life right now, so develop the momentum to succeed right now. Do not wait, thinking that you are not ready for this. Develop the momentum today, tomorrow, and for the rest of the moments, days, and years of your life. By so doing, when you go into the bardo, you will be a person of increasingly superior faculties, thus progressing to enlightenment itself.

"In the beginning, it is difficult to remain for very long," Gyatrul Rinpoché continues, "This experience is, however, identical to the experience you have in between thoughts."[67] That is, "this experience" refers to the experience of nonduality. That fresh moment in between thoughts—when a previous thought has ended and just before the second thought begins—is resonant with the experience of the nondual space of pristine awareness. The reason you may not be aware of that now is because there are a multitude of thoughts arising so quickly that the moment in between them remains unnoticed.

❖ Brief Meditation: Examining the Character of Unborn Awareness

https://wisdomexperience.org/alan-wallace-dzokchen-meditation-9/

Pause for a moment, without needing to adopt a particular position. Swiftly settle body, speech, and mind in their natural states.

Resting in that stillness, can you observe a thought? Does that thought come to an end? Then, can you observe the next thought as it arises?

Can you clearly identify the interim space, that quiet space, after one thought has ceased and before the next thought has arisen, in which you are vividly, discerningly aware of being aware? That clear, quiet awareness is where rikpa resides. Although such identification is simple, it probably does not mean that you have achieved the full, unmediated, nonconceptual realization of rikpa and are now a vidyādhara. However, in that moment—and there can be many moments like that—you are, indeed, resting in rikpa. Meditate for more than thirty seconds and see how many such intervals you can identify; rest right there without modifying or doing anything at all. That place is nothing else other than a ray of rikpa, just as a ray of sunlight is still the light of the sun.

Rest there without suppressing thoughts, but allowing them to arise. The thoughts themselves are effulgences, or creative expressions, of rikpa; they do not obscure rikpa. Yet, rikpa *is* obscured when you appropriate the thoughts by thinking them and then reifying them. They then become one cloud layer after another that obscures the light of rikpa. Do not try to flick away the thoughts but look carefully for the interim space and rest in that nondual place, where there is no object and no subject, no bifurcation between apprehender and apprehended. Then you will have hopped onto the ray of rikpa. Simply by resting and not doing anything, you will eventually flow right up the sunbeam into rikpa itself.

Padmasambhava talks about this effortlessness, saying,

> To introduce [pristine awareness] by pointing it out forcefully: it is your very own present consciousness. As it is this very unstructured, self-luminous consciousness, what do you mean [when you say], "I do not realize the mind itself"? [As] there is nothing here on which to meditate, what do you mean [when you say], "It does not arise due to meditation"? When it is just this direct awareness, what do you mean [when you say], "I do not find my own mind"? When it is just this uninterrupted clear awareness, what do you mean [when you say], "The nature of the mind is not seen"? When it is the very thinker of the mind, what do you mean [when you say], "It is not found by seeking it"?[68]

The clarity of awareness is always present—there is no need to "find" the mind. Simply rest, without doing anything at all. Know that the spear of discerning intelligence and the ferocity of Dorjé Drolö is not directed at you. Rather, it is focused on delusion and protecting you from delusions that obscure your own pristine awareness.

Take a moment to rest in this direct, spacious clarity, and from that place, dedicate the merit of this meditative session to your own perfect awakening, so that you may help all others achieve the same. ❖

Further Determining the Nature of the Apprehended and the Apprehender

In order to fathom more fully the apprehender, Gyatrul Rinpoché instructs on a method to use when your own mind distracts you from recognizing rikpa. This classic analytical strategy of examining the origin, location, and destination of thoughts can help you see more clearly the actual nature of the apprehending mind. He states: "You've already been able to come to terms with the fact that concepts arise from the mind. Now you must find where the mind originates, where it exists, and where it finally ceases."[69]

The mind generates thoughts, so that is where they originate. You can observe those thoughts, and thus observe the mind, as discussed earlier. In order to "find where the mind originates," you look for the generator of the thoughts, the thinker. From where does the mind emerge? It would, in fact, take a lifetime to find the mind's origination, where it exists, and where it comes to end. When considering the full extent of your mind in this lifetime, it starts at conception and ends at death. However, when you are first conceived (the first moment of having a mind in this lifetime), consider from where it came. Then during the course of your life, investigate where it is located. Finally, at the last moment of your life (the moment after which you do not exist as a human being anymore), in that last moment of mind and of being this sentient being, where did that mind go? You would not be able to complete that meditative investigation until your death, and you may have even started a bit late since you probably weren't meditating when you were conceived. That is no problem, and you can simply come back to the present moment for this investigation.

Similarly, saṃsāra did not begin at the Big Bang, thousands of lifetimes ago, or many cosmic cycles before. When looking for how saṃsāra came into being, look right into this present moment. Right now, as much as any time in all of your previous lives, is when saṃsāra begins. Every single moment that you slip into dualistic grasping, saṃsāra begins. This becomes a more practical way to examine and find where the mind originates, where it exists, and where it finally ceases—look at what's happening right now, from moment to moment. Right now there is a mind; from where did it come? Where is this sentient being's mind located? If it is real, it must be somewhere. Then, from moment to moment, it both arises and passes. For example, every time you awake, it arises; every time you fall asleep, it passes. In the interval between waking and sleeping, it is continuously arising and passing from moment to moment.

"Similarly," Gyatrul Rinpoché continues, "try to understand where discursive thoughts originate, where they exist, and where they cease."[70] He is applying this analytical strategy in two complementary ways: trying to find the mind and trying to find discursive thoughts generated by that mind. Both ways shed light on the actual nature of the apprehending mind, doing so with respect to the activities of the mind. Asking questions, for example, "Where do discursive thoughts come from, where are they located, and where do they go?" is one profound way of determining the nature of the apprehending mind, because this investigation serves as the basis of designation of the mind for almost everything you do. Then, going deeper into that which is apprehending the movements of the mind, you ask of it, too, "Where do you come from, where are you located, and where do you cease?" Both of these are ontological probes.

In the close application of mindfulness to the mind there is a phenomenological approach, as the Buddha counsels in the *Satipaṭṭhāna Sutta*: "In this way, one abides regarding the mind internally ... externally ... internally and externally. One abides contemplating the nature of arising ... of passing away ... of both arising and passing away in regard to the mind. Mindfulness that 'there is a mind' is established in one to the extent necessary for knowledge and continuous mindfulness. And one abides independent, not clinging to anything in the world."[71] The Buddha says in his discourse that as you are observing mental events arising, review the factors of origination: In dependence upon what causes and conditions do mental events occur? From moment to moment, does your mind arise? If so, what triggered it? Was it seeing a person, a memory, feeling a tactile sensation? From what or where did it come? Then, while it is present, is it permanent or impermanent? Satisfying or unsatisfying? Is it you or not you? Is it yours or not yours? By examining the factors of dissolution, you ask how, from moment to moment, do these emotions, thoughts, and memories dissipate or vanish? This is a phenomenological approach, while the ontological probe asks if they are real, where they originate, where they are located, and where they cease.

To conclude this analysis, Gyatrul Rinpoché comments, "If, through the process of examination, you are totally unable to find the mind and what you have found instead is just like the sphere of space itself—open, like looking into a vast, empty space—yet you are unable to express it, then you are on the right track."[72] This is encouraging that when you look for the mind and cannot find it, look at what you *do* find: an openness, "like looking into a vast, empty space," that is inexpressibly beyond the realm of thoughts and labels. He is telling us right here that it is enough to be on the right track. It is enough to go in the correct direction with a pure motivation and clear, genuine guidance. How many people are on the right track to achieving enlightenment, even in one lifetime? How many people have all of the leisure, freedoms, and endowments to achieve enlightenment? However, knowing that you have leisure, freedoms, and endowments to practice should not give rise to even one iota of a sense of superiority because you are *not* superior. Instead, it can give rise to a massive sense of gratitude, rejoicing, and compassion to want to help all others who are suffering without a path to freedom. It is possible right now to be on the right track and to have confidence in that. This is what Gyatrul Rinpoché means when he says that "you are on the right track."

He continues: "However, this experience of emptiness is not the negation of everything, falling to the extreme of nihilism, believing there is nothing."[73] Emptiness, or *śūnyatā*, does not imply an emptiness of meaning. Do not think for a moment that if you realize this phase that somehow it will rob you of your compassion for other people as they will become merely insubstantial, ephemeral appearances, and, therefore, unworthy of compassion. That is nihilism, in which case you completely missed the point, as emptiness is *not* a sheer nothingness.

By contrast, regarding this experience of emptiness, he says, "It is an experience that is very open; and, within that openness, there are many, many possibilities."[74] This is something in which to rejoice! There are so many possibilities that most people have never imagined—the possibilities that you could reach the path, achieve bodhicitta, and be free of all mental afflictions!

His Holiness the Dalai Lama once commented that when you realize the actual nature of the mind, you are realizing nirvāṇa, and to realize nirvāṇa is to know that you can be completely, irreversibly free. This freedom is a knowing that you can abide and dwell timelessly in immutable bliss. Further, when you come to know the actual nature of your mind, it is essentially the same as knowing the actual nature of anyone else's mind. From this place, as soon as you emerge from meditative equipoise, the desire to share the profound possibilities with others arises. The compassion that arises here is so immense and is far beyond the compassion that is realized from achieving śamatha.

In this section, once again there are instructions in terms of striking the vital points in meditation that are similar from phase to phase, and identical to the meditation instructions given at the beginning of the text. This instruction will come up repeatedly. Although it looks the same, you will see that in each phase, it is imbued with deeper and deeper realization. In principle you could, as Düdjom Rinpoché said, achieve śamatha by striking the vital point of the mind, for example—that would be enough. Bear in mind, though, that if you are engaging in śamatha practice authentically within the Buddhist context, there will be more, as it will be imbued with taking refuge, the four revolutions in outlook, bodhicitta, the spirit of definite emergence, the four immeasurables, and guru yoga. That does not necessarily come to mind when simply resting in awareness, but that would be the undercurrent of practice.

On the path of śamatha, there is no corresponding view of reality. In other words, you do not have to be a Buddhist or believe in reincarnation, God, buddha nature, or anything else; it is simply a technique that comes with no strings attached. That is, it's not necessary to adopt any particular worldview to achieve this, and you do not need to have achieved bodhicitta. It is simply a resting in awareness in the flow of your mental continuum. By so doing, in that concise way that he explained, rest right there, and allow all the convolutions, constrictions, tightness, and warping of your mind to release themselves. As you are resting in that awareness, an approach is to apply one antidote after another to mental afflictions as they arise—one antidote for greed, one for lust, another for craving, hostility, jealousy, and so forth—which can be a good approach. In Śāntideva's *Guide to the Bodhisattva Way of Life*, he gives a whole pharmacopoeia of remedies for individual mental afflictions.

On the other hand, in this practice, you come to a simplicity in this stage of completion of your practice, where you are plainly and simply resting. From there, as mentioned, you see that if you do not appropriate mental afflictions or reify them, then they release themselves. This is like lying on your back and seeing a thick fog above, and then, when the sun rises, the fog dissipates without your having done anything about it. In this practice you may be lying in the supine position, with your body resting in its natural state, watching all of the mist of the mind dissipate and release itself, revealing the clarity of awareness shining brightly. It was always shining brightly, but now, without gripping so tightly to appearances, you can see it. On the path of śamatha, with no particular view, your mind dissolves into the substrate consciousness. Then the light of self-illuminating mindfulness arises, the sheer luminosity of the substrate consciousness manifests, and, thus, you have realized the substrate consciousness. You could simply dwell there, enjoying the bliss, luminosity, and nonconceptuality, but if you do, then you are not going any further than that.

This is the time to bring in vipaśyanā—to investigate and determine the nature of the phenomena around you. With that awareness of the dream-like nature of phenomena, imbued now with this wisdom gained through examination, reflection, contemplation, and investigation to the point of certitude, and with the view of the Middle Way, the emptiness of inherent nature of the world, you then come back and rest in the union of śamatha and vipaśyanā. You are resting, but now that simple resting is imbued with the view of emptiness of the world of all external objects. This view is liberating because it is a direct route to the union of śamatha-vipaśyanā, with vipaśyanā directed toward the nature of apprehended objects.

The next phase is about realizing the emptiness of the inherent nature of the mind that is apprehending the emptiness of everything else. You probe inward to the origin, location, and destination of the mind: Does it have characteristics or not? Does it exist or not? Can you find it or not? You probe, penetrate, and pierce until you have this experience exactly like Gyatrul Rinpoché and Düdjom Rinpoché have described. That is, they tell you what it is like to succeed, and you do so for a few moments at a time, but it is unsustainable. Then you return to this and continue to familiarize yourself with it. In this familiarization, you are still resting in awareness, but it is now imbued with the realization of emptiness of inherent nature of the world around you, and then infused with the realization of the emptiness of inherent nature of your own mind. You see that both the world around you and your mind are empty of origin, empty of location, and empty of destination. This transcends the categories of existence and nonexistence. It transcends time, and then, fundamentally, it transcends the very bifurcation of subject-object. Now simply rest here in the knowing of this empty and luminous nature that is unborn emptiness and unborn luminosity. In this way, you have found the apprehender. As you can see, in each of these phases, the method looks virtually the same, but it is imbued with deeper and deeper insight.

Crossing the Threshold into Vipaśyanā

How do you cross the threshold from śamatha into vipaśyanā? In order to enter fully into vipaśyanā and be able to investigate more effectively and deeply the actual nature of apprehended objects and the apprehending mind, thereby further preparing you to cut through to pristine awareness, you must first have the essential and solid foundation of śamatha so that your mind is serviceable. Regarding the actual achievement of śamatha, Jé Tsongkhapa writes,

> Once the rapturous pleasure of the mind has disappeared, the attention is sustained firmly upon the meditative object; and you achieve śamatha that is freed from the turbulence caused by great pleasure.[75]

And, in his *Śrāvakabhūmi*, Asaṅga adds that when the physical and mental pliancy and quiescence gained from the achievement of śamatha arises,

> having taken delight in the extraordinary mental joy in superb mental engagement, there is supreme mental pleasure in accompanying the meditative object. At that time, that is called *the mind*.[76]

So, one of the benefits of achieving śamatha is that now you have a mind. Before you achieve śamatha—when the mind is still prone to hedonism, malevolence, excitation, laxity, and afflictive uncertainty—it is a stretch to say that you have a mind; it is more accurate to say that the mind has you. It is like a five-year-old kid walking a Great Dane, and the dog sees a rabbit and takes off. Who is taking whom for a walk here? The child intended to take the Great Dane for a walk, but it turns out the Great Dane is taking the child for a run. Do you often feel that your mind is speeding along, while you are just trying to keep up, all the while being tormented, stressed, blown away, bewildered, and battered as a result of it? In such a situation, why would you say "I have a mind"? Would a mosquito on top of Mt. Everest say "I have a mountain"?

So what do we do with all of these thoughts? Returning to Düdjom Rinpoché's commentary, he advises, "closely observe by chasing down the origin from which they first arose, where they are now, and where they finally cease." These instructions describe something you *do not* do when practicing śamatha. Some contemporary teachers of vipaśyanā—or in Pāli, *vipassanā*—and "mindfulness" teach a practice that focuses on maintaining a nonjudgmental awareness and simply being present and mindful. This is not vipaśyanā as the Buddha taught it, either in the Pāli canon or in the Mahāyāna sūtras, and it is incorrect to describe it in that way. Vipaśyanā by definition in the Buddhist tradition always entails an element of *inquiry*. Hence, by inquiring into, investigating, and analyzing the actual nature of reality, insights will arise that do not necessarily occur by passively witnessing whatever is coming up.

Vipaśyanā is beyond śamatha; to *fully* enter into vipaśyanā, you must first achieve śamatha. As Karma Chakmé Rinpoché writes,

> Thus, once you have cultivated śamatha by itself, then the greater the śamatha, the greater the creative power and fine qualities of vipaśyanā. If śamatha is weak, the power of vipaśyanā will be weak, just as little rain falls from a small cloud, or a small flame burns from a small piece of wood.[77]

Whether or not you have already achieved śamatha in the past, when you are meditating and not simply resting in the substrate consciousness, then thoughts are still likely to arise. In this particular case, if many thoughts flow forth unimpededly, then you are to enter into the practice of vipaśyanā. In the spirit of inquiry, closely observe whence they first arose, and examine from where these thoughts occur.

Toward the end of the last century, the mind was considered the agent, the *doer*, and it was understood to arise in dependence upon the brain. Soon, neuroscientists started saying that the *brain* is the agent. While materialists often get away with making these broad claims, in reality, their experiments have only shown that there are *correlations* between brain activity and subjective experience. What is the nature of these correlations? This is still a mystery. Those who say "the mind is what the brain does" have never actually discovered that. If they had, they would have solved the mind-brain problem—the mystery of how subjective experience and neural phenomena are related and interact—but this problem is still hotly debated by scientists and academics. Trying to trace consciousness back to the brain has thus far proven to be a futile pursuit, driven by materialistic dogma, not empirical facts.

Rather than simply assuming that thoughts must emerge from the brain, closely observe and look directly at the thoughts themselves. This is the close application of mindfulness to the mind itself. This is *smṛtyupasthāna*, or *satipaṭṭhāna* in Pāli, the close application of mindfulness, which is the foundational Buddhist phenomenological approach, exploring how mental events *appear*. Here, we are taking this foundational practice a step further, extending it from a phenomenological inquiry to an ontological inquiry. Instead of asking how mental events are *perceived*, we are now asking, How do mental events actually *exist*?

When thoughts arise, rather than passively witnessing or simply noting them as you do in śamatha, the pith instructions are to "closely observe by chasing down the origin from which they first arose." The "thoughts" to which Düdjom Rinpoché is referring consist of a multitude of mental activities: desires, emotions, memories, fantasies, impulses, discursive thoughts, and whatever else arises in the space of the mind. Watching the mind is like being a birdwatcher in a lush forest observing a bird emerging from the trees. In such a situation, an ornithologist would inquire, From where did this bird come? What are its habits? Where is it going? Likewise, in the practice of vipaśyanā you investigate from where thoughts come, their location, how they influence other phenomena and are influenced by them, and where they go in the end. As for their special origins, do the thoughts come from in front of you, from the side, above, or below? Do they come out of your heart or your head? Watch these movements of the mind when they arise and find out if you can trace them back to their origin. It is worth investigating for yourself and not merely thinking about it or relying on what you read in the media or what other people say.

This practice goes beyond śamatha, crossing the threshold into vipaśyanā. Once a thought or any movement of the mind has arisen, ask, Where is it now? Simply because the mind and brain are correlated does not mean that they are located in the same place, any more than a light switch exists in the same place as the light. They are correlated, but the light switch is not in the light. Why should you think that thoughts are located inside the head simply because there are specific neural activities correlated with specific thoughts, emotions, and so forth? Carefully scrutinizing the first arising of thoughts and where they are located in a spirit of inquiry, you will see that eventually thoughts are going to pass and will not be there anymore. Where do they cease? Where do they go? What happens to them? Do they suddenly turn into nothing right where they are, or do they dissolve into the ground from which they first arose? These are fundamental, scientific questions that can also be asked of the earth, galaxies, and molecules. Everything is in the process of change. This process of inquiry is vipaśyanā on the nature of thoughts.

❖ Meditation: Vipaśyanā on the Actual Nature of the Mind

https://wisdomexperience.org/alan-wallace-dzokchen-meditation-10/

Relax and loosen any arousal from words, concepts, and so forth. Drop your shoulders and let your awareness descend into the body, down to the ground of this quiet, nonconceptual field of somatic sensations. In a similar manner, let your awareness quiet down. Rest your body in a state that is relaxed, still, and vigilant.

Then, strike the vital point of speech by allowing your respiration to flow unimpededly. Releasing all grasping, and neither going outward nor inward, rest your awareness in its own place—utterly at ease, still, and luminous.

Remain in this stillness and intentionally let the light of your awareness illuminate the space of the mind, the sixth domain of experience. Withdraw your attention from the five physical sense fields and deliberately let the light of your awareness shine upon the space of the mind and whatever arises within it—thoughts, images, and all movements and activities of the mind. Be discerningly mindful of them from moment to moment. This is called "taking the impure mind as the path," or "settling the mind in its natural state." This is śamatha focused on the mind.

Clearly distinguish between the stillness of awareness and the movements of the mind. Sustain the ongoing flow of self-knowing awareness, the ongoing cognizance of being aware.

With discerning mindfulness and intelligence, arouse an interest in the range of movements and activities that arise in this space of the mind. Be aware of any objective appearances, such as mental images and discursive thoughts. Be aware of any subjective impulses, such as desires and emotions. These are all movements of the mind. It is like going into a forest and becoming vividly aware of the full range of flora and fauna within this natural habitat. Get to know the forest of your mind by watching closely.

Now, bring in the sharp spear of investigation and inquiry, resting in the stillness of awareness. Sustain that flow to the best of your ability and, while so doing, focus your attention intensely and piercingly on the space of the mind and whatever arises within it. As soon as something emerges, such as a discursive thought or a mental image, closely observe, From where does it come? How did it first appear?

In order not to reinforce the delusion of thinking your mind is inside your head, let your eyes be open, at least partially, and vacantly rest your visual gaze in the space in front of you. This creates a sense of spaciousness and openness, so that you are not locked inside your head. Within this openness, selectively focus on the domain of the mind. This domain is not small, nor is it inside your head; it has no center and no periphery. Attend closely to the space of the mind, and as soon as something arises, examine it carefully. Do these phenomena of the mind exist? They indeed have causal efficacy within the domain of obscurative reality. If they exist, whence do they originate? Once such phenomena have arisen, continue to observe them by closely applying mindfulness to thoughts, emotions, or other mental events. Where are they located? Do you see any evidence that they are behind your eyes and inside your head? Is there any evidence that they are arising elsewhere in your body, such as your heart, gut, or limbs? Might they instead be located outside of your body in physical space and, if so, where? If they are located only in mental space, where is that mental space? Does it have a physical location? Observe closely. Such examination gives rise to insight and knowledge.

Emotions and desires arise, and eventually they disappear. You used to feel one way, and now you do not. You used to want something, and now you do not. Sometimes a cascade of thoughts and mental images rush in, but then there is a brief interlude of silence. When these movements of the mind vanish, where do they go? Do they disappear right where they are? How do they go? Do they gradually fade out, or are they suddenly no longer there? Examine closely.

There is a lot of knowledge about the origins of distant galaxies and where they are located. As the universe continues to expand, what is its destiny? Will it continue to expand until everything goes dead cold, or will the universe begin to contract once again into a singularity? Much is known about the external world because we have been looking carefully with the appropriate technology; however, little is known scientifically about the origin, location, and destination of our own minds. The reason for this is because we have been looking elsewhere or simply not looking at all, letting our reductionist beliefs override our own first-person experience. This inner domain remains a great mystery to the modern world, but only because we have not devised the appropriate technology or science to explore it successfully. We can, however, do so now—and the mysteries will be revealed. Clarity comes by observing closely, by following the Buddha's own injunction: Come and see for yourself.

Bring this meditation to a close by dedicating the merit of this session to the realization of your greatest aspiration, so that you may achieve perfect awakening for the benefit of all beings. ❖

An Integration of Eastern and Western Influences

Elaborating further on determining the actual nature of external apprehended objects and the internal apprehending mind, let's bring this root text—Düdjom Rinpoché's commentary and Gyatrul Rinpoché's later commentary, both written in the twentieth century—more fully into the twenty-first century. Specifically for people educated in modern academia, the aim is for there to be a full integration of the Dharma with every aspect of our thinking and behavior, so that our understanding of Dharma is thoroughly contemporary and, thus, practical in life as it rises to meet us in this day and age.

We have all been conditioned and influenced profoundly by being raised in Eurocentric civilizations with the associated modern worldviews and academia. If these timeless teachings of Düdjom Rinpoché and Gyatrul Rinpoché are going to come into full dialogue with our own minds as we are situated here in the modern world, then there need to be bridges across these two worldviews. How do these texts relate to the things learned through education and the experiences of living in a Western culture?

It is helpful to return repeatedly to the root text and to Düdjom Rinpoché's commentary in order for a fuller integration process to take place as an interplay between these traditional teachings and our modern worldview.

To supply context, we will examine classical phenomenology and epistemology in Buddhism. In addition, we will trace the history of the Prāsaṅgika Madhyamaka view and its evolution, outlining the revolution in quantum physics over the past century, and delineating the progression of modern Western philosophy, mapping it onto modern science. We will also look at how, over the past thirty years, the paradigm of scientific materialism has come under increasing scrutiny. In light of Düdjom Rinpoché's Dzokchen view, we are asking the big questions: What is real? What is really out there? What is really in here?

The Actual Nature of the Internal Apprehending Mind

Bear in mind the dense paragraphs that Düdjom Rinpoché presented in "Determining the Internal Apprehending Mind." Each line has been addressed, but we will revisit this to show contextually what the Dzokchen view of the actual nature of the internal apprehending mind is, and how it can easily be confused with things that it is not. As a reminder, Düdjom Rinpoché states: "yet, apart from being the delusive appearances of one's own mind, in actuality, nothing whatsoever is determined to exist."

The foundational philosophical views of Indian Buddhism—Vaibhāṣika and Sautrāntika—are rooted in metaphysical realism, which assume there is an objectively existing reality *out there*, independent of anybody looking at it. That is, there are causal interactions in the real world when nobody is there to see them, and these include objective contributing conditions for our subjective experience. For example, regarding the sense of sight, there is a physical faculty in dependence upon which visual perception arises. If the retina, optic nerve, or significant parts of the visual cortex are damaged, then there will be either a distorted visual perception or no perception at all. When the physiological basis is damaged or completely destroyed, the sense of sight will follow suit. In this view, there must be a physical faculty first.

Buddhism has never fallen into the pit of materialism. For sensory perceptions to arise, it is not enough for there to be the objective contributing conditions from the physical environment and the physical sense faculties in our brains. Physical processes are not enough to bring about sensory experiences, or qualia. For example, the colors you see are subjective impressions and are not *out there* in physical space. This was recognized in Buddhism centuries ago, for example, in the Sautrāntika view. The subjectively apprehending aspects of the mind, or *dzin nam*, and objectively apprehended qualia, or *zung nam*, arise in dependence upon the physical contributing conditions, but they do not emerge from them. There must be a third factor, and that is the continuum of consciousness from which specific modes of perception and qualia arise, conditioned by external and internal physical influences. Qualia have no physical attributes and cannot be measured physically. Qualia are neither located in physical space outside the body nor inside the head. They are simply correlated with brain processes but are not equivalent to them, nor do subjective experiences arise as emergent properties from the brain. There has to be something nonphysical that both transforms into these qualia and into the awareness *of* the qualia.

That "nonphysical" is the flow of consciousness. Fundamentally, mental consciousness is conditioned in the brain by external physical influences and then emerges as derivative forms of sensory consciousness.

Three factors are necessary for the perception of sensory qualia and for the awareness of qualia to arise: the objective contributing condition, the physiological faculty, and the flow of consciousness. Simply put, in order to have a visual awareness of the red color of a shirt, for example, there needs to be a shirt, the visual cortex, and a flow of consciousness. In deep, dreamless sleep, the only kind of consciousness that is active is mental consciousness. Within a dream, you are seeing facsimiles of visual forms and sounds. Imagine being asleep and dreaming with your mental consciousness, when a man in waking life comes to you wearing a red shirt and shouts, "Wake up! The house is on fire!" The first thing you hear is his voice, experienced with auditory consciousness that emerges from the preceding moment of mental consciousness. Then you open your eyes and see his red shirt. That first moment of visual perception arises from the prior moment of mental consciousness that was then conditioned by the visual cortex and manifested as visual consciousness. The qualia of colors and the awareness of them are both nonphysical.

Physical things do not turn into nonphysical things, but both kinds of phenomena influence each other. For example, a thought (nonphysical) can influence a behavior (physical), just as one's own and others' behaviors influence thoughts. Classical Buddhist epistemology says that physical things do not transform into mental things, nor do they give rise to nonphysical emergent properties. According to physics, all emergent properties of physical entities are themselves physical. Likewise, the nonphysical can transform into nonphysical, so that a stream of consciousness can become configured, conditioned, and turn into a derivative form of consciousness. For that to happen though, you need a flow of mental consciousness.

Buddhist Epistemology

Then came the great logicians Dignāga and Dharmakīrti, who formulated the Cittamātra, or mind-only, view. They were towering figures in understanding Buddhist epistemology, and they noted that appearances are consequences, and there are various causes that give rise to them. They saw compelling evidence that one *must* have consciousness in order to experience appearances. Otherwise, if there is a corpse, and you open its eyes and shine a bright light on them, the corpse does not see anything. In modern terminology, the photons are there, the visual cortex may be freshly dead, but there is no consciousness so the corpse will not see anything. They examined this carefully and saw that all appearances—from the five fields of sensory experience—are consequences.

Advocates of the Vaibhāṣika and Sautrāntika views assume appearances arise in dependence upon what is out there—the world of atoms—as contributing conditions. However, the Cittamātrins thought about this further, and saw that all we actually perceive are appearances. Metaphysical realists assume that out there beyond the appearances, there is some absolutely objective, inherently real world that has a role in generating the causes of the appearances and accounts for the consensuality of our common experience, yet we can never see what is out there.

Nowadays, whether you are looking through the Hubble Telescope, the James Webb Space Telescope, exploring elementary particles with the Large Hadron Supercollider, using a microscope to observe neurons, or anything else, everything you see consists of appearances, but you never see what is out there prior to the appearances—what is objectively causing them. Philosophically, this is called "the black box problem." How do we know what is out there in the external world, as it exists prior to any sentient being looking at it with a consciousness that illuminates all appearances? What is there prior to and independent of anybody's perceptions? Every time you look— whether with the most sophisticated present-day technology, the power of samādhi, naked-eye observation, or by listening with your ears—all you ever get are appearances. The universe as it exists, independent of appearances, is a "black box"—it is not findable with any of our sense faculties. These Buddhist epistemologists, Dignāga and Dharmakīrti, said that the whole external world is a black box. We know only the mind—or awareness and appearances—so anything apart from this is unknowable. We directly know we are aware, and no evidence or reasoning could ever be presented that would be so compelling and persuasive to say that we are not conscious. What about the external world independent of the mind and appearances to it? They concluded that you can never directly look inside the black box of the external world, whether you are clairvoyant, looking with your physical senses, or with samādhi. There are only more appearances—mental appearances and sensory appearances.

According to this theory, there is no way of inferring external causes that are contributing to the arising of the consequences or effects manifesting as appearances because we do not know what might be out there independent of appearances. You can imagine countless things filling that black box, and you may think they are all physical, but there will never be a consensus. There is the knowledge that a cause is always necessary for the production of an effect, but you cannot infer a cause based upon an effect if nobody has ever seen the cause producing the effect. Dignāga and Dharmakīrti then analyzed how one can infer causes on the basis of effects to see whether it is necessary to affirm the existence of an external world independent of experience to account for the commonality of the intersubjective experiences of sentient beings.

This attempt to infer causes based on effects is something you do every day. A classic example given in Buddhist philosophy is that when seeing billowing smoke rising into the sky from over a hill, you conclude that it is not fog, not mist, and not a dust storm. Having seen fire produce smoke on many occasions, and then finding invariably that when there is smoke, there is fire, you deduce with certainty that there must be a fire that is producing smoke. By using the power of inference, on the basis of the effect, you can now definitively infer the presence of fire as its cause. There are countless other examples where you can validly infer a cause based upon the effect.

However, these two logicians, Dignāga and Dharmakīrti, argued that in order to make that inference and have it be anything other than a guess, a belief, or an assumption, you or someone else must have *seen* the cause upon which you are seeking to infer. Not only that, but you must have seen it generating the effect, and there must be extremely compelling reasons to draw the conclusion that that effect does not occur without that prior cause.

Turning to this external world that presumably exists independent of appearances, has anybody actually seen what is out there producing appearances? Is it God, cherubim, seraphim, the Big Bang, atoms, quantum entanglement, or anything else? All we see are appearances. People have visions of

God, but has anyone *seen* God creating the universe? If no one has ever seen beyond the veil of appearances, or looked into the black box of nature and seen what is out there contributing to the emergence of appearances, and if no one knows with certainty that appearances never arise without there being that external, objective world or agent (that objective contributing condition), then no one has ever looked beyond the veil of appearances. If this is the case, then no one knows whether intersubjective appearances can possibly arise without there being an external world or creator.

Dignāga and Dharmakīrti asserted that it is not just that we do not *know* anything about the independently existent external world, but that it is *unknowable*. The definition of something that is existent in Buddhist epistemology is that it is knowable by valid cognition; that is, it must be knowable either by way of direct perception or by way of cogent inference. It does not have to be already known, otherwise, we would never learn anything new. Nonetheless, we can neither perceive what is beyond appearances, nor cogently infer what is beyond appearances for the aforementioned reasons.

Then they drew this astonishing conclusion: There is a fair amount of commonality in our experiences, as we all can bump into a table, see a bird flying into the same tree, and so forth. Although it makes common sense to believe there must be a world out there independent of appearances, there is still nothing we can say with certainty about it, for to say anything at all is just to project into the black box according to one's particular theistic beliefs, Buddhist beliefs, materialistic beliefs, or any other beliefs. Dignāga and Dharmakīrti concluded that there is no way to have a valid cognition of what lies out there independent of appearances. There is no reason to believe that there is an external world out there. It is unknowable in principle, and to insist that whatever is out there must fit into our human conceptual construct called "physical" is groundless conjecture and quite limited.

Besides, what is even meant by the word "physical"? In the twenty-first century, it includes dark matter and dark energy. There is nothing known about these things, which is why they are called "dark," yet they are still thought to be inherently physical. The causes of the inexplicable degree of order in the physical universe and the fact that space-time is expanding have never been seen. This is a powerful philosophical point, and this is why the Cittamātrins say that the only things we know are appearances and the mind that is aware of, observes, and perceives appearances; therefore, reality consists only of the mind—mind-only—and appearances to it. Thus, the whole of reality is like a dream. Within a dream, over there you may see a truck driving toward you, and it is over here that you perceive it. Yet, in this view, "over there" does not exist—apart from appearances—because everything is within the mind.

Dignāga and Dharmakīrti said that those who assert the existence of an external world are placing the whole ontological burden of reality (which accounts for the commonality of our experiences across species) on the external world made of matter and atoms. Yet, there is no way of positing the existence of an atom or anything else out there independent of appearances. The Cittamātra view says that we experience an intersubjectively validated world, and the projections of atoms, particles, waves, and fields are unnecessary and unverifiable.

An Evolution in Science

This is a revolution that completely guts all of Christianity-based science—from Copernicus up to the eminent nineteenth-century physicist James Clerk Maxwell, a devout Christian—which assumes that God created everything. He was here before we were, and theologically inspired scientists were trying to get a God's-eye view of what was out there before humans, and what is out there now that we are here. There was a strong theological motive behind most of the great founders of modern science—Copernicus, Galileo, Newton, and Kepler were all devout Christians and quite a number of them were theologians as well.

The existence of atoms as fundamental to the universe has even been called into question by some of the leading physicists of our time. For example, Max Planck, the founder of quantum mechanics, declared: "As a man who has devoted his whole life to the most clearheaded science, to the study of matter, I can tell you as a result of my research about the atoms this much: There is no matter as such!"[78] In a similar vein, the contemporary Nobel laureate in physics Steven Weinberg writes: "In the physicist's recipe for the world, the list of ingredients no longer includes particles. Matter thus loses its central role in physics: All that is left are principles of symmetry."[79] Another Nobel Prize–winning physicist, Richard Feynman adds, "It is important to realize that in physics today, we have no knowledge of what energy *is*."[80] While scientists know a great deal about matter and energy within the context of human experience—independent of all appearances—the nature of space-time, matter, and energy is indeterminate and can be affirmed only conventionally. However, despite their merely nominal status, they evidently still do have causal efficacy.

Collective Karma

Dignāga and Dharmakīrti have shown that we cannot know anything about the external world that is independent of appearances, but we may still feel there must be a universe out there since there is a commonality of experiences among human beings and animals. Are we not seeing and experiencing the same world in different ways? And if so, how do we account for our common, collective experience?

We share a lot of collective karma from past lives that is now coming to fruition in our intertwined streams of the substrate consciousness. Collectively, we are creating the worlds we experience with a lot of overlap, but not a complete overlap—for example, nobody else has my perspective on reality, and vice versa. This resonates with the following comment by the physicist Thomas Hertog, who was a protégé of Steven Hawking:

> You can think of that quantum reality a bit like a tree. The branches represent all possible universes, and our observations—we are part of the universe, so we are part of that tree—and our observations select certain branches, and hereby give meaning, or give reality, to our past in a quantum world.... Quantum theory indicates we may *not* be mere chemical scum. Life and the cosmos are, in the quantum theory, a synthesis, and our observations now give in fact reality to its earliest days.[81]

In other words, our observations create different realities through the meanings we impute upon them. This, in turn, gives meaning and reality to the earliest days of life and the universe, as well as to the collective experience of our current reality as a whole. Although, as mentioned, individually we have our own personal observations that are informed by our individual past karma, which then shape "my perspective," which is different from "your perspective."

Dignāga and Dharmakīrti believed that all the causes of appearances are to be found in the mind and its karmic imprints. They were relying on the direct discovery of the Buddha, as well as many accomplished contemplatives before and after him who discovered the continuity of consciousness from lifetime to lifetime and the coherence of cause and effect across lifetimes. The Buddha asserted the existence of individual karma and collective karma stored in the mindstreams of sentient beings. By the power of the collective karma of animals of a specific species, of human beings, of devas and pretas, and so forth, we are all experiencing quite different worlds relative to each class of sentient beings. This accords with the Buddha's contemplative discovery, succinctly expressed in Vasubandhu's *Abhidharmakośa*: "The myriad worlds emerge from karma."

To illustrate this, it is said that if you take a glass filled with fluid, each being will experience it differently: A human being sips it and experiences it as water. A deva sips it and tastes ambrosia. A preta sips it and tastes pus and blood. The only common denominator is that they all experience it as something fluid. What is the nature of the fluidity that is common to a myriad of perceptions? It is collective karma.

Further, according to Buddhism, it is by the power of karma—individual and collective karma across species and intraspecies—that we are reborn as a human being or an animal with an array of experiences in common. The whole ontological burden of reality that accounts for commonality is not placed on some invisible world that you imagine to be physical; it is placed on something you actually *know* exists—that is, the mind and the imprints stored in the mind, many of which are intersubjective. As our actions and perceptions are intersubjective, so is our karma.

The Black Box of the Mind as an Agent

Where Cittamātrins found the external world to be nonexistent and concluded that only the internal world of the apprehending mind exists,

Düdjom Rinpoché calls this into question. Based on the Prāsaṅgika Madhyamaka view, Düdjom Rinpoché turns the spear of discerning intelligence inward toward the internal apprehending mind. He asserts that the internal cause of appearances—the mind that observes, experiences joys and sorrows, thinks, meditates, plunges into the whirlpool of saṃsāra, and then tries to ascend along the path of enlightenment—cannot be inferred on the basis of resultant appearances, for the mind as it exists in and of itself is also a black box; that is, it cannot be found by means of ontological analysis. This view shatters the fundamental assumption of Cittamātrins—namely, that the mind alone is ultimately real.

When you look for the mind that is the agent, the observer, and so forth, what do you see? As you are looking for the mind, see if you can find the mind that is really there, the agent, the doer, the creator of saṃsāra—called in Tibetan *kun jé gyalpo*, the "all-creating sovereign." Can you find the all-creating sovereign of your own mind? Is it any more findable under analysis than is the external world as it really exists out there, independent of appearances?

Piercingly search for the mind, not only with samādhi, but with discerning, radiant, fierce intelligence, like the blazing sword of Mañjuśrī that cuts through appearances, trying to identify that which is aware of the appearances. What do you see? There are only more appearances. Who has ever seen the mind as something *in here*, real, and inherently existent? Who has ever seen the mind generate a thought or an appearance? Appearances are always illuminated by consciousness, but who has seen the mind that is generating and observing the appearances—the mind that exists prior to and independent of appearances, and has its own self-existence? Who has seen the mind generate qualia, thoughts, or anything else?

In that bifurcated view of reality—objects "over there" and subjects "over here"—nobody has actually seen the self-existent objects out there, as Dignāga and Dharmakīrti demonstrated. Similarly, the same blade with which you repudiated an inherently existent objective world out there can be can turned inward so that you are able to invalidate the inherent existence of a subjective mind in here. Both are equally unfindable.

In this way, the *Ratnakūṭa Sūtra* states,

Consider this, "While thoroughly experiencing the mind, what are those minds that become attached, or hateful, or deluded? Do they arise in the past, future, or present? Any mind that is past has vanished. Whatever is in the future has not come. Whatever arises in the present does not last." Kāśyapa, the mind is not found to be present inside, or outside, or both inside and outside. Kāśyapa, the mind is formless, undemonstrable, intangible, devoid of a basis, invisible, unknowable, and without any location. Kāśyapa, the mind has never even been seen, is not seen, and will never be seen by any of the buddhas. . . . Kāśyapa, even though one looks for the mind everywhere, it is not to be found. Whatever is unfindable is unobservable. Whatever is unobservable does not arise in the past, or in the future, or in the present. Whatever does not arise in the past, or in the future, or in the present really transcends the three times. Whatever really transcends the three times is neither existent nor nonexistent.[82]

No buddhas of the past, present, or future have seen or ever will see the mind. If the buddhas cannot see it, do you think you have? The black box is of a real mind *in here* that is the real observer and the agent that exists independent of appearances and is not equivalent to awareness but is the agent that is aware.

If the great advocates of the Prāsaṅgika Madhyamaka view—such as Buddhapālita, Candrakīrti, Śāntideva, Sakya Paṇḍita, Atiśa, and Jé Tsongkhapa—say that both the world of apprehended objects and the apprehending mind as they exist in and of themselves are unknowable in principle, then what remains? You might be tempted to conclude that none of these exist at all. However, just because they cannot be found by means of such ontological analysis, does not mean they don't exist at all. How can the mind not exist at all if you came to that conclusion using your mind? The mind cannot deny its own existence.

Conventional Reality and Conceptual Designation

As you can see, the Prāsaṅgika Mādhyamikas reject the conclusion that there is no external world in the same way that they refute the nihilistic conclusion that the internal world of the mind doesn't exist. Conventionally speaking, the world out there is populated by objects, but how do they come into existence? Certainly they arise in dependence upon prior causes and conditions, and each object is dependent for its existence on its own constituent parts and attributes. However, the existence of all objects and subjects also depends on the conceptual designations of them. Nothing exists by its own nature, independent of being conceptually imputed upon a basis that is not that entity.

To elaborate this point, the conceptual mind is crucial in the "birth" of objects and subjects because, in and of themselves, the many parts that compose something never become a whole without the conceptual mind designating them as such. For instance, the eight planets, the sun, and the various moons around different planets never become one thing. When we speak of a solar system, there is one solar system in our immediate vicinity. It is one solar system, but the many planets, sun, and the moons around the planets never fuse into one thing called a "solar system," and yet, how does one solar system come into existence? This is because the conceptual mind looks upon the planets, sun, and moon, and upon that basis, designates the term "solar system." The whole is imputed upon the parts, but it is neither equivalent to any or all of those parts collectively, nor does it exist independently from them.

The power of conceptual designation is absolutely critical, but it leaves you with only a nominally existent external world, nominally existent space and time, and nominally existent mind and functions of the mind. Yet, these objects and these subjects, in a manner of speaking, do exist, and have causal efficacy, but none of them are *inherently* real. This is widely acknowledged in Tibetan Buddhism among the great scholars and adepts, and is the ultimate interpretation of the Perfection of Wisdom sūtras and the Middle Way view of Nāgārjuna.

It is revolutionary to say that there is nothing inherently out there or in here, and that everything exists in dependence upon conceptual designation. Moreover, the very demarcation, or borderline, between "out there" and "in here" is purely imaginary and simply designated, like the border between two countries. This is the Prāsaṅgika Madhyamaka view that Düdjom Rinpoché is coming to in the next section of the text. Having concluded his examination of the nature of external apprehended objects, he then turns to the internal apprehending mind and concludes that that, too, is not inherently existent.

In sum, advocates for the Prāsaṅgika Madhyamaka view within the Sūtrayāna context conclude that the external world and the internal world *are* existent—albeit conventionally, relatively, and nominally existent—but they do not *inherently* exist. From here, the Dzokchen masters like Düdjom Rinpoché are going to thrust the spear even deeper. Since you speak of things as conventionally and relatively existent, then they *do* exist. You determine that something conventionally exists by consensus within a group of language-users until it is proven otherwise. That is also how science progresses: collective consensus. For example, scientists agreed that there is absolute space and time, until it was proven otherwise by compelling reasoning and empirical evidence. Currently physicists say that there was never absolute space and time because they have accepted Einstein's relativity theory.

His Holiness the Dalai Lama has commented that there are three criteria by which you can determine that something exists conventionally: (1) Something is known to worldly convention (i.e., it is commonly agreed upon as existing in the first place). (2) The known phenomenon should not be invalidated by any other valid cognition, which may include one's own later cognitions. For example, you may perceive something and think it to be the case, but your next perception of the phenomenon may ultimately invalidate it as a false perception. Similarly, it could be invalidated by valid cognitions of a third person. (3) The known phenomenon must not be invalidated by ultimate analysis. In this way, it is collective agreement that further allows objects and subjects to take birth in the conceptual realm as being conventionally existent.

Ultimate Reality and Pristine Awareness

How can we begin to make the shift from conventional, obscurative reality to ultimate reality? Dzokchen asserts that the perspectives of sentient beings, who reside in this obscurative reality, are radically different from that of pristine awareness. Viewed from the perspective of a sentient being, a human being and the familiar world of subjects and objects are conventionally existent. This is true for animals as well—even though they may have very limited conceptual abilities, they, too, designate things in their own primitive ways. If one views reality from within the context of a conceptual framework, one labels everything in sight and many things that are out of sight, like dark matter or dark energy. That is a way of viewing reality by means of a conceptual grid and a dualistic mind. However, there is an alternative: You can view reality from the deeper perspective of pristine awareness, which has never been conceptual, never conceptually designates anything at all, and which transcends all conceptual categories, including that of existence and nonexistence.

If you are viewing reality from this perspective, which was the perspective of Düdjom Rinpoché, the words "existent" and "nonexistent" do not mean anything because they are concepts that are merely defined by human beings. Pristine awareness certainly is not a human being's awareness, as there is nothing human about it. From this perspective, the ultimate reality of how things *actually* exist does not fit into these little conceptually fabricated cubicles of existence and nonexistence. The so-called outer and inner worlds are indeterminate—they are neither really existent nor really nonexistent.

There is a sequence that begins from the metaphysical realism of the Abhidharma that methodically asserts a real external world, real sensory faculties, and a real mind in dependence upon which appearances, thoughts, and mental states arise. Then, according to the Cittamātra view, the external world was swept away—it does not exist at all. From there, we go to the Prāsaṅgika Madhyamaka view: The external world exists, however, everything that is posited to exist out there has only nominal existence. Then we come to Dzokchen and the perspective of pristine awareness, which transcends all conceptual frameworks entirely and views all of reality from the perspective of pristine awareness. This is an evolution within Buddhist thought from the classical framework of the Abhidharma to the Cittamātra to the Prāsaṅgika Madhyamaka to Dzokchen. In this hierarchy, the former is more primitive than the latter. As we can see through this progression of thought, what was once considered to be valid cognition turns out to be invalid, allowing for a revolution that transforms reality as we know it.

Scientific Developments of Reality

Is there anything comparable in physics, where valid cognition and collective agreement have shape-shifted former understandings into scientific discoveries? By reflecting in this way, we can come to see that things that seem to be solid are, in fact, quite changing. One example is the view of space. In physicists' view of space in the late nineteenth century, there was a virtually ubiquitous, unanimous assertion that was in accordance with Newton's view that space and time are absolute. Physicists at this time added to that the insights from electromagnetism by James Clerk Maxwell, Hans Christian Ørsted, Michael Faraday, and so on. They asked how one can account for the phenomena of light waves colliding with each other, giving rise to interference patterns of waves. The logic is that there cannot be water waves with no water, or air waves with no air. Likewise, they assume you cannot have interference patterns unless there is a medium in which light waves move. There must be a subtle, physical medium permeating space, otherwise, it was inconceivable that light waves could propagate and create interference patterns. There was no empirical evidence for such a "luminiferous ether," as they called it, but they were absolutely sure it must exist. Light and space would be unimaginable and unintelligible without such an ether.

These scientists all agreed upon this until in 1887, there were two physicists by the names of Michelson and Morley who devised an ingenious experiment that determined beyond any reasonable doubt that if there is an ether, then the effects of the ether should appear. It was a definitive experiment that was designed to reveal empirical evidence that would conclusively support the existence of this hypothetical ether. This experiment, deemed the Michelson-Morley experiment, came back with a negative result. It is not that they didn't find the ether, but rather that it could not possibly exist because had it existed, it would have given rise to a different result as light moved through it. Essentially, they found its unfindability, and finding that something does not exist is no easy task. And yet, two years later, the renowned physicist Lord Kelvin expressed the general attitude of physicists at that time by saying, "One thing we are sure of, and that is the reality and substantiality of the luminiferous ether." Further, Sir J. J. Thomson, the recipient of the 1906 Nobel Prize in physics, declared that all mass and kinetic energy is composed of the ether. Despite this, Michelson and Morley's conclusion paved the way for a different means of viewing reality as it was once known. All that remained was absolute space, but then there was no explanation for the propagation of waves and interference patterns because the ether was gone.

The certainty of absolute space and time then, too, dissolved when, in 1905, Albert Einstein discovered special relativity, and ten years later his general relativity theory emerged. Absolute, inherently existent matter and energy were proven nonexistent as well because their magnitude varies depending on the initial frame of reference. In 1938, Einstein asserted, "All assumptions concerning ether led nowhere! The experimental verdict was always negative."[83] His relativity theory presented a big shift in physics that went from the belief in absolute space or time to a relative, yet inherently existent space and time that warps, woofs, curves, and so forth—that is, its existence is objective and inherent, but not absolute or invariant across all frames of reference.

Then emerged quantum cosmology and quantum mechanics as a whole. The director of the Institute for Advanced Study, Robbert Dijkgraaf, said that space itself has disappeared. In support of this, Nima Arkani-Hamed, also from the Institute for Advanced Study, declared,

> Many separate arguments, all very strong individually, suggest that the very notion of spacetime is not a fundamental one. Spacetime is doomed. There is no such thing as spacetime fundamentally in the actual underlying description of the laws of physics. That is very startling because what physics is supposed to be about is describing things as they happen in space and time. So, if there's no spacetime, it's not clear what physics is about. That's why this is a hard problem.[84]

It was a huge advance in science to discover that there is no inherently existent space or time.

Descartes's Influence

A key point in Western philosophy is also worth exploring because it, too, has greatly influenced the modern worldview. We cannot turn our backs on René Descartes and the later evolution of Eurocentric philosophy, deeming them as unimportant. It is meaningful to understand the impact not only of science but of some of the Western philosophies that have inevitably influenced, shaped, and developed the media, education, and the minds of billions of people. Even if the people involved in these sophisticated, philosophical pursuits are not Buddhists, remember the bodhisattva motivation: As Śāntideva says, bodhisattvas are willing to learn anything to be of service to sentient beings. Carrying with you this motivation, let's explore a key point in European philosophy in order to get a more expansive bird's eye view of how conventional reality changes with fluctuating human conventions.

According to the great natural philosopher and brilliant mathematician René Descartes, the external world out there manifests in space (*res extensa*). In other words, physical things have extension and volume; that is, they have size in space. This is one category of existence that he saw as inherently real. Then there is the internal world (*res cogitans*), which is the internal world of the mind. Descartes said that this internal world is not physical and has no spatial extension—for example, in physical space, there are not big minds and little minds—but, despite this, the internal world is also real. Therefore, he posited that both the external and internal worlds are real, yet separate and distinct from one another. Clearly, the world out there is real, for if you throw a rock at somebody, it hits them, and they feel it. Your emotions and mind are also real, as you can think, understand, experience sensory perceptions, and have will. In his view, the mind, although real and inherently existent, is fundamentally different from the body. Descartes completely embraced this dualistic view that both the physical and the mental—the body and the mind—exist, but as separate and incompatible entities. Yet, he was never able to provide a compelling explanation for how two separate, inherently existent domains of reality could causally interact. He further speculated that the entryway to the brain—in order for the immaterial soul, mind, or consciousness to influence the body, and vice versa—was by way of the pineal gland, despite having no evidence for this claim.

Moreover, reality has never been able to fit inside the two mere conceptual categories of mind and matter, let alone being reduced solely to materials. Reality has always been pluralistic because, as Hamlet suggested, "There are more things in heaven and Earth, Horatio, / Than are dreamt of in your philosophy." In this way, there are many things in heaven and earth that are neither matter nor mind; for example, semantic information, mathematical equations, the laws of nature, qualia, time, and people.

Descartes' fundamental error was to reify objective phenomena extended in space and reify mental phenomena not extended in space, which led him to be stumped with the problem of an immortal, nonphysical soul somehow interacting with the physical world—that is, the "ghost in the machine," where the machine is the body being operated by the ghost of the mind.

The Rise of Materialism

Arising in the mid-nineteenth century, the implausibility of the Cartesian dualistic view of the mind and body had become increasingly evident to the scientific community, especially in light of evidence supporting the conservation of matter and energy, which appeared to preclude the possibility of nonphysical phenomena having any causal efficacy in the natural world. The mind and consciousness became relegated to emergent properties of matter, and the physical world alone was regarded as inherently real. Thus, by the power of this view, materialism came to dominate Eurocentric civilization.

This firm assertation of the innate materiality of things in the external world was entirely unquestioned among scientists until the advent of quantum mechanics. The materialist view has dominated the media, academia, scientific community, and many publications therefrom, almost without exception, relegating the subjective mind to being either nonexistent or illusory. Eliminative materialists insist that subjective experience does not exist at all, with equally preposterous denials of the very existence of consciousness, qualia, and introspection. The mind is either dismissed as being nonexistent because it is nonphysical or as being illusory and existing only as an illusion. Meanwhile, the validity of subjective experience in general and introspection in particular has been disparaged in comparison to the cold, hard facts of objective science. It is also written off to be merely epiphenomenal, where all of subjective experience is simply fluff generated as a byproduct of the brain. In this way, if the mind and subjective experience are taken to be real, then they are nothing other than the brain or brain function, for which there is no evidence whatsoever. The materialist view is such that real existence of the mind can be admitted *only if* it is equated with physical dispositions for behavior or with neurological activity. Therefore, if it is not physical and cannot be measured scientifically, then it is not real and plays no significant role in the natural order of things. Dogmatism stupefies—whether it's religious, political, or philosophical—and the dogmatism of scientific materialism is no exception.

Emerging from materialism, physicalism asserts that everything is contingent upon the physical in order to exist. This empirical view says that only what you experience with the five senses, augmented by way of technology, exists. Empirical evidence is always "out there." Based on this, if the only evidence that counts is physical evidence, you will perforce have to be a physicalist, and then reality is composed only of what you can measure. Thus, empiricism is confined solely to physical phenomena, completely abolishing the existence of any nonphysical phenomena. These very limited notions are closely tied to and influence the pragmatic expressions of hedonism and consumerism in our modern culture. Materialism is like a parasite that has latched onto science (falsely assuming the authority of science itself) and, thereby, infected all of modern society as a whole. It lies at the root of many of the catastrophes that humanity has inflicted upon ourselves, other species, and the entire natural environment. Like many other lethal parasites, sooner or later it winds up killing its host, which in this case is human civilization as we know it.

A Quantum Reality

Scientific materialism has been under assault with the rise of quantum physics, especially in the field of quantum cosmology. This is principally due to the influence of the towering figure of the world-class physicist John Archibald Wheeler, who was the counterpart of the groundbreaking physicist Richard Feynman, both in the latter half of the twentieth century. John Wheeler applied the principles of quantum mechanics, but rather than seeing the quantum mechanical system as something quite local that you have to protect from outside influences, he took a bold leap instead. Working with a postdoctoral student of his, Bryce DeWitt, he applied Schrödinger's wave equation—the fundamental equation for making calculations in quantum mechanics—to the whole universe, thereby imagining the whole universe as a quantum system. They created an equation, known as the Wheeler-DeWitt equation, to adapt to the entire universe so that it is not something *within* the universe, but is the *whole* universe. In this way, Wheeler and DeWitt applied Schrödinger's equation to the universe, viewing it as a quantum system that is purely objective and inherently existent. As such, time naturally drops out of the equation. They then found the implication that if the universe did consist of objective, inherently existent space, time, matter, and energy, there would be no change; nothing would interact with anything else, and everything would be frozen. If we think of the universe as a quantum system, independent of any observer, then the universe and everything within it would be static and immutable. Their overall conclusion that space and time have no objective, inherent existence was drawn two millennia ago by Nāgārjuna, based purely on philosophical analysis and contemplative insight.

John Wheeler further underscored the complexity of the situation and introduced such terms as a "self-observing universe." The objective reality doesn't say "now"; it doesn't say anything at all, for it is not conscious. However, an observer who must be conscious, has to look upon the world and say "now" in order to speak of the past and the future relative to now. Without a "now," there is no past, present, or future though. The observer is a necessity in order to make the split between subject and object. The subject then has to be present to give life to the objective world—to make change, to transform, and to evolve. Stanford theoretical physicist Andrei Linde comments on this point, saying,

The universe becomes alive (time-dependent) only when one divides it into two parts: a subjective observer and the rest of the objective universe, and the wave function of the rest of the objective universe depends on the time measured by the observer. In other words, the evolution of the universe and everything in it, including life itself, is possible only with respect to the observer.[85]

What Do We Know?

What *do* we actually know, and not merely imagine or impute such as an inherently existent external, physical world? As Düdjom Rinpoché writes, "apart from being the delusive appearances of one's own mind, in actuality, nothing whatsoever is determined to exist. Appearances do indeed appear, but real things are not real. Regard these simply as illusory apparitions." The external world that gives rise to sensory appearances is independent and indeterminate, for it cannot be determined either really to exist or really not to exist. The internal world of the mind that is aware of all appearances and generates all mental activities, is also independent of these cognitions and is indeterminate in the same way. What *do* we know? Appearances and awareness. Yet, when we look for the objective sources of those appearances, they prove to be unfindable; likewise, the mind that generates the appearances and is aware is also unfindable. This brings us back to knowing only the field of experience of *pratītyasamutpāda*—of dependently related events.

❖ Meditation: Vipaśyanā on the Actual Nature of the Mind as an Agent

https://wisdomexperience.org/alan-wallace-dzokchen-meditation-11/

Relax and release all concepts and mental stimulation. Let your awareness descend nonconceptually into this expansive somatic field. Settle your body in a state that is relaxed, still, and vigilant.

When attending closely and concentrating, there may be some pressure, ambition, hope, or fear. This contraction around desire and aversion often inhibits and disrupts the natural flow and rhythm of the breath. This is counterproductive for relaxing the nervous system, as stress and exhaustion will likely ensue from such efforts. In this case, keep returning to a state of ease by settling your body, speech, and mind in their natural states as many times as needed throughout the course of the day. Settle your respiration in its natural, effortless rhythm. Allow the body to breathe in the way it knows best.

If there is a conceptual storm on the ocean of your mind—waves crashing, winds howling on the surface of your mind—dive deep, down into awareness itself. Submerge beyond the turbulence, the comings and goings of the mind, and into the simple, unmediated, unelaborated experience of being aware. Rest there in awareness itself, in a state that is relaxed, still, and luminously clear.

With your eyes at least partially open and your gaze resting vacantly in the space in front of you, continue relaxing in this flow of self-illuminating, self-cognizing awareness—the knowing of knowing, the most indubitable knowing you may ever experience.

In the mode of śamatha, simply rest in the flow of that ongoing awareness of being aware without inquiring into or having any interest in the appearances within awareness. Relax in the unmediated, nonconceptual experience of being aware of being aware. There is no reason for consciousness to remain a mystery if you set out to explore it rigorously from a refined, first-person perspective.

If you find yourself getting a bit lax or spaced out because there is nothing to do, then peripherally and effortlessly maintain an awareness of the flowing in and out of the respiration. As you are breathing in, draw your awareness right in upon itself. Withdraw from all sensory and mental appearances, right into the very experience of being aware, which is unelaborated and unclothed with appearances. Concentrate there and sharpen this awareness, focusing your attention as the breath flows in. Then, as you breathe out, utterly relax and release awareness into space, where there is no object, no referent, no thought. Simply release awareness into an open, objectless expanse while gently sustaining the flow of awareness of awareness. Arouse and release in this way with each in-breath and out-breath.

As you withdraw your attention, turn it in upon itself and probe more deeply, more piercingly, into your own immediate experience. As you invert your awareness, seek to discover *who* or *what* is the agent that is inverting and releasing awareness. It is not happening by itself, or simply because instruction was given to do so. *You* decided to do so. Your mind, it seems, is inverting and releasing attention. What is the nature of that agent that can be called the mind? When you invert your awareness more deeply, seek out and try to identify: What is the mind that is the agent, that is meditating, that is inverting and releasing the flow of attention? Seek it out as you breathe in. Then, as you breathe out, relax and totally release into this objectless expanse. Then, as you inhale again, rise to the challenge again and try to discover what is the nature of this agent that is controlling the flow of attention. What is the nature of the mind? Does it have characteristics? If so, what are they? Can you find this mind that is the agent? Look carefully, gaze piercingly inward, and then relax, seeing what you see.

As you are looking inward, come in with a command: "Mind, show yourself! I know you must be in here somewhere! Something is controlling the flow of attention, and you are the primary candidate!" Keep looking for the mind in this way. What does it look like? What are its characteristics? Does it have a shape or a color? Look for it, but do not exhaust yourself, then relax again.

The attention is not inverting and releasing without reason. Something is controlling it. The flow of attention is an instrument; so what is wielding the instrument, directing it inward and outward? When you invert your awareness, appearances arise; but are they in fact appearances and characteristics of the mind that is the agent, or are they merely appearances, and not characteristics of something else? Look more deeply. What is the mind without characteristics; the mind itself? *Cittatā* is the Sanskrit word for the actual nature of the mind—but what *is* that?

If you see appearances, ask, Are they, in truth, appearances of the *mind*, or are they simply empty appearances signifying nothing and having no referent apart from themselves? If you see no appearances, can you conclude that the mind is unknowable in principle and does not exist at all? Is there nothing that is inverting and releasing the attention? If so, what would that imply? Pause for a moment without doing anything at all—just be aware.

Do you have a sense that there is something or someone "in here," someone or something from your side that is not *doing* anything but is simply observing, watching, and being aware? Is there a subject in here that is observing? Can you sense, intuit, or feel it? Isn't it the mind that observes and is aware?

Return briefly to the oscillation between inverting and releasing the attention. Set in motion, as if on cruise control, the turning of the awareness inward—but now, piercingly try to inwardly find and identify the mind that is observing. Does it have any characteristics? Search for that which observes mental and sensory appearances, and then release. Search again, and relax.

If the mind exists, either as an agent or as an observer, it must have characteristics by which it can be known. If it is otherwise—if the mind cannot ever be known by way of its attributes—then saying "it exists" means nothing. What are the mind's characteristics by which you can identify it as agent and observer? If time and again you discover nothing—no appearances, no content, just space—you cannot conclude that there is no observer, because then there would be no observation or awareness. When you investigate deeply, you thrust the spear of your wisdom so that the very constructs and categories of existence and nonexistence melt away. All that remains is space and the sheer luminosity of awareness itself. Rest in that place with no object or subject, no outer or inner, no words or concepts.

Bring this meditative session to a close by dedicating this virtue and merit to the realization of your most meaningful aspirations, and to your own perfect awakening for the sake of all sentient beings. ❖

3. Identifying the View of the Nature of Existence

TURNING AGAIN to the root text, still under the subsection on "Coming to Conviction by Means of the View," the next phase is "Identifying the View of the Nature of Existence." The "view" here is part of the Buddhist triad of view, meditation, and conduct that goes right into the heart of Dzokchen. Düdjom Rinpoché's root verse states,

> Emptiness and luminosity are the actual Drowo Lö.
> Do not seek it elsewhere; just this naked,
> self-emergent, pristine awareness
> is the great, omnipresent lord of saṃsāra and nirvāṇa.
> Return to this great, primordial place of rest.

"**Drowo Lö**" refers to Dorjé Drolö, the wrathful manifestation of Padmasambhava. "**Emptiness and luminosity are the actual Drowo Lö**," who is symbolically depicted as wrathful in appearance and riding upon a pregnant tigress. If you have a vision of Dorjé Drolö, as did both Düdjom Lingpa and Düdjom Rinpoché, then that is how the vision appears. As for the *actual* nature of Drowo Lö, it is the emptiness and luminosity of your own mind, the emptiness and luminosity of pristine awareness.

In the verse, Düdjom Rinpoché is bringing us back to the method of primordial rest, of release, of abiding without modification. You employ this method to identify the *actual* Drowo Lö, the emptiness of inherent nature—the actual nature of your mind. This actual nature is pristine awareness, unborn and luminous. This "**self-emergent, pristine awareness**," which is found in this present moment, is described in the root text as "**the great, omnipresent lord of saṃsāra and nirvāṇa.**"

It is commonly noted in the Dzokchen teachings that the ground of becoming—the wellspring and locus of all appearances for every being in the six realms of saṃsāra—is pristine awareness, which transcends everything in the phenomenal world of saṃsāra.

Your own substrate consciousness is individual—that is, it is not a collective unconscious—and carries with it your own individual karmic imprints, predilections, and spiritual momentum from past lives. This substrate has no center or periphery and is private yet not bounded. It is not located in your country or your hometown, your head or your body. Your substrate is vaster than the full extent of space known by modern cosmology with its two trillion galaxies. That space includes only the physical world in the desire realm and does not include the form realm or formless realm, whereas your own substrate encompasses all of that. Your substrate is the womb of your entire phenomenal world of saṃsāra and of yourself within saṃsāra. In Tibetan, the substrate is called *kunshi* (*kun gzhi*), or *ālaya* in Sanskrit. The substrate is the basis of everything—the foundation, ground, and source of everything in saṃsāra. Likewise, in Pāli, bhavaṅga is the ground of becoming of your entire phenomenal world that emerges from it. Further, it is the mental factor of mentation—or *manas* in Sanskrit—that manifests and crystalizes this ground and makes it distinct.

The first verse of the *Dhammapada*, a classic set of aphorisms of the Buddha in the Pāli canon, states, "All phenomena are preceded by mentation, issue forth from mentation, and consist of mentation." However, when it comes to the ground of saṃsāra *and* nirvāṇa, your substrate is *not* the ground of nirvāṇa, but is only the ground of your saṃsāra. Additionally, "**self-emergent, pristine awareness**" does not arise in dependence upon causes and conditions that play out through time; rather, it is spontaneously and timelessly displayed. This pristine awareness is "**the great, omnipresent lord of saṃsāra and nirvāṇa.**" As a further note, in Dzokchen, Samantabhadra is the personification of primordial consciousness and is said to be the ultimate ground of both saṃsāra and nirvāṇa. Some Christian theologians depict God as the ultimate ground of being, as well. So, at this point, it is difficult to say that the Buddhist Great Perfection is theistic, atheistic, or nontheistic, for it does not fit neatly into any of those categories. Without concern for any of these conceptual frameworks, simply "Return to this great, primordial place of rest."

As a reminder, Düdjom Rinpoché's commentary said, "if awareness appears nakedly and serenely, free of any recognition of an essential nature of appearances and awareness—unmediated, inexpressible, inconceivable, unobservable, empty and luminous, without an object—then you have internalized the instructions." In this way, you have cracked open the door and begun to view reality from the perspective of pristine awareness. Now, simply rest here.

Düdjom Rinpoché's commentary on his root verse states,

> In this way, one recognizes that which is free of all characteristics elaborating an apprehender and apprehended objects; one recognizes the primordial character, empty of any inherent nature of its own, the place of rest that is originally pure and inexpressible by thoughts or words; one recognizes the natural display of primordial consciousness, which is luminous, radiant, and unimpeded—spontaneously actualized as the great, omnipresent lord of saṃsāra and nirvāṇa.

Here we see that there was no point in time when pristine awareness became pristine, became aware, or became awakened, because it is timeless and has never been unawakened. Pristine awareness has never been the obscured awareness of sentient beings. Right now, as you are reading, your own pristine awareness is aware of itself. This is called "self-knowing primordial consciousness," or *rang rikpé yeshé* (*rang rig pa'i ye shes*) in Tibetan. Your own pristine awareness not only knows itself, it also knows every thought you experience, every sorrow with which you are burdened, every joy in which you rejoice, your hopes and fears, and what it is like for you to be embodied; it is aware of everything you are aware of in every single moment. It is utterly, fully aware of you as this human being. Pristine awareness is aware of you whether or not you are aware of it.

This whole text is about becoming aware of who you have always been and who you are now, and realizing that, in reality, when you look closely, you have never been a sentient being. This radical idea represents the Dzokchen view. The whole sense of being a sentient being is like having a very firm conviction about something, without having investigated the matter thoroughly. You are completely convinced of your own identity as a sentient being, without ever doubting it for a moment. What makes you so certain, when everything you identify with is not really you or even yours? What if you had such a conviction, such a certainty that you would bet your life on it, and it turned out that the entire basis of your certainty was misleading. Everything on which you based that conviction was constructed on a mound of lies and misinformation, yet you were so convinced that the lie was true that you wouldn't even question whether or not it was a lie. That is the degree of conviction you have right now that you are a sentient being. Yet, the basis of your total certainty consists solely of delusive appearances. That said, there is a perspective from which it is true to say that you are a sentient being, which veils your deeper, actual nature as an already awakened buddha.

Düdjom Rinpoché continues,

> Moreover, one recognizes the mode of existence of the unconditioned place of rest, the primordially inseparable union of the two. Primordially awakened and naked, this self-emergent primordial consciousness rests in itself.

When Düdjom Rinpoché writes, "the primordially inseparable union of the two," he is referring to the apprehender and the apprehended. Further, "primordially awakened and naked" describes the way that primordial consciousness is unelaborated, unadorned, and conceptually and primordially unveiled. At the beginning of practice, you come to the facsimile of this by resting in the stillness of awareness and observing the movements of the mind without wavering or being drawn away. When you are drawn away, you release your grasping and come back again and again. Through such practice, you may gain some realization of emptiness—whether of the external world or the internal mind—and then you waver and lose it. This may happen because you get caught up in distracting thoughts, or perhaps the fog of reification starts creeping in again, darkening the sky of the mind.

Your mind is thus always on the move, though primordial consciousness has never been on the move. Because primordial consciousness is timeless and nonlocal, the very notion that it moves is a categorical error; it has no meaning. In contrast to pristine awareness, the substrate consciousness does appear to move, as Nāgārjuna writes,

> When iron approaches a magnet, it quickly spins into place. Although it has no mind, it appears as though it did. In the same way the substrate consciousness has no true existence, yet when it comes [from a previous life] and goes [to the next], it moves just as though it were real, and so it takes hold of another lifetime in existence.[86]

It is like watching a 3D movie and feeling dizzy as the camera creates the illusion of movement, while, in actuality, you are sitting still in a mounted seat. Similarly, the substrate consciousness isn't really moving anywhere, but it gives the impression of doing so. However, for pristine awareness, there is not even the illusion of movement, as it is nonlocal and timeless. This "self-emergent primordial consciousness rests in itself" primordially and is stable, for it never changes from its own nature into anything else. It transcends the very categories of coming and going, which is one of the seven qualities of a vajra. The categories of transition and change are transcended here, just as are the categories of existence and nonexistence, arising and passing, and so on. Furthermore, it is easy to think that because you have your own pristine awareness and I have my own pristine awareness, then there must be two different pristine awarenesses. There are eight billion people on Earth, so are there eight billion pristine awarenesses? If this question arises for you, then you are still trying to try to wrap your conceptual mind around pristine awareness by quantifying it. But pristine awareness doesn't fit into any conceptual categories; it transcends them.

Düdjom Rinpoché continues,

The recognition of this enlightened view of the extinction of all phenomena is the view of the Great Perfection, which transcends cognition. Manifestly realize this by identifying it just as it is.

When Düdjom Rinpoché writes, "The recognition of this enlightened view," he is pointing to the view of a buddha, the view of pristine awareness. When you come to the culminating phase of Dzokchen, all impure appearances of saṃsāra are extinguished forever without trace, dissolving into the actual nature of reality, the *dharmatā*. These impure appearances include all of saṃsāra, the six classes of sentient beings, the three realms, everything that appears to and emerges from the substrate consciousness, and all appearances generated by karma and *kleśa*, or mental afflictions. This is the view of the Great Perfection, and it transcends anything cognition can possibly imagine.

Thus, when he writes, "The recognition of this enlightened view of the extinction of all phenomena is the view of the Great Perfection, which transcends cognition. Manifestly realize this by identifying it just as it is," he is referring to the fourth and culminating vision in the practice of tögal, the direct crossing over.

INTERLUDE:
The Four Visions of Tögal and Buddhahood

I N ORDER to give some context to Düdjom Rinpoché's commentary
in the last section—"The recognition of this enlightened view of the
extinction of all phenomena is the view of the Great Perfection, which transcends cognition. Manifestly realize this by identifying it just as it is"—let's
now discuss the four visions in the sequential practice of the direct crossing
over, or tögal, into the spontaneous actualization of buddha-mind.

The Four Visions of Tögal

Düdjom Lingpa, in his commentary to *The Sharp Vajra of Conscious Awareness Tantra*, discusses the fourth vision, writing,

> With the extinction of the outer delusive appearances and all
> inner habitual propensities for delusive conceptual mindsets and
> mental factors, and with the extinction of all the secret visions of
> the clear light, you cross over into the absolute space of the inef-
> fable, actual nature of reality.[87]

In tögal, an array of four sequential visions arise in which your whole experience becomes increasingly filled with pure visions of the divine, the five
Buddha families, their entourages, and so on. These pure visions reach their
culmination when they dissolve and are extinguished. This is the extinction
of the secret visions of the clear light, whereby a final crossing over follows.

With the first vision of the direct perception of the actual nature of reality, you cross over to the first *āryabodhisattva* ground, or bhūmi, and become a vidyādhara. As you progress to the second, third, and finally the fourth vision, you cross over from one āryabodhisattva ground to the next. Having achieved the first āryabodhisattva bhūmi with the first vision, you continue in the practice to the second vision, known as "progress in meditative experience," by which you cross over to the fifth āryabodhisattva bhūmi. With the realization of the third vision, known as "reaching consummate awareness," you cross over to the eighth bhūmi. Finally, with the realization of the fourth vision, the "extinction into the actual nature of reality," you cross over to the tenth bhūmi, the final bodhisattva ground of a vidyādhara. From here, you are now right next to enlightenment. You are in the concluding phase of your practice of tögal, and of the entire path of Dzokchen where even those pure visions, which have manifested and are now complete, also dissolve, and you make the final crossing into the absolute space of the ineffable, actual nature of reality.

In this final phase—the extinction into the actual nature of reality—the "extinction" refers to the dissolution of all the pure visions that sequentially arise along the path of tögal, freshly emerging and manifesting more and more fully until they are complete. All of this entails a profound purification of your mind and a drawing forth of all of the power, wisdom, and compassion of the buddha-mind, such that they are all spontaneously actualized. Once your whole experience is filled with these pure visions, then their work is done, and they also dissolve. Everything dissolves into dharmadhātu, the absolute space of phenomena. This is the extinction of all appearances into the actual nature of reality, the dharmatā.

Regarding this extinction, Düdjom Lingpa says that it can occur either gradually or suddenly. In the first case, he says, "extinction occurs gradually for anyone who has come to the culmination of the four visions."[88] This way involves gradually moving through the four visions, which build more and more fully until they finally dissolve and are extinguished. This is the classic way of accomplishing tögal for those who have already accomplished the phase of cutting through to the original purity of pristine awareness, and by so doing, have gained the direct perception of the actual nature of reality and have become a vidyādhara. With that as a basis, such a person may move gradually through the visions from there.

Düdjom Lingpa then proceeds to explain the second way this extinction into the actual nature of reality occurs, saying, "just from having begun to familiarize themselves with seeing the visions of the direct perception [of the actual nature of reality]." That is, they see ultimate reality in the first vision, then they familiarize themselves with it by resting there in the direct perception of the actual nature of reality "without reliance on the stages of progress in meditative experience and reaching consummate awareness."[89] Here, Düdjom Lingpa is referring to the second vision of progress in meditative experience and the third vision of reaching consummate awareness. By resting and familiarizing themselves solely with the first vision, everything unfolds from there.

Yangthang Rinpoché mentioned that those who have cut through to the original purity of pristine awareness and dwell there with śamatha, vipaśyanā, and the Dzokchen view can achieve perfect enlightenment in twenty years by practicing tögal. However, according to Düdjom Lingpa, this is the gradual way. The other possibility is simply to dwell in the direct perception of the actual nature of reality without relying on the stages of the second and third visions. Such a one can come to the culmination and achieve perfect enlightenment right there and then.

Clear Light, Pure Visions, and Buddhahood

Düdjom Lingpa wrote that people who are exceptionally gifted with supreme wisdom or very sharp faculties may go to the first vision of the direct perception of the actual nature of reality; that is, they may rest in pristine awareness that is unmediated, nonconceptual, and nondually realizing the dharmadhātu, or the absolute space of phenomena. *The Sharp Vajra of Conscious Awareness Tantra* continues, "The initial moment of consciousness emerges as a vision of the clear light, manifesting as a sight for the eye of wisdom."[90] The clear light is nothing other than pristine awareness and is not due to any ordinary sensory faculty, but rather is a vision that is the direct perception of the actual nature of reality.

It is important to note that what you are realizing here is unconditioned and timeless, and the awareness with which you are realizing it is unconditioned and timeless. Therefore, nominally speaking, there is a perfect symmetry between object and subject because primordial consciousness and the absolute space of phenomena have never been separate; they are primordially, eternally, and timelessly of the same nature, undifferentiated, and co-extensive. In this phase of the practice, when you have achieved this first vision, you are then resting without mediation in pristine awareness, fully supported and suffused with śamatha and your realization of the emptiness of all phenomena including both apprehended objects and the apprehending mind. Having achieved this vision, you are now a vidyādhara. From there, without engaging in the specific further visionary practices of tögal, you may directly cross over to the fourth vision—the vision of the extinction of phenomena—into the actual nature of reality, or dharmatā.

Becoming a Buddha

But crossing over into the actual nature of reality is not the end; you don't simply rest there in the dark for the rest of eternity with all appearances having vanished. What it means is that all *impure* appearances have vanished irreversibly and will never return. From your perspective, you will never experience impure appearances again, nor will you ever be in saṃsāra again. To your own awareness, all appearances of saṃsāra are completely finished. As such, all appearances—including those pure appearances that were arising sequentially along the four visions—dissolve into emptiness, into the absolute space of phenomena. Then, pure appearances arise again, and you manifestly actualize the state of buddhahood. You are now imbued with the two aspects of primordial consciousness: the primordial consciousness of knowing reality as it is, and the primordial consciousness that perceives the full range of phenomena. You have just realized reality as it is, and you continue realizing dharmadhātu—the totally unmediated, nonconceptual, nondual realization of nirvāṇa, dharmatā, and dharmadhātu, which now continues timelessly.

In actualizing the state of buddhahood, you are not simply an arhat who is dwelling in nirvāṇa, but rather, you have manifestly actualized the state of perfect awakening. In this awakened state, there arises both the experience of the primordial consciousness of knowing reality as it is, and the realization of the primordial consciousness that perceives the full range of phenomena. From your side, from your dharmakāya, pure appearances continue to arise; for example, pure appearances of other buddhas and of pure lands. Now you have pure visions—you abide within an environment of appearances that are unadulterated, creative expressions of pristine awareness. However, you are also experiencing the primordial consciousness that perceives the full range of phenomena. This means that since you are now a buddha, your awareness of phenomena is unimpeded throughout the three times and throughout all of space. As a buddha, you are now aware and perceive the appearances that are arising to every sentient being.

A buddha is aware of impure appearances because they are aware of what is arising in the minds of sentient beings. A buddha's perceptions of these impure appearances and experiences are nondual from those of the sentient beings who are perceiving them. Furthermore, a buddha is perceiving these only because sentient beings are perceiving them. In other words, a buddha is not looking from somewhere else in order to see and perceive what you see and perceive; otherwise, a buddha would be trapped again in dualistic grasping. If a buddha were residing in a pure land and looking from afar at you while having some clairvoyant but remote viewing of your experiences, then that would be a dualistic grasping that manifests as clairvoyance. This is not the case. Rather, a buddha is aware of every thought, every emotion, every feeling, every experience you have in the past, present, and future. A buddha's awareness of your experience is of the same nature as your perception and experience of appearances.

What is the difference, then, between a buddha's awareness of whatever you are experiencing right now and your experience of whatever you are experiencing right now? If you are a sentient being within saṃsāra, then you are perceiving all these experiences as being "out there." Essentially, you are apprehending objects and reifying them. When mental afflictions arise, you experience them as mental afflictions, and they afflict your mind because you appropriate and reify them. Buddhas are experiencing everything you are experiencing right now from your own perspective and from the perspective of each sentient being. A buddha is seeing what you are seeing from your perspective, and thereby knows what it is like to be you—to feel uncertain, to have low self-esteem, to be anxious, afraid, upset, and so on. Yet, a buddha is seeing these appearances—appearances of your mind, body, other people, and so forth—not only without appropriating or reifying them, but also as empty of inherent nature and as spontaneous, creative displays of pristine awareness, of dharmakāya.

Everything a buddha experiences that is arising in your body, mind, and experience is viewed from the perspective of pristine awareness. A buddha's awareness of your own experience is not other than your own pristine awareness's experience of these experiences. Once you become a buddha, appearances are generated by your own dharmakāya without mediation and from your own perspective: pure appearances, buddha fields, other buddhas, and so forth. There is even mind-to-mind transmission from one buddha-mind to another, which is one of the kinds of transmission of Dzokchen.

As an analogy, think of a laptop that is about to upgrade to a new operating system. Before you can use a new operating system, the old operating system with all of its bugs and glitches has to be shut down irreversibly and trashed without a trace. Once the laptop is totally shut down, all appearances on the screen vanish, and then the laptop is upgraded. If the laptop represents you as a buddha, then, from your perspective, when the laptop is restarted after the upgrade, what you see on the screen are all pure appearances. But simultaneously and inconceivably, you are aware of the impure appearances as they appear to sentient beings who have not yet received the upgrade. In other words, you completely understand them and know what they feel. Your compassion is nondual; you wish that each sentient be free from suffering and the causes of suffering—from *their* perspective. Being enlightened, however, you also know that these suffering beings are misidentifying themselves as being sentient beings, and they therefore need your help to realize who they actually are. Buddhas are here, helping you now, and when the day arrives that you no longer appropriate the body, mind, or appearances of an impure sentient being, then you, too, will cut through. Thus, your mindstream will be utterly nondual and indivisible from that of a buddha.

Becoming a buddha is not the end of the path; once you are a buddha, your work has only begun. When you were a sentient being, you needed to exert great effort and were limited in your abilities to serve the needs of each sentient being in accordance with their own specific needs, proclivities, desires, and so on. However, now that you have broken through your very existence as a sentient being and are a buddha, you continue to manifest all kinds of enlightened activity spontaneously, effortlessly, inconceivably, and all-pervasively—enlightened activities that are peaceful, expansive, powerful, and ferocious.

This is what Düdjom Rinpoché is referring to in this penultimate stage, immediately prior to achieving perfect enlightenment: "The recognition of this enlightened view of the extinction of all phenomena is the view of the Great Perfection, which transcends cognition. Manifestly realize this by identifying it just as it is." The final thing you experience as a sentient being is the dissolution, or the extinction, of all phenomena, whereby impure appearances never return. After achieving enlightenment, pure appearances are displayed spontaneously by your dharmakāya, and you continue to manifest by way of sambhogakāyas and nirmāṇakāyas for as long as sentient beings remain. You will effortlessly, spontaneously, and infinitely continue to manifest these until every sentient being is free. This fruition is what the aspiration of bodhicitta is intended to achieve—it is "the Great Perfection, which transcends cognition."

❖ Meditation: Examining the Origin, Location, and Destination of Apprehended Thoughts and of the Apprehending Awareness

https://wisdomexperience.org/alan-wallace-dzokchen-meditation-12/

Find a comfortable position and strike each of the three vital points of the body, speech, and mind.

From that stillness, observe the movements of the mind. As you grow increasingly familiar with sustaining that stillness, do so without entanglement or appropriation. Slip into the mode of śamatha of taking the mind as the path—a simple witnessing of the movements of the mind.

From here, cross the threshold into vipaśyanā, whereby you examine closely whence each thought, image, and movement of the mind emerges. What is its origin?

If your mind is wandering, you will notice this after it has already occurred. In order to be aware as a thought arises without first getting caught in it, you must hover in the immediacy of the present moment, and of the stillness of your awareness. In this manner, the first moment a thought, image, or mental impulse arises, you are already there. You are there where it appears and can thus observe whence it emerges. Once you have observed a mental object arise, investigate where it is located.

Soon after witnessing a mental event arising, it vanishes; it may only last a second or two. If you have been tracking it with your awareness when it first arose, keep following its whole trajectory from it being present to when it vanishes. When it comes to its conclusion and vanishes, ask yourself, Where does it go? How does it cease?

You have been apprehending the mind moment by moment, observing thoughts, images, and desires, one event after another. Now turn your attention inwards and apprehend the apprehender. Are you not already aware of being aware of the one who is aware? Don't you know that you are aware, that you are a subject, that the mind is a subject? Seek out this apprehender. Trace the thoughts back to their origin. Trace awareness back to its origin, to that which is aware.

This mind is not always present. When you are deep asleep, there is no human mind in sight anywhere. When you die, this human mind will not continue on after death. It had a beginning, it has an interim, and it will have an end. From day to day, it has a beginning every time you awake, become conscious, and have a human mind again. Similarly, it has an end every time you fall into deep, dreamless sleep. From moment to moment, the mind is arising. Where is the beginning of this moment of mind right now, and from where did it come?

Right now in this finite present moment, penetrate right into that interim of the present moment of mind with a razor-sharp spear and see where it is located. Does it have characteristics? In each moment and each pulse of mind, there is an end before the next moment has begun. From moment to moment, frame by frame, if this were a movie, how does it end? Where does that present moment of mind go? How does it dissolve?

One thought arises after another, one image after another. From this stillness of your awareness, in the immediacy of the present moment, observe closely where a thought has arisen and where it vanishes. In that interlude before the next movement of the mind, there is a space-time interval; that is, there is an empty space and time, a moment that is not filled or veiled with thoughts. Identify this interval and rest where there is no thought to latch onto; apart from awareness, there is nothing else.

There is no object and, therefore, there is no subject, just as there is no right without a left and no up without a down. Rest there in that emptiness devoid of object and subject; rest in that emptiness that is wide awake, luminous, and clear. This is how you identify rikpa. It is right here and right now in that emptiness.

Is it possible simultaneously to achieve śamatha, vipaśyanā, and cutting through in this way? Come and see for yourself.

Bringing this meditative session to a close, dedicate the merit to your realization of this Great Perfection, to manifest enlightenment in this lifetime, and thus to heal the world. ❖

B. Practicing by Means of Meditation

Düdjom Rinpoché now discusses the second item within the threefold rubric of view, meditation, and conduct in this section entitled "Practicing by Means of Meditation." His root verse on this topic says,

> Take as the path naked, empty awareness—
> consciousness of the present moment,
> in which the past has ceased
> and the future has not arisen.

This is the essence of Dzokchen meditation. By realizing the view, you are realizing rikpa and viewing the whole of reality from that perspective. Having cut through to the original purity of pristine awareness, Dzokchen meditation is nothing other than simply dwelling in that view.

In his commentary on this verse, Düdjom Rinpoché writes,

> Recognize for yourself that the dharmakāya is none other than this great, empty, luminous, self-emergent pristine awareness, which transcends cognition.

What is the meaning of "self-emergent" (Tib. *rangjung*; *rang byung*)? Let's explore this, first, by turning to Nāgārjuna, for in order to understand the actual nature of reality and all phenomena—including the potential for self-emergence—an understanding of causality is key. According to Nāgārjuna's Madhyamaka view as interpreted by Candrakīrti, all conditioned phenomena are understood as dependently related events (*pratītyasamutpāda*) in that they are dependent upon (1) their prior causes and conditions, (2) their constituent parts and attributes, and (3) the conceptual designations made upon them. Nāgārjuna's "king of reasonings" is that all phenomena are empty of inherent existence because they are dependently related events. If things were inherently existent, each entity would be self-contained and independent and would, therefore, not causally interact with anything else, so the world would be "frozen"—with no causality, movement, or change.

Taking this a step further, Nāgārjuna applies ontological analysis to causality in order to probe into its emptiness of inherent existence. Nothing ever arises from just one cause, although we sometimes mistakenly think this happens (e.g., "He makes me so mad!"). Instead, there must always be a primary cause (e.g., a seed) and myriad cooperative conditions. Those causes and conditions are many, and if they were inherently existent, they would be inherently many; however, many things cannot inherently become one thing. Bear in mind that Nāgārjuna doesn't refute causality, since dependent origination lies at the core of the Buddha's teachings, but he does refute *inherent* causality—that things inherently arise from themselves or from something else. Using the example of a sprout of wheat, he asks whether it emerged (1) from itself, (2) from something else, (3) from both, or (4) from neither. Going through that fourfold reasoning, or *tetralemma*, you see that that sprout didn't truly arise from itself, because that would have been redundant, for it is already there. It also didn't inherently arise from any one cause or from a multitude of causes and conditions, for those other things don't objectively, inherently lose their former identity and turn into the effect of a sprout. Further, it does not emerge from both itself and other phenomena, for if it doesn't truly emerge from itself and it doesn't truly emerge from something else, then it cannot possibly, truly emerge from both. Nor does it emerge from nothing at all, for "nothing" has no causal efficacy. Then it becomes apparent that, aside from conceptual designation, phenomena don't really come into existence at all.

It is important to note that with his tetralemma, Nāgārjuna is analyzing causality within the context of saṃsāra, within time, and within conditioned existence. From this place, he asks the aforementioned series of questions when something like a sprout arises. The conclusion of this analysis is that there is no point in time when, objectively, by its own nature, a sprout is not existent and then comes into existence. Keep in mind that the category of "self-emergent" does *not* go against Nāgārjuna's refutation of things arising from themselves as their sole cause, because when phenomena are self-emergent, they have simply been unveiled, as they were already there all along.

In this way, rikpa, or pristine awareness, spontaneously manifests as thoughts and appearances, which are "self-appearances" from the perspective of pristine awareness. Everything you experience while resting in pristine awareness consists of and is perceived as creative displays that are primordially pure and of the one taste of pristine awareness. Pristine awareness, either before or after you ascertain it, does not come freshly into existence because of your practice or because of the instructions of your meditation guide or a text. In one moment you have not yet realized it, and then in another moment, you do. It does not emerge in dependence upon causes and conditions, but, rather, it manifests spontaneously. That distinction is crucially important, as it means that it was already there, timelessly.

A simple analogy is that of clouds obscuring the sun, and then suddenly there is a break in the clouds. Hypothetically, since it wasn't there before and now it is, one might wonder what the sun did in order now to manifest. Yet, of course, the sun did not do anything at all. It was already there behind the clouds; now it is merely unveiled. Thus it is for the creative activity of pristine awareness. There is no cause and effect, no temporal sequence, and certainly no effort; yet, the creative displays of pristine awareness are suddenly there. From the perspective of pristine awareness, you are resting in timelessness. From this place, the creative displays are self-emergent and do not depend upon anything else; they are suddenly and simply actualized.

From the perspective of a sentient being, in one moment you have not realized rikpa, and then in another, you have. On the one hand, it makes sense to say that you were able to identify rikpa thanks to years of reading, studying, practicing, purifying, and receiving pointing-out instructions from a lama. From your side, it may *seem* like this realization occurred in dependence upon causes and conditions, such as encountering Dzokchen guidance and so forth. However, to reiterate, rikpa is self-emergent in the sense that when it is actualized, suddenly, it is there. From the side of pristine awareness, which is atemporal, there is no sequence of cause and effect.

This is a crucial point. Therefore, "Recognize for yourself that the dharma-kāya is none other than this great, empty, luminous, self-emergent pristine awareness, which transcends cognition." No matter how hard you think about it, your cognition will never be able to wrap itself around pristine awareness.

Düdjom Rinpoché continues with the meditation instruction. He gave the pointing-out instruction in the prior pith instructions on "Identifying the View of the Nature of Existence," and now he is explaining how you sustain that view in meditation, within the triad of view, meditation, and conduct:

> Do not construct or alter anything in the momentary conscious-ness of the present, in which past thoughts have ceased and later ones have not arisen. By so doing, settle your ordinary conscious-ness in its natural, unmodified state, uncontaminated by thoughts concerning the three times, resting in the fourth time that tran-scends the three times. Come to the firm conviction that apart from this there is nothing whatsoever upon which to meditate.

This is what Düdjom Rinpoché means when he advises that when resting in the stillness of awareness right now, in the interval between when "past thoughts have ceased and later ones have not arisen," in the place where there is no dualistic grasping—no object to grasp onto, and therefore no subject who is grasping—right there, is rikpa. That is one way to cut through your conditioned mind to the unconditioned.

By not constructing or altering anything in this place, "settle your ordi-nary consciousness in its natural, unmodified state." Here, "ordinary con-sciousness" refers to the consciousness that is already there. This is why the term "ordinary consciousness" is sometimes used as an equivalent to rikpa. It is the consciousness that is already there before you start layering elabo-rations, grasping, and so forth onto it. Again, rikpa is not something to be achieved or acquired *later*—it is already here.

As for it being "uncontaminated," it can never be contaminated, though you can certainly veil it with mental elaborations. In this way, "uncontam-inated" here means unveiled. Düdjom Rinpoché identifies that veiling, or contamination, saying, remain "uncontaminated by thoughts concerning the three times." The three times are the past, present, and future. "Ordinary consciousness," here referring to pristine awareness, itself is unborn, unceasing, unconditioned, trans-temporal, and knows ultimate reality since it knows nirvāṇa, which also transcends time. Nirvāṇa is not located in the past, present, or future; it is not confined in a momentary "present" that is bracketed between the past and the future. It is timeless. In that sense, pristine awareness transcends the three times, and it is said to dwell "in the fourth time."

Now, a śrāvaka arhat who realizes nirvāṇa realizes the dharmadhātu, which, again, transcends the three times. Since nirvāṇa is timeless, unborn, and unceasing, then the bliss of realizing nirvāṇa is an immutable, unborn, and unceasing bliss. When this practice of resting in pristine awareness comes to its fruition, its culmination in perfect buddhahood, pristine awareness manifests fully and simultaneously in the primordial consciousness that perceives the full range of phenomena. In this regard, pristine awareness is dwelling "in the fourth time that transcends the three times" of the past, present, and future. It not only transcends, but it pervades the three times, which is a state unique to the mind of a buddha. No one but a buddha has an all-pervasive, unimpeded perception of the full range of phenomena, saṃsāra, impure appearances, and pure appearances. No one but a buddha knows the perspective of every other buddha, of every vidyādhara, of every bodhisattva, and also knows what it is like to be in a hell realm, deva realm, and everything in between in the past, present, and future.

Düdjom Rinpoché advises, "Come to the firm conviction that apart from this there is nothing whatsoever upon which to meditate." This technique of meditation is a profound, radical not-doing—for example, not doing anything with your body, such as circumambulating stūpas or reciting mantras. Simply do not do anything at all with your body. To elaborate, *The Enlightened View of Samantabhadra* describes three modes of nonmodification, saying,

> Motionlessly rest your body without modification like a corpse
> in a charnel ground, silently rest your voice without speaking,
> and luminously rest your mind without modification in its own

place. It is crucially important to apply yourself to these three points, devoting yourself to practice without faltering throughout the three times. Post-meditative practice entails allowing all your behavior to be unmodified, while moving and resting, without diverging from your natural state.⁹¹

The key here is to rest your mind in its natural state, like space that is utterly devoid of activity. In other words, you take the nine modes of coarse, medium, and subtle activities of body, speech, and mind, and completely release these activities into space, coming to rest right where you are. These nine modes of activity are as follows: *The activities of body*: (1) outer activities of walking, sitting, and moving about; (2) inner activities of prostrations and circumambulations; and (3) secret activities of ritual dancing, performing mudrās, and so on. *The activities of speech*: (4) outer activities, such as all kinds of delusional chatter; (5) inner activities, such as reciting liturgies; and (6) secret activities, such as counting propitiatory mantras of your personal deity. *The activities of mind*: (7) outer activities, such as thoughts aroused by the five poisons and the three poisons; (8) inner activities, such as mind training and cultivating positive thoughts; and (9) secret activities, such as dwelling in mundane states of dhyāna.

This is the meditation technique of tekchö, or cutting through, and it entails nothing whatsoever apart from this. You are resting without doing anything, without desiring anything, without modifying anything, and without striving for anything. It can be said to be "the perfection of contentment," which is utterly not doing anything at all. Then, in that way, the floodgates open, and a wellspring of the realizations, the siddhis, all-encompassing compassion, and the myriad abilities of dharmakāya flood in. Thus, the mental obscurations of a sentient being have been purified and cleared, and you are thus able to rest in buddha-mind.

Düdjom Rinpoché continues his instruction, saying,

Come to the indwelling, confident freedom of nakedly realizing that whatever arises and everything that appears is a display of the dharmakāya, empty awareness, free of cognition. Upon this basis, settle your consciousness in a state of effortless relaxation, like space, free of extremes.

The term "free of extremes" means the complete absence of conceptual constructs or elaborations that grasp onto the following pairs of "extremes" as real: (1) existence and nonexistence, (2) arising and passing, (3) coming and going, and (4) being one or plural.

Düdjom Rinpoché continues,

> At that time, [outwardly,] even though the objects of the six senses do appear, let your awareness be self-illuminating, utterly naked, and free of grasping. Inwardly, let your mind be devoid of conceptual, analytical excursions and withdrawals, nakedly self-awakened. In between, awareness rests in its own place, and without being bound by antidotes, awareness remains uninterruptedly with the gaze straight ahead, uninfluenced by good or bad objects, and uncontaminated by grasping. Without letting cognition intrude with its remedies for countering obstacles, directly recognize the vividly clear aspect of cognizance. Sustaining awareness in this way—unobstructedly and nakedly— is a distinctive characteristic of the Great Perfection.

This passage describes open presence resting in pristine awareness. In this state, there is no censorship, no withdrawal, no focusing, and no directing the attention away from or toward anything. You are resting in timeless, atemporal pristine awareness and allowing the light of your pristine awareness to flow out in all directions unimpededly. This light illuminates all of the six fields of perception.

Letting your awareness be "utterly naked, and free of grasping" means to let it be unelaborated and uncloaked by any of the activities of the mind. "Inwardly, let your mind be devoid of conceptual, analytical excursions and withdrawals" describes the mental process akin to going out on a trip, returning, thinking about the trip, and returning again—setting out on one

conceptual trip after another. These conceptual, analytical trips and ruminations are to be released. From this place of letting go, devoid of analytical outward and inward voyages, be "nakedly self-awakened." In this state,
outwardly, all the senses are open, and inwardly, all the senses are devoid of
conceptual excursions.

There is outward and there is inward, and then there is "in between."
From this in-between place, "awareness rests in its own place, and without
being bound by antidotes, awareness remains uninterruptedly with the gaze
straight ahead, uninfluenced by good or bad objects." You are experiencing all appearances as being of one taste: no good, no bad, no influence, no
desire or aversion. Everything is uninfluenced, unwavering, and timelessly
still.

Further, he states, rest in this place in a way that is "uncontaminated by
grasping. Without letting cognition intrude with its remedies for countering obstacles, directly recognize the vividly clear aspect of cognizance.
Sustaining awareness in this way—unobstructedly and nakedly—is a
distinctive characteristic of the Great Perfection." This is distinctively
Dzokchen meditation. As Düdjom Rinpoché instructed earlier, "Do not
construct or alter anything"; simply rest in awareness. Since you have internalized the view of the Great Perfection, this sitting and doing nothing—
this "nonmeditation," as it is called—is thoroughly imbued and saturated
by the view of the Great Perfection. There is nowhere to go from here; there
is nothing to achieve or for which to aspire.

Gyatrul Rinpoché comments here: "According to this rediscovered treasure from the wrathful emanation of Guru Rinpoché, Dorjé Drolö, open
luminosity is the nature of Dorjé Drolö."[92] He is clearly identifying this as
a *terma* revealed to Düdjom Rinpoché by Dorjé Drolö, a manifestation of
Guru Rinpoché. Bear in mind that luminosity is the *creative*, sambhogakāya aspect, whereas the *empty* aspect of pristine awareness is dharmakāya.
Sambhogakāya is the luminous aspect manifesting in these spontaneously
self-emergent displays. Then, manifesting out of the sambhogakāya, all
manner of emanations of nirmāṇakāya of the four kinds arise spontaneously, effortlessly, and unimpededly as pure expressions of dharmakāya.

Your consciousness has two distinctive, defining characteristics: luminosity and cognizance. It is the luminosity of your own awareness right now, your ordinary consciousness, which makes manifest all appearances. This luminosity also gives rise to and manifests as the creativity of the human mind, carrying with it all manner of ingenious ideas, music, literature, art, technology, and science. All the creativity of your own consciousness consists of displays of the luminosity of your own consciousness. The other defining characteristic of your ordinary consciousness is cognizance, which is simply knowing. The luminosity illuminates and makes manifest appearances, while the cognizance of your own consciousness right now is that which enables you to know. The culmination of this creativity and knowing is that the luminosity of primordial consciousness perceives the full range of phenomena while the cognizance of dharmakāya, or pristine awareness, knows dharmadhātu, reality as it is. These two terms—luminosity and cognizance—are profoundly coupled; they are inseparable. This open luminosity is the manifest nature of Dorjé Drolö. Gyatrul Rinpoché continues,

> This refers to the [manifest] nature of the mind of all buddhas, which is the nature of all meditative deities, of all lamas, ḍākinīs, and true objects of refuge. In order to realize that nature, you do not need to search any place other than within yourselves.[93]

Sustaining the View through Meditation

Since Dzokchen meditation consists of nothing more than sustaining open presence while resting in pristine awareness, the instructions here build upon the instructions given in the previous section on "Coming to Conviction by Means of the View," but now it's all about sustaining that view through meditation.

This type of meditation is authentic "open presence" that is open in all directions—outwardly, with all six doors of perception fully open, and, inwardly, being totally free of all grasping and of the coarse, medium, and subtle activities of body, speech, and mind. There have been yogis in the past who have settled their minds in their natural state in the substrate consciousness and who erroneously think they are resting in open presence in the empty, essential nature of pristine awareness, beyond concepts. In this way, they are confusing śamatha with Dzokchen nonmeditation, which is a huge mistake. This was a problem that goes back for centuries in Tibet. In *The Vajra Essence*, the Lake-Born Vajra explains that this is very common in regard to śamatha, stating, "The state that becomes manifest, in which the appearances of self, others, and objects have vanished, and in which there is an inwardly focused grasping to the experiences of vacuity and luminosity, is the *substrate consciousness*."[94]

From this place, you are simultaneously aware of the vacuity of the substrate consciousness and the luminosity revealed by self-illuminating mindfulness, the fourth kind of mindfulness. This vacuity and luminosity are indivisible and co-extensive. This is a state in which "the appearances of self, others, and objects have vanished." The only object is the sheer vacuity illuminated by the substrate consciousness. As the Lake-Born Vajra says, "Some teachers say that the substrate to which you descend is the 'one taste' or 'freedom from conceptual elaboration,' but others say it is ethically unspecified."[95]

There, you have descended to the substrate, and some teachers tell yogis who have slipped into the substrate and come out that this is the "one taste," but the "one taste" is way beyond śamatha; it is the third of the four yogas of Mahāmudrā. The yoga of one taste is viewing the whole of reality from the perspective of pristine awareness and seeing all appearances—evil, sublime, beautiful, ugly, virtuous, nonvirtuous—as equally empty of inherent nature and as primordially pure expressions of pristine awareness. Resting in the substrate consciousness, however, is not freedom from conceptual elaboration, nor is it the yoga of one taste; rather, it is ethically unspecified.

The Lake-Born Vajra concludes here, "Whatever they call it, in truth you have come to the essential nature [of the mind]."[96] Note that this resting in the substrate consciousness is the *obscurative* essential nature and not the *ultimate* essential nature of the mind. The yogis who come to rest in the substrate consciousness and realize *that* as the obscurative essential nature of the mind have not yet fathomed *primordial* consciousness, which is the ultimate essential nature of the mind. From the obscurative essential nature, you are now realizing the sheer luminosity and cognizance of consciousness. The mysteries of consciousness within conditioned reality are revealed to you. It is like holding a cup of tea and knowing clearly what it is. There is no mystery about the cup or the tea. Similarly, obscurative consciousness—conditioned consciousness, the human mind, the substrate consciousness—is no more a mystery. Those who have achieved śamatha have fathomed it, let alone an authentic Dzokchen practitioner who enters into the practice of cutting through and then cuts through to pristine awareness.

Impure Śamatha and the Way to Pure Śamatha

"Impure śamatha" entails resting in the vacuity of the substrate, which seems to correspond to the Theravāda view of the bhavaṅga. The bhavaṅga is the ground of becoming that arises right after you perceive the "counterpart sign" in the practice of śamatha. The classic Theravāda teachings elucidate on how you gradually achieve śamatha with the preliminary sign, the acquired sign, and the counterpart sign, the final of which is a sign, or an appearance, that arises from the form realm and from simultaneous access to the first dhyāna. For example, in the practice of mindfulness of breathing, first the preliminary sign is the tactile sensations of the breath at the nostrils or above the upper lip. Then the acquired sign will arise which is a purely mental sign that is somehow symbolic of the element of air. Focusing on that, the counterpart sign of the air element then breaks through. The great Theravāda commentator Buddhaghosa writes in his classic work *The Path of Purification (Visuddhimagga)*:

> The counterpart sign appears as if breaking out from the acquired sign, and a hundred times, a thousand times more purified, like a looking-glass disk drawn from its case, like a mother-of-pearl dish well washed, like the moon's disk coming out from behind a cloud, like cranes against a thunder cloud. But it has neither color nor shape . . . it is born only of perception in one who has obtained concentration, being a mere model of appearance.[97]

The counterpart sign is considerably subtler than the acquired sign. When that counterpart sign arises, your mind has crossed the threshold over into the form realm. You have achieved śamatha and access to the first dhyāna.

In most cases, having had a glimpse of that extremely subtle archetypal form of the air element, its subtlety is such that you cannot retain it. Since you cannot hold on, you lose it and then you fall back into the bhavaṅga, back into the substrate. You do not go unconscious, but you are not conscious of much. It is like being in a lucid, dreamless state—there is no sense of the passage of time, and so on. It is "impure" śamatha because it is not self-illuminating. In the Theravāda tradition, once you have achieved that, then it is encouraged to come out and start practicing vipaśyanā or return to practicing śamatha. Having achieved access to the first dhyāna, your five obscurations are subdued, and then you have access to the five dhyāna factors. However, the five dhyāna factors are not as robust as they could be if you were to return to śamatha, regain access to that very subtle, quintessential archetype of the air element, retrieve it, focus on it, achieve śamatha on that, and then fully achieve the first dhyāna. You are not encouraged to remain in the bhavaṅga indefinitely, as it would not take you further toward the path to enlightenment. It would be akin to resting in deep, dreamless sleep.

At the beginning of this subsection, Düdjom Rinpoché said: "Come to the indwelling, confident freedom of nakedly realizing that whatever arises and everything that appears is a display of the dharmakāya, empty awareness, free of cognition. Upon this basis, settle your consciousness in a state of effortless relaxation, like space, free of extremes." To reiterate, it is crucially important to know that when you are resting in rikpa, you are approaching the state of becoming a vidyādhara, where the realization is utterly unmediated. At this point, you have achieved śamatha, vipaśyanā, and have identified rikpa, but your realization of emptiness is still veiled by conceptualization. It is like seeing the sun, but through the clouds of conceptualization. You are seeing it, yet not without mediation. Likewise, you have identified pristine awareness, but are still identifying it with your mind. There are still the veils of dualistic grasping even though you are on the right track, resting there in the achievement of śamatha with a degree of realization of emptiness and a degree of realization of rikpa. Now, though, you must familiarize yourself with it continuously. Then as you gain deeper and deeper realization, you see clearly and eventually nonconceptually, without mediation. You have the realization of empty awareness that is naked and free of cognition, or activities of the dualistic mind. You realize that all phenomena, external and internal, are empty of inherent nature, which is the cognizance that is knowing reality as it is. Yet, the other aspect of primordial consciousness is seeing all appearances that arise as displays of primordial consciousness. This is analogous to perceiving the full range of phenomena.

The first point here is a realization that "whatever arises and everything that appears is a display of the dharmakāya." This is indicative of Dzokchen and Mahāmudrā, where you are not only seeing appearances as empty, but are seeing them from the perspective of pristine awareness and as displays of your own primordial consciousness. From here, the whole notion of "obstacle" becomes a term without a referent, for displays of pristine awareness could never obstruct you on the path to enlightenment.

Thus, "empty awareness, free of cognition" is the essential nature, the emptiness, of pristine awareness that is dharmakāya. The luminous realization that "whatever arises and everything that appears is a display of the dharmakāya" is the sambhogakāya as the unborn luminosity of the dharmakāya and its unimpeded compassion as the nirmāṇakāya. In other words, that luminous aspect which is the manifest nature of pristine awareness is sambhogakāya. The sambhogakāya—specifically when you come out of meditative equipoise and into the post-meditative state—manifests spontaneously and unconditionally in all manner of ways as nirmāṇakāya, which is unimpeded, unconditioned, spontaneous compassion.

Düdjom Rinpoché concludes the subsection on "Practicing by Means of Meditation" with the following words: "Without letting cognition intrude with its remedies for countering obstacles, directly recognize the vividly clear aspect of cognizance. Sustaining awareness in this way—unobstructedly and nakedly—is a distinctive characteristic of the Great Perfection." That is, without trying to fix things when there are no obstacles to fix, simply recognize the vivid, clear aspect of cognizance, which is also the luminous aspect of pristine awareness. Again, do not conflate pristine awareness with the substrate consciousness. It could be a real problem if you are at the initial stages of practice in śamatha and already think you are resting in rikpa. It is an obstacle to think you know something that, in fact, you do not actually know. As long as you think your ignorance is knowledge, you will be unable to overcome ignorance and, thus, gain true knowledge.

Further Notes on Open Presence

As mentioned in the previous section, Dzokchen meditation consists of sustaining open presence while resting in pristine awareness. Considering the centrality of open presence in Dzokchen, it would be worthwhile to pause here to consider what open presence is, and what it isn't.

It would be a mistake to think that the Dzokchen practice of open presence is the same as the mindfulness practice of simply resting in the present moment in a nonjudgmental way. Equating these two practices implies that open presence contains no view, no conduct, no preliminary practices, no renunciation, and no bodhicitta. Some may equate open presence with *zazen* or mindfulness practice; some see it as being the essence of all meditation. Similarly, some popular Dzokchen teachers dilute open presence down to just being moment-to-moment, nonjudgmentally aware of anything that arises. All of these popular misconceptions fundamentally misunderstand what open presence actually is and tend to override or ignore its richness and profundity.

One of our best authorities on open presence is Sera Khandro (1892–1940), a ḍākinī, a woman, an accomplished treasure-revealer, and the spiritual partner of one of the sons of Düdjom Lingpa, Drimé Özer. In her definitive commentary to Düdjom Lingpa's revealed text *Buddhahood Without Meditation*,[98] entitled *Garland for the Delight of the Fortunate*,[99] Sera Khandro, speaking for the whole Dzokchen tradition, not just the Düdjom lineage, discusses open presence in the context of four aspects: (1) view; (2) meditation; (3) pristine awareness, or rikpa; and (4) appearances and mindsets. Addressing these four sequentially, she begins by saying,

(1) Regarding the view of open presence, the great uniform pervasiveness of the view transcends intellectual grasping at signs, does not succumb to bias or extremes, and realizes unconditioned reality, which is like space.[100]

Here, Sera Khandro is asserting that open presence must be imbued with the view of emptiness and must realize "unconditioned reality"; otherwise, it is not Dzokchen open presence. This is the *view* of open presence.

Sera Khandro continues,

> (2) Regarding the meditation of open presence, just as the water of the great ocean is the same above and below, whatever arises is none other than the nature of ultimate reality. Just as water is permeated by lucid clarity, in ultimate reality there is no saṃsāra or nirvāṇa, no joy or sorrow, and so forth, for you realize that everything dissolves into uniform pervasiveness as displays of clear light.[101]

As you are resting in authentic open presence, you realize all appearances arising as primordially pure displays of dharmakāya. Your whole world is divine, and this is the *meditation* of open presence.

Sera Khandro then clarifies the meaning of open presence in pristine awareness:

> (3) Regarding open presence in pristine awareness, just as the supreme mountain in the center of this world system is unmovable, pristine awareness transcends time, without wavering even for an instant from the nature of its own great luminosity.[102]

This luminosity is unborn, unwavering, and primordially still, which is pristine awareness itself.

However, there are all the appearances and mindsets of open presence that manifest—appearances not only of the surrounding environment by way of the five physical sense doors, but the movements of the mind, states of consciousness, mental activities, thoughts, and so forth. She addresses these, saying,

> (4) Regarding open presence in appearances and mindsets, all appearing phenomena are naturally empty and self-illuminating. They are not apprehended by cognition, not grasped by the

mind, and not subdued by awareness. Rather, they dissolve into great uniform pervasiveness, so they are liberated with no basis for acceptance or rejection, no bias for luminosity or emptiness, and no doubt as to whether they are or are not [this or that].[103]

How do you see the appearances of the activities of the mind, that is, the mindsets? They are naturally empty, of course, but what is it that causes them to manifest? Does pristine awareness shine a bright light on them, like a projector on a movie screen? This would imply a kind of duality: appearances over here and pristine awareness over there. Rather, it is nondual, and thus, all appearances are self-illuminating. When viewing appearances and mindsets from the perspective of pristine awareness, there is no preference, as "they are liberated with no basis for acceptance or rejection." Without preference, there is nothing to grab onto; everything is of "one taste." Thus, there is no distinction between luminosity and emptiness, and there is no ambivalence or doubt.

Summing up the essence of Dzokchen open presence meditation, Gyatrul Rinpoché says,

> This luminous, open experience, which is the self-originating nature of one's mind, does not need to be searched for as a separate meditation experience. You should not consider that you're trying to create an artificial experience. It is simply recognizing and remaining directly introduced to your own nature.[104]

❖ Meditation: Vipaśyanā as the Prelude to Authentic Open Presence

https://wisdomexperience.org/alan-wallace-dzokchen-meditation-13/

While in a comfortable posture, strike the three vital points of your body, speech, and mind.

Very briefly and gently, calm the turbulence of your conceptual mind by resting in the stillness of awareness and counting seven breaths—one count for each full cycle of the respiration. In between the counts, let your mind be quiet. As far as possible, have just seven thoughts during the seven cycles of respiration, beginning with thinking the number "one," up to "seven."

With your gaze resting vacantly in the space in front of you, your eyes soft and unfocused, your mind utterly at rest, and your awareness resting right where it is, engage in the first practice that Düdjom Rinpoché teaches in the context of śamatha: Simply rest in the self-knowing flow of awareness without being distracted by appearances, thoughts, and so on, and without grasping onto or identifying with any mental impulse. Rest in the utter simplicity of the sheer luminosity and cognizance of your own awareness.

While resting continuously in awareness, open all of the six doors of perception. Let the light of awareness flow out unimpededly in all directions. Be aware of all manner of appearances—sensory appearances from the surrounding world, mental appearances of thoughts, images, and so on—and see them for what they are. See them nakedly, without projecting upon them any conceptual constructs, and without appropriating or reifying them. See all of these appearances for what they are; they appear, but they are not really there. They are neither here nor there; they are just where they are. See them as empty, as mere appearances, all the way through. These sensory and mental appearances come and go as movements of the mind. Observe all these movements, the comings and goings of appearances, from the stillness of your awareness.

As the Buddha said to Bāhiya, recorded in the Pāli canon, "In the seen, let there be only the seen; in the heard, let there be only the heard; in the tactilely sensed, let there be only the tactilely sensed; and in the mentally perceived, let there be only the mentally perceived."[105] Likewise, see all appearances nakedly, without elaboration.

All around you is a field of emptiness—albeit, not a nihilistic emptiness; it is filled with possibilities. It is up to you what you observe, how you designate what you observe, and, thereby, how you actualize the world around you. Ultimately, it is your mind that constructs your experience of the world that you inhabit.

Now, turn your awareness inward upon the movements of your own mind. Briefly examine where these movements, thoughts, desires, and so on originate. Moment by moment, where are they located and where do they go? In observing nakedly the activities of the mind, do not identify with, reify, or appropriate them. Practicing in this way is the direct path for freeing yourself from the bondage of the mind. Become lucid with respect to your mind, and you can thus become fearless and invulnerable with respect to your mind. Simply know it as it is.

Then, turn your awareness increasingly more inward. Withdraw from the apprehended mind and into the mind that is apprehending—the mind that observes, meditates, and does all manner of things. Invert your awareness right in upon the mind that is turning inward on itself—the mind that is the agent—and see what you see. Does it have any characteristics that you can identify?

From moment to moment, as it arises and passes, can you see from where it comes, where it is located, and where it goes? There must be a mind, otherwise you would be mindless and unable to meditate. Yet the mind is not static and unchanging. Rest contentedly in that nonfinding, in that open space with nothing apprehended and no apprehender. Be content in that utter simplicity.

During the intervals between thoughts, rest in this stillness that is unelaborated awareness. Continue to rest there when thoughts arise without allowing these thoughts to cause your awareness to waver even the slightest bit. See these thoughts and any other appearances as expressions of your own awareness, as not existing by their own nature, as indeterminate and neither existent nor nonexistent. In utter and sublime stillness with all the sense doors open, remaining attentive, discerning, and nonconceptual, view how all appearances are empty; the mind is empty. Rest in this open space that is permeated by the luminosity of awareness, this space of infinite potential and possibilities, where all that is actualized consists of expressions of your own awareness. Relax right there quietly, without doing anything at all.

Bring this meditation session to a close by dedicating the merit in accordance with the prayers of the bodhisattvas, so that you may achieve perfect awakening in order to tirelessly help all others do the same. ❖

C. Sustaining Continuity by Means of One's Conduct

WITHIN THE TRIAD of view, meditation, and conduct, the next subsection of the text addresses conduct. Just as the practice of meditation is simply about sustaining the view that has been identified, likewise Dzokchen *conduct* refers to everything you do when not in meditative equipoise, or formal meditation. What type of lifestyle—what way of life, or conduct—is there to completely support, nurture, and sustain the realization you have gained by first identifying the view and then sustaining it by the practice of Dzokchen meditation? How do you sustain that realization when off the cushion so that it becomes completely continuous through every moment, both during meditative equipoise and during the post-meditative state?

Düdjom Rinpoché's root verse begins,

In this way, if you achieve stability through familiarization,

You have begun to achieve the unwavering continuity of "**stability through familiarization**" while in meditation, but it must not stop when you come out of meditation. You cannot break that flow and continue on the path to awakening unless you sustain the familiarization process continuously, both on and off the cushion.

Düdjom Rinpoché then writes in his commentary:

> While in meditative equipoise, utterly release into this self-illumination, without contaminating the primordial

consciousness of naked, empty awareness with grasping or clinging. During the post-meditative state, without grasping, decisively ascertain everything that appears as being luminous and
empty, like illusory apparitions or the appearances of a dream.

The "self-illumination" mentioned here has strong parallels with śamatha.
Specifically, the fourth and culminating type of mindfulness in śamatha
is the self-illuminating mindfulness discussed earlier in the section on the
four types of mindfulness. This self-illuminating mindfulness is inwardly
directed mindfulness of the substrate consciousness, which is the *obscurative* ground of your mind. Here, though, you are releasing utterly into the
self-illumination of *pristine awareness*, or primordial consciousness. Here,
Düdjom Rinpoché says to "utterly release into this self-illumination, without contaminating the primordial consciousness of naked, empty awareness
with grasping or clinging." In other words, there is still the possibility that
the old habitual propensities for grasping and clinging can creep in, especially when you are off the cushion and engaging with other things. Your
practice now is to release into this self-illumination, this "primordial consciousness of naked, empty awareness," without contaminating or veiling it
"with grasping or clinging."

Further, "During the post-meditative state, without grasping, decisively
ascertain everything that appears as being luminous and empty, like illusory apparitions or the appearances of a dream." At a more superficial level,
this is the same approach to post-meditation that one has after achieving
śamatha. The difference here, however, is that now you are seeing appearances as being luminous displays of pristine awareness and not just appearances arising in the substrate, empty of substantiality. When you come out
of meditative equipoise in śamatha, you see all the appearances around you
as insubstantial, but that doesn't mean you have realized the emptiness of
inherent nature of all appearances and objects of the entire phenomenal
world. In ascertaining all appearances as luminous and empty, and in seeing them as "illusory apparitions or the appearances of a dream," you then
become totally lucid in the waking state. The key here is to avoid having this
lucidity slip away in the conduct of your post-meditation. This unwavering
lucidity is a taste of what the Buddha said of his own experience when he

was asked if he was a human being, and he responded, "No, I am awake." That is, he no longer regarded himself as the human being that *you* see in your nonlucid state, but rather, he was awake and totally lucid.

In dream yoga, as you become lucid, you are not *fully* lucid until you fully fathom the nature of the dream as a dream. Likewise, those in the first phase of being a fully matured vidyādhara corresponding to the first vision are lucid, but not yet thoroughly lucid since they are still prone to grasping or clinging. In viewing all phenomena in the waking state as if they were appearances in a dream, it is important not to conflate dreams you had while sleeping with this dreamlike experience in the waking state. You know the difference between the two even while you see how profoundly similar they are.

Düdjom Rinpoché continues his analysis of the post-meditative conduct of Dzokchen, saying,

> By taking this as the spiritual path, periods of meditative equipoise and post-meditative states will merge indivisibly. As all appearances will manifestly release themselves, thoughts will arise as aids to meditation.

When he says, "By taking this as the spiritual path," "this" refers to the practice just discussed of seeing all appearances as being "luminous and empty, like illusory apparitions or the appearances of a dream." Through this practice, he says, "periods of meditative equipoise and post-meditative states will merge indivisibly." This merged state is the whole point. It is the same for the āryabodhisattva on the sūtra path: You plunge into the depths of meditative equipoise in a nonconceptual, unmediated realization of emptiness in which there are no phenomena appearing at all, and then emerge from meditation and see all appearances as arising from emptiness and dissolving back into emptiness. Once this emptiness is seen, you plunge back into meditative equipoise and then reemerge into the post-meditative state repeatedly, in and out, in and out. Through this simple practice—which comprises the basis of "conduct" in the context of Dzokchen—any distinction between your realization while in meditative equipoise and your realization while in the post-meditative state fades and dissolves, until the two are indivisible.

At this point, what is one to do about the arising of thoughts as you move from meditation to post-meditation? Düdjom Rinpoché says, "As all appearances will manifestly release themselves, thoughts will arise as aids to meditation." Thoughts for a beginner *obscure* the natural luminosity of the substrate consciousness, obscure your insight into emptiness, and in early phases, they may also obscure glimpses of pristine awareness. Now, however, you are dwelling so deeply in pristine awareness that when thoughts arise, you see them clearly as creative displays of pristine awareness, effulgences of dharmakāya. Accordingly, rather than obscuring, obstructing, or afflicting anything, thoughts actually arise as aids to your meditation.

Düdjom Rinpoché's commentary then addresses the problem posed by the arising of thoughts, saying,

> If you are afflicted by thoughts, piercingly focus your attention
> on whatever roving thoughts arise. By so doing, thoughts will
> vanish without a trace, just as waves disappear into water.

Even at this advanced stage, thoughts can still disturb you. Therefore, at an even deeper level, when thoughts arise, do not focus on the referent of the thought, but rather piercingly focus your *pristine* awareness right into the nature of the thoughts themselves. By directing your attention in this way, "thoughts will vanish without a trace, just as waves disappear into water." Here, parallels are seen clearly from the very early phase of working with thoughts as they arise.

As you approach the substrate consciousness, when thoughts or movements of the mind of craving and attachment arise, peer into them simply with your mental awareness of a sentient being. By so doing, you pierce right through to see the three salient qualities of the substrate consciousness. Cutting through the toxicity of the afflictive and disturbing qualities of the mental affliction of attachment, or craving, you thus see bliss. When thoughts of hatred or hostility arise, instead of looking at the object of the hatred, focus right in upon the mental affliction of hatred; pierce directly through its toxicity to something that is pure within the substrate consciousness—its luminosity. Likewise, when you are practicing śamatha and the mind becomes dull, pierce right into the dullness; do not appropriate or identify with it, but instead go straight into the dullness and see nonconceptuality. In Dzokchen, you are not simply pointing the spear of your ordinary consciousness, but rather are pointing the spear of *pristine awareness* and cutting through to the ultimate ground of any mental affliction, thereby seeing from this perspective that they are in no way afflictive. They are simply expressions of dharmakāya, and specifically, the five facets of primordial consciousness.

Tertön Sögyal Lerab Lingpa, a teacher of the Thirteenth Dalai Lama, commented,

> By resting the mind in its natural state, sensations of bliss may arise, such as pleasant physical and mental sensations, experiences of luminosity, such as the clarity of consciousness, and experiences of nonconceptuality, such as the appearance of empty forms, as well as a nonconceptual sense that nothing can harm your mind, regardless of whether or not thoughts have ceased.[106]

As you become deeply familiar with settling the mind in its natural state, even if thoughts and images arise, you will know they cannot possibly harm you as you rest in the safety and stillness of awareness. Your practice, which on the surface looks so similar to śamatha, is now imbued with the unwavering insight that whatever appearances arise—including thoughts, emotions, feelings, memories, intentions, desires, and whatever else comes up in the mind—they have no basis. They are not rooted in reality but are appearances all the way up and all the way down. They are without essence, nothing but empty appearances. They arise spontaneously and effortlessly, and they dissolve and release themselves effortlessly. Witnessing the insubstantial nature of appearances in this way, you then know beyond any shadow of a doubt that this sentient being's mind can no longer harm you.

Düdjom Rinpoché concludes this section on conduct by saying,

Once the certainty arises that thoughts have no basis or root, your practice will proceed joyfully. In short, during all your activities, do not succumb to the delusive proliferations of your ordinary cognition, but, like the current of a river, continuously practice this yoga that is free of distraction and of grasping. In this way, you will come to the culmination of familiarization with the practice.

Here, he describes resting "free of distraction and of grasping" to the ruminations, thoughts, afflictions, or fantasies of your ordinary, dualistic mind. This passage correlates with the first practice taught in this text, and is why the initial phase of śamatha—settling the mind in its natural state—is included *within* the context of the Dzokchen practice of cutting through to the original purity of pristine awareness. Śamatha is not simply preliminary; it is the *first step* of Dzokchen meditation. The method of developing śamatha is similar as you progress along this path, but now your practice goes deeper and deeper.

From this deeper place, you are a vidyādhara—albeit, the first phase of being a vidyādhara is that the old habitual propensities of your ordinary mind naturally continue to proliferate. Düdjom Rinpoché advises not to succumb to that proliferation, "but, like the current of a river, continuously practice this yoga that is free of distraction and of grasping." That is, neither be carried away from pristine awareness, nor let it be veiled by dualistic grasping, since the possibility of that is still a risk. Instead, now that you have become a stream-enterer as a vidyādhara, continue "like the current of a river . . . In this way, you will come to the culmination of familiarization with the practice." Familiarization is crucial, ensuring that there is complete saturation with no lapses in resting in pristine awareness, free of activity.

The Conduct of a Buddha

At this point in the practice, you have become thoroughly familiarized with the view and meditation, and you have come to know who you truly are, recognizing your own mind as the dharmakāya. However, since you are not yet manifestly and perfectly a buddha, it is still possible to slip back into amnesia. When it comes to conduct on the basis of the view and meditation, simply put, your sole task is not to do anything a buddha wouldn't do, so that everything a buddha *would* do can manifest in your conduct. A buddha engages in all manner of activity spontaneously and effortlessly as displays of virtue in the service of all sentient beings.

So, what *wouldn't* a buddha do? What would primordial consciousness *not* do? The buddha-mind, your dharmakāya, is as vast as space itself; it is luminous, transcendent, unimpeded, and has the seven qualities of a vajra. What the buddha-mind would *not* do is shrink down to the size of thoughts, be abducted by them, and then carried away. The buddha-mind would not appropriate, identify with, or collapse down to the size of your mind or body, with thoughts of "I, me, and mine." If the buddha-mind were to do that, it would not be a buddha-mind. The buddha-mind would never be perturbed by any of the fluctuations of your emotions and desires, nor would it ever reify any of your experiences. Primordial consciousness is primordially, infinitely, and timelessly free of all mental afflictions, including the delusion of reification. The buddha-mind would never move or have the sense of being moved because of identifying with something within this field of delusive appearances.

Yet, the buddha-mind is not simply inert; it is not like space. Nirvāṇa is like space and is inert—it does not do anything and is timeless and primordially still. However, there is more to a buddha than the primordial stillness of the dharmadhātu. That is, there are the active form kāyas, or *rūpakāya*—including the rarefied sambhogakāya, which manifests only to āryabodhisattvas, vidyādharas, and other buddhas, and the four kinds of nirmāṇakāyas, which manifest to all manner of sentient beings. The buddhas train each sentient being according to each being's capacities, spontaneously manifesting enlightened activity of any of the four kinds to help subdue the mental afflictions of those they meet, leading them gently on the path to their own liberation. They are both infinitely active and primordially still.

Thus, in between sessions, do not do anything a buddha wouldn't do. When you are resting in pristine awareness, you are really not *doing* anything at all. You are *being* aware and are *being* dharmakāya; in other words, while in meditative equipoise as a vidyādhara, the empty, essential nature of your mind *is* dharmakāya. The luminous, manifest nature of your own awareness *is* sambhogakāya. In post-meditation, as you are engaging with the world and looking out upon a whole range of phenomena of the world around you, nirmāṇakāyas spontaneously emanate as expressions of omnipresent, spontaneous compassion from the depth of the empty and luminous nature of your awareness. Sitting in meditative equipoise, you are absolutely free of any activation of the body, speech, and mind of a sentient being. You become so deeply familiarized with that resting that you release any identification with being a sentient being at all. From here, the whole point is to maintain that continuity off the cushion. Thereby, whatever thoughts arise are pure expressions of dharmakāya; whatever speech arises is a pure expression of sambhogakāya; and whatever physical activities you engage in are pure expressions of nirmāṇakāya. In this way, do not do anything a buddha wouldn't do, so that everything a buddha *would* do can manifest through you without impediment or obscuration.

The conduct specified here in this text is the ultimate perfection of lojong. There are different types of lojong, with some of the most well-known being taught in Śāntideva's *Guide to the Bodhisattva Way of Life*, the Third Dodrupchen Tenpai Nyima's (1865–1926) *Transforming Felicity and Adversity into the Spiritual Path*, and Atiśa's *Seven-Point Mind Training*. These are all lojong—or mind training, mind transformation—which is focused on learning how to transform felicity and adversity into the path of awakening.

Lojong is like the six perfections in that, upon being perfected, they are transcended. For example, when you achieve the perfection of generosity, you have *transcended* generosity. Likewise, the perfection of lojong results in the transcendence of lojong: you no longer seek to train, modify, purify, or transform your mind in any way; you have transcended all that by engaging in an abundance of lojong practice and then perfecting that practice. Therefore, without seeking to train, modify, or transform your mind, rest in pristine awareness as fully as possible.

Even between formal meditation sessions, allow all mental afflictions to release themselves and dissolve back into their ground as facets of primordial consciousness. This is not to say that mental afflictions—proliferations of cognition, dualistic thought, and so forth—that still crop up after you are a vidyādhara will never arise again. But when they do arise, you will be well-prepared not to be abducted by them. You will be able to gaze piercingly into their nature and see right through the manifestations of bliss, luminosity, and nonconceptuality of the substrate consciousness. If some craving or attachment arises, turn the spear of your pristine awareness and pierce right into it; see directly into its naked nature, its core ground nature as discerning primordial consciousness. The same goes for all other mental afflictions, some of which are not intrinsically toxic or afflictive. As you peer into them, they melt right into their ground, revealing that all of these thoughts, including afflictive thoughts, are no longer able to afflict, since you are not appropriating or reifying them. They self-release—but not into nothing; they self-release back into the primordial ground, where they reveal their face as facets of primordial consciousness. As Düdjom Rinpoché says, now thoughts are acting as aids to your meditation.

This is dzokrim, the stage of completion of your spiritual practice within atiyoga, whether or not you are doing any visualizations involving the channels, vital energies, vital essences, or the cakras. This is the stage of perfection of your practice, in which you are no longer practicing as a sentient being at all. In other stage-of-completion practices—even those in highest yoga tantra, or anuyoga—there is still a striving to achieve something that has not yet been achieved, however much one may be actualizing or has actualized the personal deity. Here in this ninth yāna of atiyoga, of Dzokchen, there is no striving; you have already identified your own identity and your own nature as dharmakāya.

At this point, in contrast to the stages of generation and completion, you do not imagine that you are a buddha and that all appearances of the world around you are pure displays of nirmāṇakāya, because you have gone straight to the core. The whole point of the stages of generation and completion is to fully realize this indwelling mind of clear light. Having done so, there is no need to return to activities, striving, visualizations, and so forth, in order to realize that which has already been realized. The path of Dzokchen is a very direct, unelaborated, and quite effortless path. You do not need to imagine or visualize anything, for you are simply viewing your thoughts as displays of dharmakāya. Because you are resting in pristine awareness, you perceive your own speech and the sounds around you as displays of sambhogakāya.

For the same reason, all appearances—including the appearances of your own activities, of the surrounding world, and of other people—are naturally and effortlessly seen as displays of nirmāṇakāyas. The whole point of the stages of generation and completion is to achieve this realization. Thus, your conduct has one prime directive: throughout all activities, do not allow this flow of resting in pristine awareness to fade, do not allow the flow of pure perception to fade, and do not allow the knowing of your actual identity as a buddha to fade. This is the simple task of conduct.

Self-Arising and Self-Releasing Thoughts

These instructions on conduct might strike you as being great for advanced yogis but not practicable for someone who is still in the early stages of stilling their mind and seeing through ingrained delusions. This would be a mistake; the Dzokchen practice of conduct is directly relevant at every level of practice. Yangthang Rinpoché, in his quintessential root text *A Summary of the View, Meditation, and Conduct*, gives a clear and distinct understanding of what you can do right now; not at some later time after you have achieved śamatha, vipaśyanā, and fully identified the view. As Yangthang Rinpoché once advised to an inquiring student, do not wait in terms of śamatha and vipaśyanā practice. Do not wait in regard to seeking to identify the view, engaging in the meditation, and embracing the conduct of Dzokchen. If you wait, how long are you going to wait—until your next lifetime? This is too precious to postpone.

Focusing on conduct, Yangthang Rinpoché writes,

> Then, to give a partial account of the conduct:
> During the times when you are dwelling in meditative equipoise
>   in that way,
> when fresh thoughts suddenly emerge or else crop up
>   subliminally,
> perceive their emergence from the sphere of your own pristine
>   awareness.
> Do not follow after them, and whether they are good, bad,
> pleasurable, miserable, and so forth, do not do anything.

Rather, as soon as you see them arise, rest in the nature of just
that which has arisen.[107]

"During the times when you are dwelling in meditative equipoise in that
way," refers both to your actual periods of meditative equipoise as well as
to between-session periods off the cushion. Further, "when fresh thoughts
suddenly emerge or else crop up subliminally, perceive their emergence
from the sphere of your own pristine awareness" means that when you
see a perturbation in the flow of your mind—when you feel a surge or a
movement of something that could be born as a thought, though it is not a
fully articulated, expressed, or manifested thought—then simply watch as
these thoughts are born from your own pristine awareness. Be right there in
the instant in which they first emerge and explicitly manifest. In the present moment, when there is even the subtlest movement of the mind that
looks like it might give birth to a thought, you are right there to perceive it
with your pristine awareness. Perceive these movements of the mind during
everything you do; this is your practice. All activities—drinking, walking,
eating—are for the sake of sustaining the flow of pristine awareness. This is
exactly the case where hedonia is in the service of eudaimonia—where the
pursuit of stimulus-driven pleasures leads to genuine well-being. Everything
you do to take care of your body is for the sake of this conduct. Therefore,
when these thoughts emerge—be they explicit or subliminal—recognize
them immediately. Do *not* pursue thoughts as they emerge. Instead, remain
utterly at rest in the primordial stillness of pristine awareness where there is
no coming and going, yet observe as thoughts come and go. As soon as you
see a thought arise, just view it.

In his commentary, Yangthang Rinpoché explains that in the initial
moment of perception, you open your eyes and perceive a visual appearance for the first time. In the first instant of hearing, you hear a sound, and
likewise in the first instant of smelling, tasting, and touching. Similarly, in
the first moment of perception—including the first moment of perceiving
a mental image or a dream—it is nonconceptual. The first moment of any
mental awareness of appearances by way of the five modes of sensory perception is nonconceptual, albeit finite and brief in duration. It is an unmediated experience of whatever is appearing by way of that particular sense

door. However, in the very next instant, mental consciousness projects a net of conceptual proliferation, conceptual framing, and conceptual structuring upon these perceived appearances. It conceptually freezes and grasps at whatever is arising, and then there is a simultaneous stream of sensory perception and mental conceptualization. Visual perception does not become conceptual; it is only perceptual. Yet, it is now conjoined with conceptual mental awareness, which makes "sense" of everything. It is conceptually designating the object it sees with labels and elaborations of what it is, such as the black color of a friend's sweater. This labeling provides a sense of comfort in its familiarity, feeling that you've "got it figured out." Yet, the conceptual world is a world saturated by dualistic grasping and reification, so that the pure stream of perception—which is naked, fresh, and momentary—is veiled by and conjoined with mental consciousness. This mental consciousness slips immediately into a conceptual mode where you are then viewing everything through that conceptual lens. You are always seeing the color *of* something, hearing the sound *of* something, smelling the smell *of* something, and that something is the object you have conceptually designated. That is how you perpetuate saṃsāra.

In this practice during the phase of conduct, expand and sustain that initial moment of freshness to the best of your ability in the post-meditative state. Release the habitual tendency to make sense of everything conceptually and simply observe the tendency arise, letting it release itself as you continue streaming in a moment-to-moment encounter with whatever arises in the visual, auditory, olfactory, gustatory, tactile, and mental fields. It is all a fresh flow of perception.

Yangthang Rinpoché then raises this crucial point: Why do our mental afflictions arise? How do any of the six primary or twenty derivative mental afflictions get launched? How do they invade our minds? How do they saturate our apprehension of reality? It is because they are riding on the current of conceptualization. Insofar as you can remain in that utterly fresh, moment-by-moment *perception* of reality, including all of the six sensory fields, then the mental afflictions have no footing in your mindstream. They cannot latch onto a stream of perception. These parasitic mental afflictions find their host in the stream of mental conceptual designation; that is, in the conceptual mind, which is not by nature delusional, yet easily slips into reification that then opens the door for mental afflictions to enter. The simple, direct way of making sure mental afflictions cannot get in is to maintain the flow of perceptual awareness and not allow the overdrive of conceptualization to smother the freshness, luminosity, and purity of moment-by-moment perceptual awareness. As soon as you see these explicit or subliminal thoughts arise, "rest in the nature of just that which has arisen."

Yangthang Rinpoché continues his analysis, writing,

> By resting naturally, thoughts will disappear by themselves,
> and you will return to the pristine awareness you had experienced earlier.
> Then sustain the practice of resting naturally as before.
> Thus, whatever good and bad thoughts arise, do not fixate on them,
> but let them arise and be released by themselves.[108]

In this practice, you are seeing thoughts as thoughts and piercing right into their nature. You recognize their actual nature as displays of dharmakāya; just as they spontaneously arise, they spontaneously release with no perturbation, disturbance, or affliction. You then return to the simplicity of pristine awareness and back to the interlude between thoughts. During the intervals between thoughts, just rest—rest in the flow of pristine awareness.

Düdjom Lingpa, in his visionary treasure text *Buddhahood Without Meditation*, relates a teaching given to him by the great Dzokchen lineage master Śrī Siṃha in which Śrī Siṃha tells him,

> Although there is no outer or inner with respect to the ground of being and the mind, self-grasping simply superimposes boundaries between outer and inner, and it's no more than that. Just as water in its naturally fluid state freezes solid due to currents of cold wind, likewise the naturally fluid ground of being is entirely determined as saṃsāra by nothing more than cords of self-grasping.[109]

When you experience reality from the perspective of pristine awareness, the awareness itself and all the appearances are fluid, like water at room temperature. However, as soon as the reification of grasping or the grasping of reification sets in, then it is as if what was in fact fluid is experienced as something that is frozen, concretized, crystallized. In this way, your awareness becomes frozen as the mindstream of a sentient being. All appearances are now fixed as delusive appearances of a sentient being. Objects are then solidified as conceptually designated objects that are then reified and, thus, seen as unchanging. The goal is to unfreeze your mind, your experience, and all appearances, so that they arise effortlessly and are released.

Yangthang Rinpoché continues, saying,

> However thoughts are released, in any of the three ways, there is no difference.

That is, they are going to release themselves one way or another, so it is fine however it happens. One of the ways thoughts release themselves is called "naked release," which is done simply by recognizing the thoughts as thoughts. The second way is by the power of familiarization, whereby thoughts arise and then release, like a snake that wraps itself up in knots and then releases itself. In this case, you do not have to do anything when thoughts arise; they release instantaneously and effortlessly. The third way thoughts release themselves is in the culminating phase of self-release. In this final phase, there is no way thoughts can help or harm you, like a thief who comes to an empty house where there is nothing he can do. As a result, thoughts release themselves and then empower your realization of pristine awareness by serving as aids to your practice, as Düdjom Rinpoché has explained above. There is also a fourth type of release, and this is one in which pristine awareness constitutes "primordial release," where they are eternally released. Without any beginning, they are already released because your awareness has never been bound by them. Pristine awareness is primordially free of the constriction and bondage of thoughts, so this type of release is beyond release.

Yangthang Rinpoché discusses this self-releasing of thoughts, saying,

> The one point is that they self-arise and self-release.
> Even though thoughts occur, they arise from the expanse of the
> dharmakāya.
> Even though thoughts stop, they cease in the expanse of pristine
> awareness.
> If you know their arising does no harm and
> you know how to let them release themselves,
> you will receive a special enhancement of the view.
> When you make efforts in this way, thoughts will decrease,
> even as it does no harm to the ground of being should they arise.
> With this process, the lowest, middling, and supreme
> modes of release will gradually come.

Again, you are not *imagining* thoughts arising; you are *seeing* them arising, and that is how they appear. They are not just terminated, but they dissolve back into the open expanse of pristine awareness. The "lowest, middling, and supreme modes of release" are, respectively, the first three modes of release described above. Your insight will deepen when you recognize what otherwise could look like obstacles or mundane thoughts of an ordinary being and see them with transparency as primordially pure and of one taste. Regardless of what kinds of thoughts emerge, you see them as expressions of dharmakāya, and this view will enhance and deepen your view of reality. Then, along this path of the vidyādhara, thoughts will inevitably decrease.

There is a parallel with this method of self-release and manifest mindfulness. This is the second kind of mindfulness that occurs when you become increasingly familiar with resting in awareness, whereupon thoughts gradually subside, progressively changing from being like a cascading waterfall, to a mountain stream, to a great flowing river, to an ocean, and then to utter stillness, like Mt. Meru. Long before that happens, thoughts arise, but they do not perturb you. Although similar, this is the culmination and perfection of that śamatha practice, and yet the depth here in the Dzokchen practice of self-releasing thoughts is unimaginably greater than śamatha alone.

Yangthang Rinpoché stresses how crucial this practice of releasing thoughts is, writing,

> But if the crucial points for the modes of release are missing,
> liberation will never be attained in the end.

No matter how deep your realization is in meditative equipoise, if you allow your awareness to be contaminated in between sessions, then you will not achieve liberation. Again, there is a parallel here in śamatha practice, in which one of its inner prerequisites is completely eliminating discursive, obsessive, involuntary thoughts, including those of craving, attachment, and so on, even between sessions.

Yangthang Rinpoché continues, saying,

> Knowing how thoughts release themselves is the best conduct.
> As for the results of practicing in that way,
> mental afflictions and thoughts gradually thin out,
> clinging to the eight mundane concerns diminishes, and
> admiration, reverence, and pure vision gradually increase.

He is saying that even as a vidyādhara, afflictive thoughts will still arise, as will tendencies for clinging to the eight mundane concerns. But now you see that these afflictive thoughts and propensities are diminishing as you continue going with the current in this stream of being a vidyādhara, with the result that afflictive thoughts gradually fade, and "clinging to the eight mundane concerns diminishes, and admiration, reverence, and pure vision gradually increase."

Integrating Conduct with View and Meditation in the Post-Meditative Experience

Gyatrul Rinpoché's commentary on Düdjom Rinpoché's text provides an excellent and pithy treatment of how conduct relates to view and meditation, saying,

Conduct must be like the meditation, and the meditation must be like the view. Each one subsumes the other. Usually you consider that conduct is a post-meditative experience that occurs after your formal session. To sustain continuity with conduct is to integrate the view, meditation, and conduct indivisibly.[110]

Here, conduct is intimately connected with, and relies upon, the view and meditation. Therefore, let your meditation be infused with the view and your conduct infused then with meditation, until the demarcations between view and meditation, meditation and conduct melt away.

Gyatrul Rinpoché continues,

> Since the meditative equipoise is simply remaining in open, unmediated pristine awareness, unspoiled by grasping and clinging, totally luminous and relaxed, when you arise from that experience, you should perceive all appearances and experiences to be like an illusory display of pristine awareness.[111]

Gyatrul Rinpoché is describing how, as one goes increasingly deeper in their meditative and post-meditative practice, they begin to see that all appearances and experiences are pure, unmediated effulgences of pristine awareness, which, like their source, are equally and homogenously pure. When you see them as such, you see that they cannot possibly be inherently, objectively existent—they are simply illusory displays of pristine awareness.

Gyatrul Rinpoché then describes how this deep realization of pristine awareness will begin to permeate your entire life:

> All form is seen as the meditation deity, divine form. You may hear the essence of all sound to be that of mantra. All thoughts are understood as the play of pure awareness.[112]

For example, if your personal deity, or yidam, is Tārā—the feminine embodiment of enlightened compassion—then you will see the blessings of Tārā in all appearances everywhere you go. You will be living in Tārā's pure land. Since "All thoughts are understood as the play of pure awareness," they in no way arise as obstacles or distractions. They do not obscure anything at all, for there is nothing to obscure since they are pristinely pure expressions of primordial consciousness, buddha-mind, or dharmakāya. There are no mental afflictions anywhere in sight.

Gyatrul Rinpoché concludes,

> You may also consider that appearances in daily life are like a dream, an illusion, with no true, inherent existence.[113]

As you move about, a wide variety of appearances, people, and activities arise. Yet, the constant factor flowing like a river through all this diversity is the ongoing flow of resting in pristine awareness, of seeing all appearances as being creative expressions, or effulgences, of pristine awareness, and seeing them all as empty of inherent nature. Any distinction between your conduct in the post-meditative state and your realization while in meditative equipoise dissolves away. Conduct is your lojong for those who are devoted to practicing Dzokchen. These are the pith instructions on how to do everything when you are not formally in meditation.

Dream Yoga and Visions

In *A Summary of the View, Meditation, and Conduct*, Yangthang Rinpoché moves from discussing the arising and release of thoughts to a discussion of dreams and visions, saying,

> Dreams are apprehended, and the clear light appears.

If you are not naturally gifted for dream yoga and not easily able to recognize dreams as dreams, now you will acquire that skill. The power of pristine awareness allows dreams to be apprehended, which means that dreams are apprehended *as dreams*. You become lucid and "the clear light appears." In Padmasambhava's teachings on the practice of dream yoga in the book *Natural Liberation*, referring to identifying pristine awareness while in lucid, dreamless sleep, he says,

When you are fast asleep, if the vivid, indivisibly clear and empty light of deep sleep is recognized, the clear light is apprehended. One who remains without losing the experience of meditation all the time while asleep, without the advent of dreams or latent predispositions, is one who dwells in the nature of the clear light of sleep.[114]

In this way, you cultivate and sustain lucidity while more thoroughly comprehending the dream as a dream. When the dream fades and dissolves back into the substrate, you continue to sustain the flow of lucidity into the substrate. If you are authentically practicing dream yoga within the context of Dzokchen, then as you slip into the substrate, you uphold your lucidity of knowing that you are in deep sleep while in deep sleep. In that state, it is not difficult to cut through the veil of the substrate consciousness and ascertain primordial consciousness or realize dharmadhātu. Thus, dreams are apprehended, and with lucid dreams come the clear light.

Padmasambhava continues,

Then the state of dreamless lucidity corresponds to the consciousness dissolving into the clear light, and at that time your sleep will lucidly remain in the clarity and emptiness that is unborn and devoid of recollection. If you recognize the luminosity and emptiness of that occasion, which is free of cognition, this is called "recognizing the clear light." That is similar to the dissolution of consciousness into the clear light at the time of death, so this is training for the intermediate state between death and rebirth. The present recognition of the dream state is the real training for the intermediate state.[115]

Regarding the appearance of such visions, Yangthang Rinpoché writes,

Such are authentic fruitions of the path.
On the other hand, such things as visions of deities, receiving
    prophecies,

and the arising of extrasensory perception may or may not be
fruitions of the path.

Many people might think that it is a sign of progress on the path, and even
of achieving enlightenment, to see a deity, to have visions, to have somebody
make prophecies about you, or to experience extrasensory perception, such
as precognition, remote viewing, or knowledge of other people's minds.
When he was in Tibet, Gyatrul Rinpoché experienced all of these things. In
his memoir *Stories from the Early Life of Gyatrul Rinpoché*, he commented
that as a person who had experienced all of these siddhis, they are just useful for helping other people but not of any great meaning or value in and
of themselves. Therefore, do not get too carried away by these meditative
experiences—longing for them, wishing for them, getting excited when
they happen, clinging to them, grasping to them, floundering back and
forth in hope and fear. These experiences are not essential.

Yangthang Rinpoché concludes,

> If we cannot tell the right ones from the wrong, we will be
> deceived by māras.
> Do not wait for such things—just let them go!

If you cannot tell the difference between the right, actual signs of fruition
and the wrong signs, then you will be deceived by māras. You need to know
what the true signs are of reaching the path, and what are not. Do not wait
for visions of deities and so forth. Even if such visions arise, just let them go!

❖ Meditation: Resting in the Flow of Pure Perception

https://wisdomexperience.org/alan-wallace-dzokchen-meditation-14/

Find a comfortable posture where you can be relaxed and at ease. We see
that there is a recurrent crescendo of emphasis on relaxation, as the perfec-

tion of relaxation is achieved only by the buddhas, and the perfection of relaxation is the transcendence of exerting any effort at all. The deeper the relaxation, the less of a foothold grasping can get, which means there is less of a basis for mental afflictions and for being carried away by conceptual proliferation.

With this in mind, relax deeply in your body, further allowing the exhalation to release any tension. Now, relax deeply in your breathing by allowing it to proceed effortlessly, to flow in and out as if you were deep asleep. Completing the triad, profoundly and existentially relax your mind. Release and settle effortlessly into awareness, as you have done before. Continue to rest in the flow of unwavering stillness, in the very nature of awareness.

Now, let your eyes be open or half-closed, utterly at ease. Rest your visual gaze in the space in front of you. Soften all the muscles around the eyes, letting there be a spaciousness between your eyebrows and an openness of your forehead—your whole face resting in an expression of repose. Relax there, deepening your familiarization with the opening practice of śamatha without elaboration, or śamatha without a sign or referent.

Following in the stream of Düdjom Rinpoché's pith instructions on determining the nature of external apprehended objects located in the world around us, open all five of your sense doors as you move into vipaśyanā. Let the flow of your mental awareness illuminate whatever appearances arise in the visual, auditory, olfactory, gustatory, and tactile domains. Rest in that nonconceptual stillness in the center of it all while allowing the light of your awareness to illuminate all of these five sensory domains of experience.

Now, focus single-pointedly on the visual domain. Let your mental awareness flow along with your visual awareness. Like visual awareness, let your mental awareness be nonconceptual, such that when you see, you merely see. In the visual, appearances arise unadorned, uncloaked by concepts and words—see them for what they are. Before you slip into dualistically grasping at these appearances and habitually thinking of them as being "out there," just rest in the mental perception of visual appearances. In this way, see that the phrase "out there" has no referent. There is no inner or outer; there is just the space of awareness, the substrate, and visual appearances arising and passing.

As in the pith instructions given by the Buddha to Bāhiya, direct your awareness now to the auditory domain in this same way. In the heard, let there be only the heard. Mentally perceive just the sounds without even labeling them as sounds, let alone sounds coming from somewhere "out there."

Going directly to the tactile field, the realm of physical sensations, there is a third "cinema" in which only tactile sensations arise, without colors, shapes, or sounds. Without labeling or classifying the tactile appearances, observe them quietly and nonconceptually, seeing that these, too, are neither "out there" nor "in here." Perceptual awareness does not draw such lines between object and subject. They are intangible, insubstantial, and are merely appearances, but not appearances of something else that is really out there. They are your own appearances; they do not come from anywhere else.

Continue to rest in this nonconceptual flow of mental awareness, allowing the flow of conceptual proliferation to manifest. Allow thoughts to arise and allow the designating mind to designate as it does habitually. From this stillness, watch passively yet discerningly how the conceptual mind habitually locks onto appearances—visual, auditory, tactile, olfactory, and gustatory—and then, on the bases of designation, adds something to these immaterial, insubstantial appearances. The conceptual mind designates objects: "That's the sound of traffic; that's the color of cloth; that's the sensation in my knee," and so on. Watch how the conceptual mind designates objects on the bases of designation as a ray of appearances which are not those objects. Observe how the conceptual mind populates the world around you with objects out there in physical space. Note how these objects come into existence by the power of conceptual designation. As soon as you think "this" or "that," referring to some object out there, watch how the mind conceives the object and gives birth to it by designating it as such, creating a self-fulfilling prophecy of sorts.

Then, once the conceptual mind has designated an object out there, observe how it goes a step further and reifies the object that it has designated, viewing it as existing independently from its own side; that is, independent of the process of designation, as if the designation—the conceptual and verbal labeling—were something of no consequence and utterly superficial. It is as if the objects out there were already what they are from their own side before you designated them as such; as if they bear their own intrinsic identities. Watch how the mind reifies the object that it has imputed.

Consider how concepts proliferate in dependence upon that reification. Is it true that all mental afflictions are rooted in reification? Observe closely the activity of reification without reifying it. Notice the delusion without being deluded and rest nonconceptually but discerningly in your own awareness. Continue like this for the remainder of the meditation.

Then bring this session to a close by dedicating the merit of this practice to the swift realization of your own perfect awakening for the benefit of all beings. ❖

INTERLUDE:
An Evolution in Knowing the *Actual* Nature of Reality

B EFORE WE MOVE on to the last topic, we should pause here and take stock of where we are in the arc of Düdjom Rinpoché's root text. We have been following exactly the sequence of the root text itself, beginning with śamatha. We then turned our attention outward to the five sensory domains, to the external world of apprehended objects, and sought to determine their actual nature. This was described as vipaśyanā directed outward with the goal of viewing things as dreamlike, and we explored exactly what that means. Now, we are following the next sequence of determining the actual nature of the internal apprehending mind. Note the sequence when it comes to vipaśyanā of truly seeking to understand the *actual* nature of reality. This text is not only concerned with the phenomenal nature of reality, but also with the ontological nature of reality; that is, not just with how things *appear* but how they *actually are*. For it is only by understanding the nature of reality as it is, and not just being familiar with appearances, that we can be free of suffering and the causes of suffering. The reason why we need to know how things actually are is straightforward: it is because we are misapprehending the *actual* nature of reality and are prone to suffering. That is fundamentally the teaching of the second noble truth—which, as a reminder, is more accurately translated as the second ārya reality—which identifies the cause of suffering as clinging to that which is untrue.

An Outside-In Approach

The approach here is very straightforward: First you develop your contemplative technology—a refined, stable, clear flow of awareness—and that dissolves your coarse mind with all of its obscurations and impurities into the relatively pure substrate consciousness. You have taken the impure mind as the path, and as you purify it, you develop a suitable vessel, an instrument that is up to the task of engaging in vipaśyanā and letting that powerful contemplative science do what it is intended to do—to sever irrevocably the root of suffering. Thus, you begin with śamatha, and it is only by achieving śamatha that you directly ascertain your substrate consciousness, the obscurative nature of your mind. The Buddha also referred to the substrate as the "sign of the mind" (Pāli *cittassa nimitta*) when he stated,

> In this manner, monks, the wise, experienced, skillful monk abides in happiness here and now and is mindful and introspective as well. What is the reason for that? Because, monks, this wise, experienced, skillful monk acquires the sign of his own mind.[116]

As for practicing vipaśyanā without having acquired the sign of one's mind, the Buddha says in the same sutta that if one tries to cultivate the four applications of mindfulness without the mind being concentrated and without having abandoned the impurities, one will not acquire one's own mental sign.

So, how does one go about the contemplative science of seeking to know the actual nature of reality? It is quite evident that you start by looking outward, just as the sequence of the four applications of mindfulness begins with mindfulness of the body and other physical phenomena. You then fathom that there is nothing out there that exists by its own nature, and that it all exists only nominally—that is to say, it becomes real in our minds by being named and thought of as a thing in itself.

The Buddha made this point in the Pāli canon, declaring that a chariot, like a self, does not exist as a substantial thing apart from or in addition to its various parts. Nor is the chariot to be found among any of its individual components, and the whole heap of those parts by themselves does not constitute a chariot. The term "chariot" is something we designate upon a collection of parts, none of which, either individually or collectively, is a chariot. The chariot comes into existence only when we call those parts a "chariot."[117]

There is nothing out there existing by its own inherent nature. Just as in a dream, things appear to be out there. You can see a mountain over yonder, but there *is* no mountain over yonder because there is no "over yonder" without your designating it to be so; there is nothing over there from its own side. Therefore, the sequence starts outwardly by first fathoming that. As your externally oriented vipaśyanā is imbued with the stability and vividness of śamatha, you then turn inward to fathom the nature of the internal apprehending mind, which must be imbued with your prior insight into the emptiness of inherent nature of all appearing objects in the world around you.

It is important to make clear here that the path of vipaśyanā is not independent of the path of śamatha; they are part of a single cumulative path. You do not practice śamatha and then leave it in order to do something else. Rather, you practice śamatha and then build on it by moving on to practice *externally* directed vipaśyanā, from which you move to *internally* directed vipaśyanā, which enables you to fathom the actual nature of your own mind, cittatā. In this sequence, vipaśyanā starts with investigating the actual nature of phenomena, the dharmatā—specifically those in the surrounding environment—and you then turn to investigate the cittatā, the actual nature of your own mind.

Further, there is a sequence in Düdjom Rinpoché's text that is clearly intended for those of sharp faculties—those with a lot of spiritual momentum: that is, the approach of looking outward to external apprehended objects before turning inward to the internal apprehending mind. As a note on "sharp faculties," he is not referring to IQ. There are many people with an extremely high IQ who are quite undeveloped spiritually. In the Buddhist tradition, going back to the Pāli canon, there is the legend of Buddha's disciple Cūḷapanthaka, also known as Suddhipanthaka. He was definitely one of dull faculties in the sense that his IQ was not exceptional.

While trying to memorize verses of the Buddha, when he got to the second line, he forgot the first; then, when he went back to the first, he forgot the second. I can imagine he probably felt dismayed that perhaps he wasn't bright enough to be a suitable disciple of the Buddha. However, one day the Buddha, recognizing his plight, assigned Suddhipanthaka to sweep the ground as if he were a groundskeeper. The Buddha instructed him to imagine himself sweeping out and purifying his mind of contaminations while he was sweeping the grounds. After a long time, Suddhipanthaka said, "The ground is clean, but is my mind-ground clean?" Thereupon he achieved arhatship. This story shows that "sharp faculties" doesn't necessarily mean high IQ. When the Buddha gave Bāhiya his pith instructions, Bāhiya instantly became an arhat, not because he was intellectually brilliant but rather because he was one of extraordinarily sharp faculties: he heard one Dharma talk and he was free.[118] Nobody has a smarter buddha nature than anybody else. It is all about spiritual momentum.

This sequence of looking outward first and then turning inward is also presented by Atiśa in his classic *Seven-Point Mind Training*. His guidance is first to cultivate proper motivation by way of the four revolutions in outlook; then turn directly to śamatha, making the mind serviceable and increasing attentional intelligence; and from there, to develop the cognitive intelligence of vipaśyanā through the cultivation of ultimate bodhicitta. He does not turn to relative bodhicitta first, which has a strong association with emotional intelligence, but instead goes to ultimate bodhicitta which is the realization of emptiness. In terms of his strategy for realizing emptiness, he, like Düdjom Rinpoché, says to view all phenomena as if they were dreams. He looks outward first to realize the dreamlike nature of the phenomena around him, and then he turns inward to recognize the character of unborn awareness. Turning inward, you then fathom the reality that your mind never actually came into existence, is not really located anywhere, and does not really go anywhere.

Again, Atiśa formulated *The Seven-Point Mind Training* for a small fraction of his disciples who were of very sharp faculties. Whereas, if he gave these teachings to those who were of dull faculties, they would likely have become confused, bewildered, discouraged, or even nihilistic. Thus, for the majority of Atiśa's disciples, he wrote the first *lamrim*, *Lamp for the Path to Enlightenment,* as requested by King Jangchup Ö, a ruler of the Ngari region of Tibet, who asked him to give them something with few words but great meaning—something easy to understand and easy to practice. In general, lamrim texts provide a gradual path that starts with cultivating renunciation and relative bodhicitta, then moves to developing the six perfections, culminating in śamatha and vipaśyanā. So, in the lamrim, relative bodhicitta comes first, followed by ultimate bodhicitta. That's the broader, safer approach. However, for those who will not fall into delusion or misunderstanding—those of sharp faculties—the approach in *The Seven-Point Mind Training* is more efficient: first go outward, then turn inward.

An Inside-Out Approach

Looking at the three turnings of the wheel of Dharma, the principal purpose of the spear of prajñā in the first turning of the wheel of Dharma is not simply to understand the phenomenological nature—that all conditioned phenomena are impermanent and that all phenomena influenced by mental afflictions are unsatisfying; rather, the emphasis is on the inside—realizing impermanence, *duḥkha,* "not self," and so forth. The Buddha starts with the nature of your own personal identity, because wherever you go, there you are. Regardless of whether you change the external environment, you bring the inner delusion of your own self-grasping and reification of yourself as an individual who has five *skandhas* wherever you go.

Probing into the nature of self and realizing personal identitylessness is absolutely the core and the pinnacle of the practice of vipaśyanā in the first turning of the wheel of Dharma. The goal of vipaśyanā is, above all, to realize the emptiness of your own inherent nature, that there is no substantial autonomous agent that is separate from, but somehow controlling, the five skandhas—the five psychophysical aggregates—and whatever else you try to appropriate and take as "mine."

With the second turning of the wheel of Dharma, as Avalokiteśvara said to Śāriputra in the *Heart Sūtra,* it is not only the self that is empty, but the skandhas that make up the self—your body, feelings, recognition, mental formations, and consciousness—are also empty. The whole universe is empty, from elementary particles up to buddha-mind, or dharmakāya.

Suddenly, the emptiness of inherent nature of a self now expands to be the emptiness of inherent nature of all phenomena. The Perfection of Wisdom Sūtras are the core scriptures of this second turning of the wheel of Dharma, which were then explicated and systematized by the great Indian Buddhist philosopher Nāgārjuna. In Nāgārjuna's treatises, he goes through the whole range of categories from the Buddhist Abhidharma, from the external— such as space, time, all the six domains of experience, the formless realm, form realm, desire realm—to the internal aspects of mind, and, one by one, shows how the tendency to reify all these classes of phenomena is erroneous and nonsensical. Everything in the second turning of the wheel of Dharma regarding the emptiness of inherent nature of phenomena leads to the realization of the objective clear light, which is emptiness, the absolute space of phenomena, or dharmadhātu.

The third turning of the wheel of Dharma focuses primarily on the realization of your own buddha nature—the *tathāgatagarbha*, or *buddhadhātu*—and this is the subjective clear light. As such, this approach in the three turnings of the wheel of Dharma works from the inside out.

Other Approaches to Knowing the Actual Nature of Reality

The earliest Greek philosophers, such as Thales and Democritus, were seeking primarily to understand the actual nature of the external world. These thinkers were trying to understand the world out there without humans in it, as if our perception of it, thinking about it, and presence in the world are irrelevant to reality as a whole. They were trying to understand reality from the outside in. This was a common approach in Greco-Roman philosophy.

Then there is the Judeo-Christian tradition beginning with the Genesis account of Creation, in which a transcendent God created the heavens and the Earth, and then created Adam and Eve. The biblical account of God indicates that he is ultimately, even quintessentially, real. The prophets spoke to God as to a person, a transcendent person, one who is other than themselves, and in that way, they received God's wisdom and instruction.

Then Jesus shocked his disciples by saying that "I and the Father are one,"[119] and suddenly the external and internal are unified—they have become nondual. The great apostle Saint Paul says, "It is no longer I who live, but Christ lives in me."[120] As Christ saw the Divine within, so was his disciple Saint Paul able to do so in Christ. So there is an inversion within the Christian tradition.

Then, among the early Desert Fathers, once again there is a withdrawing from the complexities, busyness, noise, and distractions of a socially engaged way of life, and retreating into the desert in order to seek God within. In the monastic traditions of Christianity, the growing tradition of Jewish mysticism, and eventually in the Islamic traditions of Sufism, contemplatives sought to know the nature of reality by turning inward. By so doing and thereby realizing the inner light of the Divine, they realized that this inner light shines out on the world around them, thus illuminating the outer world. This is done by first fathoming the Divine within.

Fast forward over one thousand years to Galileo, who was introduced to the contemplative life when he was trained as a youth in a Camaldolese monastery near Florence. If not for his father pulling him out to go to medical school, Galileo perhaps would have stayed to become a contemplative seeking to fathom God by looking within. While in medical school, he still had a passion for knowing the mind of God and took to his new calling that same motivation, *apotheosis*: the aspiration to let your own perspective ascend and come as close as possible to the perspective of God himself. He wanted to know the mind of the Creator by way of His creation, by looking outward and understanding phenomenologically the nature of the outer world. This is akin to inferentially understanding the mind of the clockmaker by fathoming how the clock works. That was the motivation not just for Galileo, but for many other Christian founders of modern science. They turned outward in order to seek a God's-eye view of reality.

By contrast, in the latter part of the nineteenth century, there were three great pioneers of modern psychology: William James, Wilhelm Wundt, and Edward Titchener. They were instrumental in founding the introspectionist movement, which argued that if you want to understand the mind, you have to do the obvious—that is, look within because you are not going to find the mind *out there*. Nevertheless, after only about thirty years, the great dogma of materialism as advocated by behaviorists such as John Watson overrode this view, insisting that introspection plays no role in the study of the mind, which was assumed to be nothing more than a mere predisposition for behavior. They felt that subjective experience and consciousness cannot be studied scientifically and are, therefore, not real. They sought to draw inferences about dispositions for behavior by studying behavior that, unlike the mind, is objective, physical, and quantifiable.

Materialism has overwhelmingly dominated the cognitive and physical sciences ever since. They are still touting the primary intervention for psychological problems to be the external substances of drugs. But despite the billions of dollars spent on developing and marketing psychopharmaceutical drugs, not a single drug cures any mental disease. They do nothing more than suppress the symptoms of mental disease at best, often with deleterious side-effects.

This is an "outside-in" approach, and it has dominated the physical sciences since Galileo and through to the development of chemistry, biology, and so forth. Darwin looked outward and discovered evolution; Rutherford looked outward and discovered the nature of the atom; Einstein looked outward and discovered curved space-time and the relativity of matter and energy. Quantum physicists have been looking outward, only to discover that the world "out there," independent of all systems of measurement, is unknowable in principle.

There is something quite remarkable and unprecedented taking place in this phase of human history. For the first time, Eurocentric civilization is beginning to appreciate the wisdom of Asia. Modern scientists and philosophers are actually learning about the great insights of ancient Asian civilizations rather than trying to colonize them for their own financial profit. In particular, the West is encountering the wisdom of India, with its thousands of years of academia rooted in the wisdom of the Buddha and other great contemplatives, seeking to understand reality from the inside-out. Could we be approaching a Great Perfection of human history? If so, can we survive our current decimation of the environment and the proliferation of weapons of mass destruction that are developed with knowledge from modern science and could undermine human civilization entirely? Can we survive our own short-sightedness, greed, and the stupidity of misusing science and technology? To do so, we must augment our modern understanding of the mind and its role in nature by drawing on the discoveries of the great contemplative traditions of the East and West. If we can unite the knowledge of modern science and technology with such ancient wisdom, then human civilization may not merely survive, but may thrive as never before.

❖ Meditation: Determining the Actual Nature of the Apprehending Mind

https://wisdomexperience.org/alan-wallace-dzokchen-meditation-15/

Find a comfortable position and strike the three points of your body, speech, and mind. Note that in the very act of releasing and relaxing, you may also release the sense of personal ambition, of ego—the sense that *I* want to achieve. You may release self-centeredness and lighten yourself of that burden as you relax the body. Having thus released self-centeredness, attend to the breath without seeking to control it. Rest in awareness without appropriating it, without colonizing or exercising your own imperialism over the domain of the mind, without trying to conquer the mind. Rest in awareness; master the flow of your own awareness, sustaining it with the qualities of ease, stillness, and clarity.

Briefly returning to a continuation of śamatha practice, rest in the stillness of awareness and observe the movements of the mind without appropriation. As you relax more deeply into the practice, you will experience an increasing sense of ease as you lightly rest your awareness in the present moment. With that ease, there may come an increasingly subtle release of grasping, which will give rise to a greater stillness and continuity of awareness. That, in turn, may elicit a heightening qualitative vividness of attention, which allows you to detect subtler and subtler impulses in the mind, such as thoughts or a flickering of images that previously were too brief for you to discern. The ability to identify increasingly brief impulses within the mind corresponds to temporal vividness, whereas qualitative vividness entails the ability to recognize increasingly subtle images and thoughts—which may linger for only the briefest of moments—which were previously beneath the threshold of your conscious awareness. Observe these events very closely within the mode of śamatha, still without active inquiry.

Rest precisely in the present moment, attending with interest to the movements of the mind so that you are able to recognize the very birthing of thoughts, images, and other events within this mental space. You are right there watching them as soon as they emerge, as they play themselves out, and as they dissolve away.

Once you have familiarized yourself with that precision of mindfulness, then cross the threshold from śamatha into vipaśyanā. As you venture into the vipaśyanā that is inwardly directed upon the apprehending mind, when you see with razor-sharp attention a thought, an image, or any other mental activity arise, ask, From where do these thoughts emerge? Are they real? If so, they must really have come from somewhere, but where?

Once a thought, an image, or subjective impulses—such as desires, emotions, or feelings—have arisen, point the spear of your intelligence and ask, Where are these mental objects located? If they are real, they must be someplace, so closely examine and investigate their location.

Of course, none of these thoughts, desires, or emotions last indefinitely. Sooner or later they fade away. Watch what happens when you closely inspect a subjective feeling, desire, or emotion of any kind. Does it linger or does it disappear quickly? In either case, where do they go when they are gone?

Although there can be a cascade of wildly proliferating thoughts, look closely and you will see that there are intervals between thoughts—the silent space and time that is apparently devoid of content. Rest right there in the emptiness of that interval, and sustain the flow of knowing without objectifying or identifying with anything. Rest in that simple awareness.

You have been doing many things during the first half of this session— meditating in various ways, reading or listening to the guidance, and putting it into practice. You are doing it because the mind is doing it. It is the mind that is the agent, so what is the nature of that which is engaging in this meditation, observing this, inspecting that, asking this question, seeking this? Probe piercingly inward beyond the apprehend*ed* mind to the apprehend*ing* mind. Probe inward into the nature of that which is piercing inward—the mind piercing itself. What is the nature of the agent? What arises when you invert your awareness right in upon that which is inverting?

There must be an agent, for you did not perform this meditation by chance. Just because there is instruction, you don't have to follow it. There must be an agent here, so what is the nature of that agent? You may think it is you, but only because this "you" is designated upon your mind. Look right at the mind that is the actual agent upon which you designate yourself—what is that mind? Does it have characteristics by which you can identify it?

If you cannot find or identify it, then ask again, What is it that cannot identify it? Is that not the mind?

Then, let there be intervals between doing things with your mind, such as inverting, questioning, and seeking your mind. Between the activities of doing, let there be an interval when you are not doing anything with the mind at all; you are simply present. In the intervals between activities, is there not still a mind that is aware without doing anything at all? What is the nature of the mind that is aware and is an observer? Look closely.

Then, stop looking and just be aware of what is left when all activities of the mind have ceased.

Activate the mind again and set out on a search for the mind. Track down your awareness to its source—the mind that *is* aware. Seek it out persistently and tenaciously. If it is here, it must be findable. Then, cease looking and simply be aware of what is left.

Is there still a quiet, intuitive sense that there is someone or something in here that is observing, that there is a subject? There must be—otherwise, how could that subject engage in activity? How could that subject be aware of objects if there were no subject? Therefore, if there is a real subject in here, it was not always here, so it must have come from someplace. From where did it come? From moment to moment, can you identify the origins of that which you identify as your mind?

Do you have a persistent sense that "the mind is here"? If so, where is "here"?

Moment by moment, does this mind phenomenologically come into existence? Does it exist and then pass away—continuously arising and passing? When a moment of mind ceases, can you see where the mind goes? If it really exists, it must go somewhere—but where?

When you seek and find the unfindability of the mind and its origin, location, and destination, simply come to rest in the open, empty space of mind. Rest in that knowing with no further seeking.

Bringing the meditative session to close, bear in mind that Düdjom Rinpoché's counsel is to come out of meditation gently and smoothly. Let there be no abrupt transition from meditative equipoise to engaging with the world around you.

From this place, dedicate the merit of this practice to the realization of your highest, most pure ideal, and for that attainment to be for the benefit of all sentient beings. ❖

A Brief Note on Silence

There is a theme of venturing into silence in contemplative traditions around the world. It is a silence where you do not keep talking, thinking, or seeking. In ordinary English vernacular, there are all kinds of silence: a pregnant silence, tense silence, serene silence, noble silence, oppressive silence. Silence isn't just silence; silence is imbued with what you bring to it. The silence that is deep in the domain of śamatha is the silence of simple, sheer inner calm and clarity of awareness. The silence when you seek to determine the nature of external apprehended objects is imbued with insight into the emptiness of those apprehended objects. Here again, silence is emphasized at the end of the inquiry. You begin with silence but end with a richer silence that is infused with insight from the inquiry that preceded it.

D. Realizing the Fruition

THE FINAL subsection of Düdjom Rinpoché's commentary is entitled "Realizing the Fruition." The fruition referred to here is perfect enlightenment. The final phrase from the root verses reads,

once all phenomena with characteristics have been overwhelmed, Glorious Heruka will become manifest.

Samaya

"With characteristics" means characteristics of phenomena that are seen as inherently existent, impure appearances, as if they existed from their own side. When all of this has **"been overwhelmed"** by resting in pristine awareness and familiarizing yourself with this pristine awareness both on and off the cushion, then **"Glorious Heruka will become manifest." "Glorious Heruka,"** here, refers specifically to Dorjé Drolö, who is the personification of the luminosity of pristine awareness. When he becomes manifest through this luminosity, your own identity as a buddha will become manifest and, thus, your own spiritual awakening will be perfected.

Düdjom Rinpoché's commentary on this final verse begins by saying

The spontaneously actualized awakening of your own pristine awareness, which has never been deluded, is obscured by the addiction of grasping to the signs of delusive thoughts regarding adventitiously arising appearances that do not in fact exist, and you are trapped by the view of seeking to achieve enlightenment elsewhere.

The phrase "The spontaneously actualized awakening of your own pristine awareness, which has never been deluded," points to the fact that pristine awareness never becomes deluded; it is primordially awakened and free of obscurations. However, from the perspective of a sentient being, it is obscured. It "is obscured by the addiction of grasping to the signs [and referents] of delusive thoughts regarding adventitiously arising appearances that do not in fact exist, and you are trapped by the view of seeking to achieve enlightenment elsewhere."

Here, Düdjom Rinpoché is essentially describing the second noble truth, which regards the origins of suffering as arising from clinging. From the Dzokchen perspective, this clinging specifically refers to clinging to a deluded view of appearances as being other than ourselves, as existing "over there," which causes us to implicitly, nonverbally, or nonconceptually grasp onto an "I" that is "over here." That bifurcation is when our saṃsāra begins; that is how we are caught in the grip of delusion. The origin of suffering occurs every time that happens. This is why Yangthang Rinpoché advises in his verses on conduct not to start saṃsāra again in each moment. Every time we overlay perception—which does not in and of itself entail dualistic grasping—with conceptualization, conceptual designation, and reification, that is the moment saṃsāra begins. Yangthang Rinpoché said that our daunting task in the post-meditative state is to try to maintain a continuous flow of not beginning saṃsāra again. If we see that we have started creating saṃsāra again, then we should let this saṃsāra be as brief as possible by releasing our grip right away from that dualistic grasping.

This is the reality of the origin of suffering, as it is understood from the Dzokchen perspective. Pristine awareness never becomes deluded, but somehow it happens that grasping does occur, and that is when pristine awareness is obscured. That is when we forget who we are, and we identify with that which is not ourselves—our bodies, minds, possessions—as being "I," although none of them were ever "I." Like the hermit crab who is born without a shell, appropriates a shell, and then thinks "It's mine!" the shell represents our human body and mind, and how we appropriate and identify with that which was never ours, thinking, "I am a sentient being, and that's who I *really* am." In time, we become dissatisfied with being who we are and with the world as we see it, and we therefore seek transcendence and freedom. However, when we look for enlightenment, we look outside ourselves because when we look inward, we see either nothing much at all or chaos, affliction, and boredom, and surely that's not the path to awakening!

Who can rescue us from this delusion and provide us with refuge and authentic guidance? It is true that our ultimate refuge is pristine awareness, but if we cannot identify pristine awareness as distinct from our own minds, then it will be hard to take refuge in it. It is still possible, but it is not the same as vidyādharas taking refuge in their own pristine awareness and knowing this *is* dharmakāya, the ultimate refuge. In the meantime, we may seek an authentic spiritual mentor who knows the way to freedom—a guru.

Düdjom Rinpoché continues here:

> Then, due to the kindness of your guru, you identify your own face as the naturally present dharmakāya, and you continuously rest in the realization of primordial freedom.

In this context of Dzokchen, you look outward and view the guru as empty of inherent nature. From the guru's own side, there is no sentient being and there never has been. It is your own impure vision that sees someone "over there" as impure. Cutting through those veils with the eye of wisdom, you see your guru as a buddha. You first see a buddha by looking outward and taking refuge in your lama, yidam, and the ḍākinī, seeing them as primordially pure buddhas. Then, with that blessing, you imagine the guru coming to the crown of your head and dissolving indivisibly your body, speech, and mind into the body of the guru, the speech of the guru, and the mind of the guru. From this place, you venture into your śamatha and vipaśyanā practice and proceed along the path. First look outward to the guru, and then internalize this refuge.

Düdjom Rinpoché concludes his commentary by saying,

> Thus, without conjuring up some new attainment, your primor-
> dial character manifests as it is, and this is conventionally known
> as the fruition of the practice. Having mastered the state of the
> blood-drinker Heruka, the omnipresent lord of the whole of
> saṃsāra and nirvāṇa, you spontaneously actualize effortless,
> boundless, enlightened activity.

This is your job until all sentient beings are free. You are now a buddha, a
"blood-drinker" who has drunk the blood of rebirth and death.

The Fruition as Rainbow Body

Gyatrul Rinpoché provides further commentary on this final passage,
saying,

> The fourth and final step is the manner in which fruition is
> achieved. Fruition is the recognition of one's own originally
> pure, pristine awareness, free from confusion. This experience,
> which is the result of the view, meditation, and conduct, is the
> experience of enlightenment, or ultimate freedom from the con-
> fusion of cyclic existence. If your practice is strong, then even
> before your death, by realizing this nature and actualizing it
> according to these four steps, you will be liberated. Otherwise,
> [if you do not achieve perfect enlightenment in this lifetime] lib-
> eration will occur at the moment of your death or in the bardo
> state. Through the blessings of accomplishing this practice, it is
> certain that liberation will occur during one of these times.[121]

The fruition that is classically associated with Dzokchen is the manifestation of rainbow body. If you indeed achieve awakening in this lifetime,
how do you let others know of your awakening? The Lake-Born Vajra in *The
Vajra Essence* says,

By practicing in this way, those of superior faculties attain enlightenment as a great transference rainbow body, without reliance upon death or their full lifespan.[122]

While still alive and in good health, coming to this perfection and achieving
great transference rainbow body is exactly what Guru Rinpoché, Vimala-
mitra, Chetsün Sengé Wangchuk, and others did. This occurrence is quite
rare thus far in the history of the Nyingma tradition. It is a manifestation of
perfect awakening such that while you are still alive, the entire materiality of
your body dissolves, melts away, and vanishes into the energy of primordial
consciousness, which is indivisible from dharmadhātu. Your mind, which
was the mind of a sentient being, dissolves into the dharmakāya. Someone
observing you manifestly achieving great transference rainbow body would
simply see you disappear. Yet in the very next instant you may reappear,
manifesting as a human being, but without a human body or mind.

The Vajra Essence continues, "Those of middling faculties are liberated
within the actual nature of reality, without undergoing the transitional
phase of dying."[123] That is, in the dying process, the mother clear light manifests, and they are united with it. They fully realize pristine awareness, or
dharmakāya, and thus achieve the perfect awakening of a buddha by way of
dharmakāya through the dying process. The culmination of their achieving
perfect enlightenment occurs "without undergoing the transitional phase
of dying." In other words, there is no bardo for them, as they are enlightened
before the intermediate period, or bardo, even begins, and it is "within the
actual nature of reality," dharmatā.

Further, "Those of inferior faculties merge with the mother and child
clear light in the intermediate period and attain liberation."[124] This says
that they achieve enlightenment either in the bardo, where they realize the
actual nature of reality by way of sambhogakāya or, if they miss that opportunity, then they take birth in a pure land, like Sukhāvati, and achieve enlightenment there by way of nirmāṇakāya in the bardo—either in the bardo
of dharmatā of the actual nature of reality, or in the bardo of becoming.

This raises the question of how those with "inferior faculties" could
achieve enlightenment. How can you be right on the verge of achieving

enlightenment and be inferior in any way? Is the enlightenment they achieve also inferior? In short, no: they all achieve the same enlightenment. Whether by great transference rainbow body through the dying process, or in the intermediate period, the quality of enlightenment achieved is not superior, middling, or inferior—it is the same enlightenment. It is the same as with those achieving arhatship, where prior to passing away, some arhats have powerful experiences of the four immeasurables, and some have less powerful experiences; some have great paranormal abilities, and some have less. However, the nirvāṇa they realize is exactly the same, and once they shed this outer shell of their human body and mind, then the nirvāṇa in which they are all immersed is exactly the same. Here, the perfect, nonabiding enlightenment of a buddha is identical. Yet, by the power and nature of their practice, along with the power of their prayers, they will manifest differently depending on the nature of their path, while the awakening itself is the same.

The Vajra Essence continues,

> Those of the most superior faculties are liberated as a great transference body, extending infinitely into the all-pervasive dharmakāya, like water merging with water or space merging with space. Those of middling faculties attain enlightenment as a great rainbow body, like a rainbow vanishing into the sky.[125]

The phenomenon of the great rainbow body being manifested by those achieving enlightenment by way of Dzokchen has long been reported in Tibet and more recently in the last few decades in places outside of Tibet. These accounts usually describe the body of the person transforming into shimmering rainbow light and then disappearing. This "great transference rainbow body" is a way of displaying their enlightenment.

The Vajra Essence continues,

> For those of inferior faculties, when the clear light of the ground arises [the mother clear light], the colors of the rainbow spread forth from absolute space, and their material bodies decrease in size until finally they vanish as rainbow bodies, leaving not even

a trace of their aggregates behind. That is called the *small rainbow body*.[126]

There are multiple accounts in Dzokchen where this, too, has been witnessed. The person ceases to breathe, the heartbeat and all metabolic signs vanish, but instead of simply vanishing into rainbow light, their bodies decrease in size proportionally. The head decreases somewhat, but the body decreases from a full-size human being down to maybe two or three feet. If you are patient, you may see the body continue to decrease in size and then vanish entirely. That is a small rainbow body. The practice of cutting through is tekchö, which is entirely covered in this text and is sufficient to achieve this type of rainbow body.

The Vajra Essence goes on to say,

> When the clear light of the ground arises, the material bodies
> of some people decrease in size for as long as seven days. Then,
> finally, they leave only the residue of their hair and nails behind.
> The dissolution of the body into minute particles is called the
> *small transference*. For those of superior faculties, this dissolu-
> tion of the body into minute particles may occur even during the
> practice of cutting through.[127]

According to Düdjom Rinpoché, this has happened countless times historically and right into the present, as at least two of his own disciples achieved rainbow body. There are many recent accounts, not only of people staying in tukdam, or meditative practice in the period following death, for days or weeks, but of witnesses seeing this.

Düdjom Lingpa's autobiography, *A Clear Mirror*, contains numerous revealed prophecies that describe manifestations of enlightenment in this very lifetime. In one case, the ḍākinī Yeshé Tsögyal, who was the divine human partner of Padmasambhava twelve hundred years ago, appeared to him in a pure vision and gave to Düdjom Lingpa a prophecy, saying,

> You are my heart's dearest child.
> These mustard seeds, thirteen grains, are spiritual heroes

who will, in the future, during the latter part of your life,
manifest enlightenment in this very lifetime.
They will become your thirteen holy disciples
equal to Buddha Dorjé Chang, Vajra Bearer.[128]

The prophecy is saying that thirteen of his disciples will achieve rainbow body and perfect enlightenment. It was widely acknowledged in Sertar, where Düdjom Lingpa was teaching in eastern Tibet, that thirteen of his disciples did, indeed, manifestly achieve enlightenment and rainbow body.

On another occasion, Düdjom Lingpa had a pure vision in which the ḍākinī Déjé Wangmo identified these thirteen individuals and prophesied,

Regarding these and others among your students,
if they cultivate their experience in the sacred instructions of
    supreme transference
in places isolated from the domain of the eight worldly
    concerns,
and they surrender wholeheartedly to this essential practice,
one hundred male and female disciples
will surely attain the rainbow body of supreme transference.[129]

She prophesied that among the direct and indirect disciples of Düdjom Lingpa, one hundred men and women disciples in this lineage will achieve great transference rainbow body. This is yet to happen. Will it happen? Don't look to someone else; come and see for yourself.

A Great Perfection

Düdjom Rinpoché was the mind emanation of one of Guru Rinpoché's twenty-five close disciples, Drokpen Khyeuchung Lotsāwa. Khyeuchung Lotsāwa (also referred to simply as Lotsāwa) was a translator who showed remarkable and prodigious aptitude at a very early age. He learned Sanskrit with ease and was quickly chosen to be part of the group of Tibetan translators under the tutelage of Padmasambhava. Khyeuchung Lotsāwa lived as a *ngakpa*, a lay tantric practitioner, and mastered all the secret Mantrayāna teachings that Padmasambhava conferred upon him and thereby became a great siddha, a great adept. His realization and power were such that he could summon birds from the sky through his mere gaze or a gesture of his hand, by which he gave them teachings. Like others among the twenty-five disciples, Khyeuchung Lotsāwa reincarnated over the centuries as a series of realized masters who spread and deepened the teachings of the Buddha, bringing enormous benefit to beings. One such reincarnation was Düdjom Lingpa, who was the body emanation of Khyeuchung Lotsāwa. Düdjom Lingpa, following his passing, manifested as five simultaneous emanations, one being the mind emanation known as Düdjom Rinpoché.

This root text is known as a "mind treasure," a *gongter* (*dgongs gter*), which means that this brief text from Dorjé Drolö, according to tradition, was instilled from the mind of Padmasambhava into the mindstream of his disciple Khyeuchung Lotsāwa some twelve hundred years ago as a mind-to-mind transfer of teachings. It remained there dormant, century after century, incarnation after incarnation, until finally in the twentieth century, this mind treasure was opened, and then Düdjom Rinpoché wrote down what he witnessed—the teachings of Padmasambhava manifesting in this wrathful form, as Dorjé Drolö.

The culmination is that this is the Great Perfection of the Buddha-dharma. It can also be seen as the Great Perfection of the physical sciences, or a knowing of the actual nature of the physical world. Likewise, it can be seen as the Great Perfection of the mind sciences, or a knowing of the actual nature and the potentials of the mind. One can also say that it is the deepest form of mysticism for which there are resonances or parallels in the great contemplative traditions of all the major religions of the world. This ultimate nonduality between science and religion is this Great Perfection, and it is permeated by the Great Perfection of the "love of wisdom," which is philosophy.

Colophon

AT THE VERY end of his commentary, Düdjom Rinpoché provides an author statement, saying,

> Due to the encouragement of Tsewang Paljor, the teacher from Nyö, and many other aspirants to this path, I, Jikdrel Yeshé Dorjé, have composed these concise, clear instructions so that they can be easily understood firsthand. May there be victory!

May we all gain victory over our mental afflictions and obscurations!

❖ Meditation: Resting in the Great Perfection

https://wisdomexperience.org/alan-wallace-dzokchen-meditation-16/

Find a comfortable posture and turn your mind to the Dharma with the motivation of bodhicitta. Strike the three vital points of your body, speech, and mind, coming to rest in this dynamic equilibrium—utterly still, yet vigilant, clear, and energetic.

Clearly distinguish between, and simultaneously be aware of, the stillness of awareness and the movements of the mind. Slip into that stream of mindful presence, free of distraction and grasping.

In this way, compose the flow of your mindfulness, monitoring it with introspection. Achieve stability within your mindstream and, once stability has been achieved, let the mystery be revealed—the mystery of the actual nature of the world of apprehended objects and the actual nature of the mind that apprehends them—and view everything as being dreamlike.

With your eyes open gently and your gaze resting vacantly in the space in front of you, open all five sensory doors to the outside world, viewing everything that arises to your mind as appearing, yet not really existent.

Then invert your awareness right in upon the apprehending mind to determine its actual nature. As you probe inward, recognize that this mind has no origin, no location, and no destination. This subjective mind is unborn.

Examine the character of unborn awareness. Recognize that, in here, no mind has ever arisen. Realize the emptiness of the origin, location, and destination of your own mind—the mind that is the basis of your existence as a sentient being. Rest in that open and free space that is beyond the duality of observer and observed, apprehender and apprehended, subject and object.

Observe the emptiness of the findability of your own mind—the emptiness of its own intrinsic identity that is nowhere to be found, not even by the buddhas. Yet, as you peer within, recognize that that open space is not only empty, but is permeated by luminosity; it is unborn, unceasing, nonlocal, and beyond time. Release into that primordial indivisibility of emptiness and luminosity. Rest in that primordial stillness with all of your six sense doors open wide, with nothing more to do.

See all appearances as empty, all of them as equally pure and manifesting as creative expressions of your own primordially pure pristine awareness. Rest in that view with nothing more. Continue like this in silence for the remainder of the session. ⁂

Dedication of Merit

Arriving at the culmination of the teachings on this root text and commentary by His Holiness Düdjom Rinpoché, let us bring to mind whatever virtue, merit, and goodness we have gained from our study and practice of these teachings, the Dzokchen view, the meditations, and our conduct both in meditation and out in the world. Further, bring to mind whatever else that may arise as worthy of dedication of merit. In light of this, dedicate the merit of this practice to the realization of our deepest and most cherished aspiration—our own perfect enlightenment for the sake of all sentient beings.

APPENDICES

1. A Brief Biography of His Holiness Düdjom Rinpoché

BY TULKU ORGYEN PHUNTSOK RINPOCHÉ

Düdjom Lingpa's immediate reincarnation was His Holiness Düdjom Rinpoché, Jikdrel Yeshé Dorjé, according to the incarnate lineage of the Düdjom tradition.

In the past, Düdjom Rinpoché was Rikdzin Nüden Dorjé; in the future, it is said, he will be born as the Sugata, Möpa Tayé; while in his lifetime he manifested as the representative of Padmasambhava, Drokben. His Holiness's previous incarnations have included some of the greatest gurus, yogis, and scholars—among them are Śāriputra, Saraha, and Khyeuchung Lotsāwa.

It was said in the prediction of Urgyen Dechen Lingpa, "In the future in Tibet, on the east of the Nine-Peaked Mountain, in the sacred buddhafield of the self-originated Vajravārāhī, there will be an emanation of Drokben, of royal lineage, named Jñāna. His beneficial activities are in accord with the Vajrayāna, although he conducts himself differently, unexpectedly, as a little boy with astonishing intelligence. He will either discover new terma or preserve old terma [or treasure teachings]. Whoever has connections with him will be taken to Ngayab Ling (Zangdok Palri) [i.e., the island of Cāmara, the location of the Copper-Colored Mountain]."

Indeed, Düdjom Rinpoché was of royal lineage, descended from Nyatri Tsenpo, the first king of Tibet, and from Powo Kanam Depa, the king of Powo. His father, Kathok Tulku Norbu Tenzin, was a famous tulku of the Pemakö region, from Kathok Monastery; his mother descended from

Ratna Lingpa, and was called Namgyal Drölma. His Holiness was born in the Water Dragon year, 1904, early in the morning of the tenth day of the sixth month, with many amazing signs. His previous incarnation, Düdjom Lingpa, had told his disciples: "Now in this degenerate age, go to the secret land of Pemakö. Whoever relies on me, go in that direction! Before you young ones get there, I, the old one, will already be there." This came to pass exactly as predicted. He was already three years old when they recognized his reincarnation. Since His Holiness was a direct emanation of Düdjom Lingpa, he could remember his past lives clearly.

Phuktrul Gyurmé Ngedön Wangpo and Lama Thupten Chönjor, two of Düdjom Lingpa's students, came to Pemakö and enthroned him. Gradually the disciples of the previous Düdjom arrived. His Holiness was taught reading, writing, and the five common sciences, and he studied many texts and commentaries. As he was taught, the power of his awareness blazed like fire! Whatever he learned, he could comprehend through a mere indication. It is said by Lama Könrab that at the age of five, he started discovering terma.

He studied for sixteen years with Phuktrul Gyurmé Ngedön Wangpo, who was a holder of the teachings of the previous Düdjom. He also received the "rediscovered teachings" of the previous Düdjom from Jedrung Trinlé Jampa Jungné of Riwoché. Ngedön Wangpo said to him, "The Terdzö represents the activity of Khyentsé and Kongtrül. I have given this teaching five times and you will give it ten times. The deep teachings of the previous ones have been offered as a mandala in the hands of the 'Wealth Holders.' Now, as I have obeyed my teacher's orders, likewise use your experience for the sake of beings."

His Holiness said that, while very young, he always had various visions, and his karma to discover the deep treasures awoke. At thirteen, he met Guru Rinpoché (with his divine partner) in person, and after having received the legacy of the self-appearing teacher, who is not a human being, the wisdom ḍākinīs gave him the yellow papers and he wrote down these mind treasure teachings.

Then he started benefiting beings, and as his teachers prophesied, he gave the empowerments and transmissions of the Vajrayāna throughout Tibet. His Holiness wrote about twenty-three volumes of various gongter (mind treasures) and treatises, all of which have been published. He also collected all the Kama teachings (oral transmissions) of the Nyingma lineage, as Jamgön Kongtrül had collected the terma teachings.

In Pemakö, he established many new monasteries for both *gelong* (ordained monks) and *ngagpa* (yogis), and regrouped many texts. In the Kongpo region, he reconstructed the Thadül Buchu Lhakhang; he erected the tantric center of Lama Ling; at Tso Pema, he established a retreat center; in Orissa (now called Odiśa), he established Düdül Rabten Ling; and in Kalimpong, he founded the Zangdokpalri Monastery. In North America he established many Dharma centers, named Yeshé Nyingpo, as well as many retreat centers; in Europe he established Dorjé Nyingpo in Paris, and Urgyen Samyé Chöling Meditation and Study Center in Dordogne, France. Further, many other Dharma centers around the world were under his guidance.

Whenever he gave teachings in Tibet and India, great teachers came to receive them. Among all the high lamas, there are none who did not receive teachings from him. They all had great confidence in his realization. So numerous were his disciples that they cannot possibly be counted. Nyingmapas from Tibet, Bhutan, India, Ladakh, and all around the globe were his students.

Lodrö Tayé, who led a life encompassing the activities of one hundred tertöns (treasure revealers), has said that Möpa Tayé (Düdjom Rinpoché's future incarnation) will have the activity of one thousand buddhas. That this great being will perform the activity of all his previous lives and have many disciples is all due to the power of his own bodhicitta and prayers of aspiration.

The Düdjom Lineage

As previously mentioned, Düdjom Lingpa revealed the lineage known as Düdjom Tersar, consisting of many texts and twenty-two volumes of teachings. He stated that these teachings were especially profound and appropriate for these degenerate times. Following this fresh and undiluted path, thirteen of his disciples attained rainbow body in their own lifetimes, and a thousand others attained the level of *rikdzin* (Skt. vidyādhara), or "awareness holder."

His Holiness Düdjom Rinpoché also revealed about twenty-three volumes of various mind treasures and treatises, all of which have been published and are available today.

The Düdjom Tersar lineage, from Düdjom Lingpa and Düdjom Rinpoché, is fresh, vivid, and direct, with no loss of meaning, words, or blessing. These teachings, from Guru Rinpoché to Düdjom Rinpoché and then to us, are a direct, short lineage. Therefore this lineage is uncontaminated and has not degenerated through broken samaya. The blessings and attainments are immediate.

Padmasambhava's tradition is the Early Translation Great Perfection School and Düdjom Lingpa is the chariot of the essential true meaning. May his profound treasure doctrine be maintained without waning through study and practice until the end of cyclic existence.

2. A Brief Biography of the Venerable Gyatrul Rinpoché

BY SANGYÉ KHANDRO

From *The Generation Stage of Buddhist Tantra.*

THE VENERABLE Gyatrul Rinpoché was born in the year of the Wood Ox, 1925, in Szechuan Province, China. Born into a noble family, he spent a happy childhood with parents and family members for his first eight years. In his eighth year, Rinpoché was formally recognized as the reincarnation of Sampa Kunkyab, taken to Dhomang Monastery (an important branch of Palyul Monastery), enthroned, and placed under the strict care of his root guru Tulku Natsok Rangdröl and other tutors. Rinpoché was recognized to be a tulku by Khyentsé Chökyi Lodrö and his root teacher Tulku Natsok Rangdröl, as well as Palyul Chöktrul Rinpoché of Tarthang Monastery.

Once enthroned at Dhomang Monastery, Rinpoché began many years of formal study and training. As a young man, he maintained constant company with his root guru Tulku Natsok, spending many years with him in solitary retreat, moving from one isolated location to another. Rinpoché studied under some of the greatest Nyingmapa mahāsiddhas of this century and carried with him all the blessings and knowledge that he received directly from his teachers.

Due to the onset of the Chinese invasion of Tibet, it was foretold that Rinpoché should flee his homeland, and his principal teachers even gave the details of his future work propagating the Dharma in foreign lands. Tulku Natsok Rangdröl, who was one of the five emanations of His Holiness

Düdjom Rinpoché—that of enlightened activity—stayed behind, explaining that it was his karma to remain. After one year of tremendous hardship on the road to freedom with a crowd of almost two thousand, Rinpoché crossed over the Nepalese border to safety with only two hundred survivors.

In the years that followed, he worked in the service of His Holiness the Dalai Lama as well as His Holiness the Karmapa. Later in 1972, His Holiness the Dalai Lama and His Holiness Düdjom Rinpoché chose Rinpoché as the Nyingmapa representative to accompany the first group of Tibetans who were sent to resettle in Canada. After arriving in the West, Rinpoché traveled extensively around the United States and Canada at the invitation of Tibetan and Western disciples alike. In 1976, when His Holiness Düdjom Rinpoché visited the West for a second time, he asked Gyatrul Rinpoché to be his spiritual representative on the West Coast. Rinpoché accepted this position out of his great devotion for Kyabjé Düdjom Rinpoché and since that time, maintained his loyal devotion to Düdjom Rinpoché by establishing several Yeshé Nyingpo centers in the United States, including Tashi Chöling in the Siskiyou Mountains near the border of California and Oregon. This site was consecrated by His Holiness Düdjom Rinpoché and has hosted many great lamas, as well as two major lineage empowerments given by Kyabjé Penor Rinpoché. The retreat center presently consists of several hundred acres of isolated forest land and a four-story traditional temple. Rinpoché also established Orgyen Dorjé Den in Alameda, California, Yeshé Nyingpo Mexico in Ensenada, Baja California, and Dorjé Ling in Portland, Oregon.

Rinpoché spent over forty years traveling and teaching in the West and in 2023 entered parinirvāṇa at the age of ninety-eight. Rinpoché remained in a meditative state for several weeks, and there were many marvelous signs of his enlightenment. He was widely known for his skillful ability to explain the Vajrayāna path in simple terms, and for his noble qualities of unfailing humor and compassion.

3. An Autobiographical Sketch

BY ALAN WALLACE

I WAS BORN IN Pasadena, California. My father was a Baptist minister and theologian. From the time I was a young boy until I went to university at the age of eighteen, I became familiar with Christianity and admired much of it—the life of Jesus, his teachings, the emphasis on ethics, love, and compassion. As His Holiness the Dalai Lama has so often commented, these are central themes of all of the great religions of the world. Simply as a person growing up and going to church every Sunday for many years, I learned a lot.

However, even as an adolescent, I found that I simply could not accept some of the assertions of the Christian doctrine to which I had been exposed. Buddhism has many diverse schools, from Theravāda, to the Pure Land school of Japan, to Vajrayāna, plus four schools of Indian Buddhist philosophy. In a comparable way, over the course of two thousand years, Christianity has also developed many schools that vary considerably. When I speak of my personal encounter with Christianity, this does not represent Christianity as a whole; my experience is with a very specific lineage within Protestant Christianity in America. As I was growing up, I found qualities I deeply admired, and yet there were elements of their view, assertions, and so forth, that didn't make sense to me. I felt these assertions were refuted by direct perception or by reasoning and, therefore, I could not accept them.

When I was thirteen years old and in middle school, I had a wonderful science teacher who inspired in me a love of nature and the wish to preserve the natural environment and the balance of the ecosphere as a whole. It was then that my interest turned to science, in particular biology and especially ecology, the latter of which is the study of the whole environment and its relationship with living organisms. Essentially, ecology highlights the interdependence of everything on our planet in the natural world. From that time, I aspired to become a scientist—specifically, an ecologist and environmentalist—planning to pursue this path for my whole education and career. With this goal, I continued focusing on biology, physics, and chemistry through high school and the first two years of university.

During my first two years at the University of California, San Diego, I studied science and Western philosophy. Western philosophy had many points I found to be very deep and meaningful. However, the culmination of philosophy seems to be to write a book or essay, or give a lecture, but it doesn't seem to have much practical application, nor are there many methods to test philosophical theories experientially in order to either validate or repudiate them. For me, this pursuit seemed to be purely intellectual and fundamentally dissatisfying.

By the time I was twenty, I found truths in the fact that many scientific assertions are based on direct perception, or are rooted in compelling, logical reasoning, including mathematical reasonings. What I didn't find, however, was meaning—there was nothing that gave me genuine happiness. I found fleeting pleasure in interesting scientific discoveries, but I didn't find anything that would transform my mind or bring a lasting sense of fulfillment. Science seemed to have nothing to offer if I became depressed or dissatisfied. I've studied science since then, but even at that time, it was clear to me that modern science is embedded in materialism—which says that "the universe out there is mindless and consists only of physical phenomena; ethics is whatever you say it is, so you have to improvise; human beings are only animals; and human minds are what human brains do." I found that worldview groundless, sterile, and meaningless. I also found the contentions of materialism to be as unbelievable as many things I heard in the particular version of Christianity in which I was raised, and which were refuted by experience and reasoning. Yet the scientific community seems to accept this dogma as if they're God-given truths. However, their ersatz religion is neither Christianity nor Judaism; their religion is materialism, often called "physicalism."

I also found nothing in Western philosophy to cultivate the mind, and nothing in science to bring about inner transformation or find meaning. This led to my becoming disillusioned with Western, or Eurocentric, civilization as a whole. Then came a turning point: around that age, I started picking up books on Buddhism. When I was nineteen, I took a one-year course on the culture and history of India, which included some information on Buddhism, albeit very thin and superficially presented. After two years at UC San Diego, I desperately wanted a change of environment. I was fluent in German, as I'd lived part of my childhood and adolescence in Switzerland, so I enrolled in the junior-year-abroad program from the University of California to spend my third year at the University of Göttingen in Germany. The summer before the academic year began, I hitchhiked around Europe, and while staying at a youth hostel in the Swiss alpine village of Grindelwald, I picked up a copy of W. Y. Evans-Wentz's book *The Tibetan Book of the Great Liberation*, which included an English translation of Padmasambhava's teachings on Dzokchen, the Great Perfection. It was love at first sight! Although I comprehended very little of these esoteric teachings, I was deeply, intuitively drawn to them as to nothing else.

As my summer of touring Europe was coming to a close, I found myself in the Norwegian port city of Bergen, and on the morning before I set out on the journey south to Göttingen, I wrote in my journal, "I need to find a wise old man to give me personal guidance." That afternoon, while standing on the side of the long road between Bergen and Oslo, an old man driving a black Volkswagen Beetle pulled over and offered me a ride. He was a long-term resident of Norway, though of German origin, and he spoke English. I shared with him my interest in Buddhism, whereby he responded that he was a Buddhist monk, ordained in Nepal, and had been given the monastic name Sugata. We immediately fell into a lively conversation, culminating in his pith advice to me, "Do some good. Help the Tibetans." That was just enough guidance to lead me on the next step of my journey.

When I'd settled into my one-room apartment in Göttingen and checked out the curriculum at the university, I found that they offered no courses in ecology, and that their curriculum in philosophy was dry and uninspiring. To my enormous surprise and delight, I swiftly learned that the Indology Department at the university had requested that His Holiness the Dalai Lama appoint a Tibetan lama to teach the Tibetan language in their department, and he chose a lama named Dzongtsé Rinpoché from the Tibet Institute in Rikon. I quickly sought him out and consequently dropped all my courses in science and philosophy, focusing solely on studying classical and spoken Tibetan. I sensed that if I were to immerse myself in Tibetan Buddhism—to which I was most drawn among all the schools of Buddhism—I would need to master the Tibetan language.

After my year in Göttingen, during which I engaged deeply in reading all I could about Buddhism, on the advice of Dzongtsé Rinpoché, I spent the summer studying with a Sakya Lama named Sherab Gyaltsen at the monastery called the Tibet Institute in Rikon, Switzerland. While there, a bulletin arrived from Dharamsala, India, saying that on the first of October of that year, 1971, the Library of Tibetan Works and Archives would open, and that a one-year course in Buddhism would be offered for Westerners with English translation under the supervision of His Holiness the Dalai Lama. I told Lama Sherab Gyaltsen that I wished to go to Nepal and find an accomplished yogi under whom I could train; I wanted only to meditate, not to return to a classroom situation. Contrarily he replied, "This opportunity is too good for you to miss. Go to Dharamsala." I followed his advice, taking a charter flight from Munich to Bombay, followed by a flight to Delhi, then a train to Pathankot, the nearest railhead to Dharamsala, and finally a five-hour bus ride to Dharamsala. I had brought with me a letter of introduction to Dr. Yeshi Dhonden, the personal physician to His Holiness the Dalai Lama, from one of the monks in the monastery in Rikon. I immediately made my way to his home and clinic, and upon reading the letter, he promptly invited me to take up lodging in his home, where I lived for the next eighteen months. No one there spoke English, so it was a perfect environment for me to learn Tibetan, in which I swiftly became fluent.

That fall, I enrolled in the first one-year class at the Library of Tibetan Works and Archives, taught by an outstanding Gelukpa lama by the name of Geshé Ngawang Dhargyey. There were eight Western students in the class who gathered six days each week, and our teacher began by presenting illuminating teachings on the stages to the path to enlightenment, or lamrim. Early in my studies with him, Geshé Ngawang Dhargyey emphasized to me the importance of reaching the Mahāyāna path in this lifetime, for it is only with this degree of realization that one becomes a bodhisattva and achieves irreversible spiritual maturation. With this accomplishment, one will always be a bodhisattva in all future lifetimes until one becomes a buddha. I found this deeply inspiring, and it has remained my aspiration ever since.

During the first months of my stay in Dr. Dhonden's home, he assured me that I would be granted a personal audience with His Holiness the Dalai Lama when I wished. I did not leap at the opportunity at first; I wanted to wait until I had a pressing question to pose to him so that I would not waste his precious time. Before long, I was met with a serious problem for which I had no solution. I had gone to study with Tibetan lamas in order to grow in wisdom, compassion, and other virtues, but insofar as my efforts proved to be fruitful, how was I to avoid cultivating a sense of superiority over others who were not devoting themselves to such a life of virtue? To put it bluntly: How could I become a better person without concluding that I'm increasingly better than others? With this burning question, I sought and was granted my first personal audience with His Holiness. He began with an analogy, telling me to imagine a homeless person who comes begging at an affluent house and, instead of being given a few leftovers, is invited to join the family for a sumptuous meal. After eating his fill, His Holiness asked me, would he feel proud? No, I responded, he would feel only grateful. He then commented that I was like a beggar who came to Dharamsala seeking spiritual nourishment. He added that the greater one's intelligence and understanding, the greater responsibility one has. His response struck right to the heart of the matter that concerned me, and I knew that I had found my root lama.

Over the early months that I lived in Dharamsala, I also became a disciple of another fine lama named Geshé Rabten, who gave me my first one-on-one meditation instruction. He was a superb scholar, a doctrinal consultant (or *tsenshab*) for His Holiness, and after completing his formal academic training at Sera Monastery in Tibet, he devoted himself full time to meditation. He lived in retreat in a cowshed on the mountainside above McLeod Ganj, the village above Dharamsala populated by around two thousand Tibetan refugees. At that time, none of us foreigners studying Buddhism in Dharamsala knew what the academic title *geshé* meant, so I asked Geshé Rabten to tell me his life story. After consulting with His

Holiness about my request, he agreed, and over a period of several months, I hiked up to Geshé Rabten's cabin and posed a series of questions to him, to which he responded by way of his Tibetan disciple Gonsar Rinpoché, who spoke some English. I was so impressed by Geshé Rabten's life story, and especially by the rigor and depth of his twenty-four years of education at Sera Monastery, that I was inspired to take monastic ordination and receive such training myself.

In another private audience with His Holiness I expressed this wish, but he responded that if I were to go to the south of India where Sera Monastery had been re-established, I would attend classes with Tibetan boys ten years younger than I, which would be awkward. Instead, he told me that the Institute of Buddhist Dialectics would soon open under his supervision in McLeod Ganj, intended primarily for young Tibetan monks in their late teens who had already received years of modern education in India. The education offered there, all conducted in Tibetan, would be much more appropriate for me, he said. I continued my studies at the Library for several more months, eventually took monastic novice vows from Geshé Rabten, and on July 6, 1973, His Holiness's birthday, I entered the first class at the Institute of Buddhist Dialectics together with about thirty Tibetan monks. Two years later, I received full monastic ordination from His Holiness.

I completed all the basic trainings in the art of debate, basic Buddhist philosophy, psychology, and logic at the institute, and then, with the encouragement of His Holiness, I temporarily withdrew from this formal education and spent about a year in meditation retreat in a cabin in the mountains above McLeod Ganj. Then when I asked His Holiness for further guidance, he encouraged me to return to the Tibet Institute in Rikon, Switzerland, where he had appointed Geshé Rabten to become abbot. I thus moved to Rikon, studied with and interpreted for Geshé Rabten there for two years and then for another two years at the Institute for Higher Tibetan Studies, which he established on a mountainside overlooking Lake Geneva. By the autumn of 1979, after almost ten years of studying Buddhism, interpreting for numerous lamas at the Institute for Higher Tibetan Studies and elsewhere, meditating, and teaching, all I wanted to do was to devote myself full time to meditation. I wrote to His Holiness, once again seeking his guidance, and he responded by inviting me to return

to McLeod Ganj to go into meditation retreat under his personal guidance. I was thrilled at this prospect and returned to India in the spring of
1980. Over the next four years, I devoted myself to a series of solitary meditation retreats in India, Sri Lanka, and the United States, training in various forms of meditation and yoga, first with His Holiness and the Tibetan
yogis Gen Lamrimpa and Jhampa Wangdü, and later with the Theravādin
monk Balangoda Ananda Maitreya Thero in Sri Lanka, the yoga master B.
K. S. Iyengar, and the accomplished yogi and teacher of Vedanta philosophy
Swami Narayan Anand in India.

By the summer of 1984, I felt the time had come for me to begin inte-
grating what I had learned and experienced over the past fourteen years of
immersion in Buddhist study and practice with the first twenty years of my
life. In particular, I wanted to learn how compatible the Buddhist worldview was with modern science. Upon returning to the United States, I
enrolled at Amherst College, where I completed my undergraduate education in two and a half years, studying physics, mathematics, the history
and philosophy of science, and Sanskrit. Immediately after my graduation,
I spent a year in solitary meditation in the eastern Sierra Nevada mountains in California. During that time, after maintaining my monastic vows
in the U.S. for the past six years and finding how unconducive American
society was to the monastic way of life, with the permission of His Holiness, I returned my monastic vows in the spring of 1987. Although I have
lived as a lay practitioner ever since, my dedication to Buddhist study and
practice has remained unaltered. During 1988, I assisted the Tibetan yogi
Gen Lamrimpa in leading a one-year śamatha meditation retreat for twelve
participants, which I had organized at Cloud Mountain Retreat Center in
Castle Rock, Washington.

In 1989, I wished to further my Western education in religion and philosophy, so I enrolled in the graduate program in religious studies at Stanford
University. In that same year, I married the Croatian Sanskrit scholar Vesna
Acimovic. I studied comparative religion and many branches of philosophy
for six years, earning my doctorate in 1995, the same year that Vesna completed her doctorate in South Asian Studies at the University of California,
Berkeley.

While I was first inspired to study Tibetan Buddhism upon reading about Dzokchen, the Great Perfection, in *The Tibetan Book of the Great Liberation* in 1970, it was not until the fall of 1989 that I first had the opportunity to receive Dzokchen teachings, granted by His Holiness in San Jose, California, just a short distance south of Stanford where I had recently matriculated. The following spring I received teachings on dream yoga from Gyatrul Rinpoché, also in San Jose. I was deeply inspired by his teachings then and increasingly as the time came when I began receiving oral transmissions and commentaries from him on Dzokchen. He has been my primary Dzokchen lama ever since. During the period from 1992–97, I had the privilege of serving as his primary interpreter, as he gave many pith instructions on Dzokchen and Mahāmudrā, which resulted in the publication of several books based on his teachings. Vesna and I lived right across from his home in Half Moon Bay, California, from 1995–97, during which we were both involved in translating multiple Buddhist texts from Sanskrit and Tibetan into English. Around this time, we accepted an invitation for both of us to teach in the Department of Religious Studies at the University of California, Santa Barbara. She taught Sanskrit, and I taught many courses on Tibetan Buddhism and language. She has remained teaching there, now as a full professor, while I left in 2001—first to go into solitary retreat for six months, then to create the Santa Barbara Institute for Consciousness Studies, and many years later to conceive of the three branches of the Center for Contemplative Research in Crestone, Colorado, Castellina Marittima, Italy, and on the South Island of New Zealand.

This summary leads me to the current day, where over these past fifty years I've come to appreciate the deep wisdom of the Buddhist tradition, which has profoundly fulfilled my longing to know reality and lead a meaningful life. Buddhism is not "just a religion." In the West, "religion" means a way of engaging with reality that is fundamentally based on faith, in the teachings of God, Jesus, the prophets, Muhammad, or founders of what the West regards as "Asian religions." Buddhism certainly includes many aspects the West deems to be "religious," but from the very beginning, it has also included philosophy and its own form of first-person, or contemplative, science. This is not "just religion," nor is it simply a philosophy or a science in the Western sense of these terms. From the age of twenty, I yearned for a deeper sense of meaning, as is often found in religion and philosophy, but also for a way to discover truths about the nature of reality, as is characteristic of science. While I never found these three fields to be deeply integrated in Western civilization, this is exactly what I found in Buddhism: a world view, meditation, and way of life that are all meaningful and true. I have found my home in Buddhism and have now come to feel at home in the West as well as in Asia.

Notes

1. Note that in Düdjom Rinpoché's commentary, this verse is relocated and discussed later on, in the section entitled, "Practicing by Means of Meditation."

2. Düdjom Lingpa, *The Vajra Essence: Düdjom Lingpa's Visions of the Great Perfection*, vol. 3, revised edition, translated by B. Alan Wallace and Eva Natanya (New York, NY: Wisdom Publications, forthcoming).

3. Ven. Gyatrul Rinpoche, *Meditation, Transformation, and Dream Yoga*, 2nd ed., trans. Sangye Khandro and B. Alan Wallace (Ithaca, NY: Snow Lion Publications, 2002), 143–44.

4. Ibid., 145.

5. Ibid., 146.

6. Ibid., 146.

7. Ibid., 147.

8. Ibid., 146.

9. Ibid., 147.

10. Ibid., 147.

11. Ibid., 150–51.

12. Düdjom Lingpa, *The Vajra Essence*, forthcoming.

13. Ibid.

14. Ven. Gyatrul Rinpoche, *Meditation, Transformation, and Dream Yoga*, 165.

15. William James, *Principles of Psychology*, vol. 1 (New York: Henry Holt and Company, 1890), 424.

16. William James, *Talks to Teachers on Psychology: And to Students on Some of Life's Ideals* (New York: Henry Holt and Company, 1899), 76.

17. "Mindfulness" is a translation of the Sanskrit term *smṛti* (Pāli *sati*; Tib. *drenpa, dran pa*).

18. *Lta sgom spyod gsum mdor bsdus.*

19. See *A Summary of the View, Meditation, and Conduct* by Domang Yangthang Rinpoché, in B. Alan Wallace and Eva Natanya, *Śamatha and Vipaśyanā: An Anthology of Pith Instructions* (New York, NY: Wisdom Publications, 2025).

20. Ven. Gyatrul Rinpoche, *Meditation, Transformation, and Dream Yoga*, 158–59.

21. Ibid., 159.

22. Ibid., 159.
23. Ibid., 159.
24. Translated in B. Alan Wallace, *Open Mind: View and Meditation in the Lineage of Lerab Lingpa*, ed. Eva Natanya (Somerville, MA: Wisdom Publications, 2018).
25. Ibid., 163.
26. Ibid., 163–64.
27. Ibid., 164.
28. Ibid., 164.
29. Ibid., 164.
30. Ven. Gyatrul Rinpoche, *Meditation, Transformation, and Dream Yoga*, 152.
31. Chapter I, verse 28.
32. Ven. Gyatrul Rinpoche, *Meditation, Transformation, and Dream Yoga*, 152.
33. Düdjom Lingpa, *The Vajra Essence*, forthcoming.
34. Ven. Gyatrul Rinpoche, *Meditation, Transformation, and Dream Yoga*, 163.
35. Ibid., 163.
36. Ibid., 163.
37. Karma Chagmé and Gyatrul Rinpoche, *A Spacious Path to Freedom: Practical Instructions on the Union of Mahāmudrā and Atiyoga*, trans. B. Alan Wallace (Ithaca, NY: Snow Lion Publications, 1998), 100.
38. Ibid., 100.
39. Ibid., 100–101.
40. Ibid., 101.
41. Wallace, *Open Mind*, 164.
42. Ibid., 164–65, translation slightly modified.
43. Ibid., 165.
44. Ibid., 165.
45. Ven. Gyatrul Rinpoche, *Meditation, Transformation, and Dream Yoga*, 164.
46. Ibid., 164.
47. Stephen Hawking made this quip in an interview with Ken Campbell on the British TV show *Reality on the Rocks: Beyond Our Ken*, which aired February 26, 1995.
48. Translated in B. Alan Wallace, *The Art of Transforming the Mind: A Meditator's Guide to the Tibetan Practice of Lojong* (Boulder, CO: Shambhala Publications, 2022).
49. William James, *Principles of Psychology*, vol. 2 (New York: Henry Holt and Company, 1890), 322.
50. *Atomic Theory and the Description of Nature* (Cambridge: Cambridge University Press, 1934), 18.
51. Quoted in Christopher A. Fuchs, N. David Mermin, and Rüdiger Schack, "An Introduction to QBism with an Application to the Locality of Quantum Mechanics," *American Journal of Physics* 82, no. 8 (2014): 749.
52. *Nova*, season 46, episode 2, "Einstein's Quantum Riddle," produced and directed

by Jamie Lochhead, aired January 9, 2019 on PBS. https://www.pbs.org/video
/einsteins-quantum-riddle-ykvwhm/.

53. Ibid.

54. Amanda Gefter, "A Private View of Quantum Reality," *Quanta Magazine*, June 4,
2015, https://www.quantamagazine.org/quantum-bayesianism-explained-by
-its-founder-20150604/

55. Ibid.

56. Hans Christian von Baeyer, *QBism: The Future of Quantum Physics* (Cambridge,
MA: Harvard University Press, 2016), 188.

57. Amanda Gefter, "The Evolutionary Argument Against Reality," *Quanta Magazine*,
April 21, 2016, https://www.quantamagazine.org/the-evolutionary-argument
-against-reality-20160421/.

58. *Wisdom Podcast*, episode 100, "His Holiness the Dalai Lama: Science and Philosophy
in the Indian Buddhist Classics," posted January 8, 2021. https://wisdomexperience
.org/wisdom-podcast/his-holiness-the-dalai-lama/.

59. William James, *The Principles of Psychology*, Vol. I (New York: Dover Publications, 1890/1950), 116.

60. Translated in B. Alan Wallace, *The Art of Transforming the Mind*, 243, translation
slightly modified.

61. Ibid., translation slightly modified.

62. Ven. Gyatrul Rinpoche, *Meditation, Transformation, and Dream Yoga*, 165.

63. Ibid., 165.

64. Ibid., 165.

65. Ibid., 165.

66. Ibid., 165.

67. Ibid., 165.

68. Karma Chagmé and Gyatrul Rinpoche, *A Spacious Path to Freedom*, 108.

69. Ven. Gyatrul Rinpoche, *Meditation, Transformation, and Dream Yoga*, 166.

70. Ibid., 166.

71. My translation. See also Anālayo Bhikkhu. *Satipaṭṭhāna: The Direct Path to Realization* (Birmingham: Windhorse Publications, 2006).

72. Ven. Gyatrul Rinpoche, *Meditation, Transformation, and Dream Yoga*, 166.

73. Ibid., 167.

74. Ibid., 167.

75. *Small Exposition of the Stages of the Path to Enlightenment* (*Byang chub lam gyi
rim pa chung ba*), translated in B. Alan Wallace, *Balancing the Mind: A Tibetan
Buddhist Approach to Refining Attention* (Ithaca, NY: Snow Lion Publications,
2005), 203.

76. Asaṅga's Śrāvakabhūmi, cited in ibid.

77. See *The Great Commentary to Mingyur Dorje's Buddhahood in the Palm of Your
Hand by Karma Chakmé*, in B. Alan Wallace and Eva Natanya, *Śamatha and
Vipaśyanā: An Anthology of Pith Instructions* (New York, NY: Wisdom Publica-
tions, 2025).

78. This quote is from a speech given by Planck in 1944 in Florence, Italy, entitled *Das Wesen der Materie* [*The Nature of Matter*].

79. Quoted in K. C. Cole, "In Patterns, Not Particles, Physicists Trust," *Los Angeles Times*, March 4, 1999.

80. Richard Feynman, Robert Leighton, and Matthew Sands, *The Feynman Lectures on Physics* (London, 1966; California Institute of Technology online edition, 2013), vol. 1, chap. 4, https://www.feynmanlectures.caltech.edu/I_04.html.

81. http://www.tedxleuven.com/?q=2012/thomas-hertog.

82. Translated in B. Alan Wallace, *Minding Closely: The Four Applications of Mindfulness* (Ithaca, NY: Snow Lion Publications, 2011).

83. Albert Einstein and Leopold Infeld, *The Evolution of Physics*, ed. C. P. Snow (Cambridge: Cambridge University Press, 1938).

84. Nima Arkani-Hamed, "The Future of Fundamental Physics," Cornell Messenger Lectures, 2010, https://www.youtube.com/watch?v=SWWBuHszyD8.

85. Andrei Linde, "Choose Your Own Universe" in *Spiritual Information:100 Perspectives on Science and Religion*, Charles L. Harper, Jr., ed. (West Conshohocken, PA, 2005), 139.

86. *Bodhicittavivāraṇa*, v. 34.

87. Düdjom Lingpa, *Heart of the Great Perfection: Düdjom Lingpa's Visions of the Great Perfection*, vol. 1, revised edition, translated by B. Alan Wallace and Eva Natanya (New York, NY: Wisdom Publications, forthcoming).

88. Ibid., 120.

89. Ibid., 120–21.

90. Ibid., 36.

91. Ibid., 170.

92. Ven. Gyatrul Rinpoche, *Meditation, Transformation, and Dream Yoga*, 168.

93. Ibid., 168–69.

94. Düdjom Lingpa, *The Vajra Essence*, forthcoming.

95. Ibid., 28.

96. Ibid., 28.

97. Buddhaghosa, *The Path of Purification: The Classic Manual of Buddhist Doctrine and Meditation*, trans. from the Pali by Bhikkhu Ñāṇamoli (Kandy: Sri Lanka: Buddhist Publication Society, 2011), Chapter IV, v. 31.

98. *Rang bzhin rdzogs pa chen po'i rang zhal mngon du byed pa'i gdams pa ma bsgom sangs rgyas*, in vol. 16 of *Collected Works of the Emanated Great Treasures, the Secret, Profound Treasures of Düdjom Lingpa* (Thimphu, Bhutan: Lama Kuenzang Wangdue, 2004).

99. *Rang bzhin rdzogs pa chen po ma bsgom sangs rgyas kyi zin bris dpal ldan bla ma'i zhal rgyun nag 'gros su bkod pa tshig don rab gsal skal ldan dgyes pa'i mgul rgyan*, in vol. 21 of *Collected Works of the Emanated Great Treasures, the Secret, Profound Treasures of Düdjom Lingpa* (Thimphu, Bhutan: Lama Kuenzang Wangdue, 2004).

100. Düdjom Lingpa and Sera Khandro, *Buddhahood Without Meditation: Düdjom Lingpa's Visions of the Great Perfection*, vol. 2, revised edition, translated

by B. Alan Wallace and Eva Natanya (New York, NY: Wisdom Publications, forthcoming).

101. Ibid., 251.
102. Ibid., 251.
103. Ibid., 251.
104. Ven. Gyatrul Rinpoche, *Meditation, Transformation, and Dream Yoga*, 169.
105. *Bāhiya Sutta* [Udāna I.10].
106. Wallace, *Open Mind*, 32, translation slightly modified.
107. See *A Summary of the View, Meditation, and Conduct*, in B. Alan Wallace and Eva Natanya, *Śamatha and Vipaśyanā: An Anthology of Pith Instructions*.
108. Ibid.
109. Düdjom Lingpa and Sera Khandro, *Buddhahood Without Meditation*, forthcoming.
110. Ven. Gyatrul Rinpoche, *Meditation, Transformation, and Dream Yoga*, 169–70.
111. Ibid., 170.
112. Ibid., 170.
113. Ibid., 170.
114. Padmasambhava and Gyatrul Rinpoche, *Natural Liberation: Padmasambhava's Teachings on the Six Bardos*, trans. B. Alan Wallace (Somerville, MA: Wisdom Publications, 2012), 164.
115. Ibid., 166.
116. *Sūdasutta*, Saṃyutta Nikāya V 152.
117. "The Questions on Conventional Names," in *Milindapañha* 3.1.1.
118. *Bāhiya Sutta* [Udāna I.10].
119. John 10:30.
120. Galatians 2:20.
121. Ven. Gyatrul Rinpoche, *Meditation, Transformation, and Dream Yoga*, 171.
122. Düdjom Lingpa, *The Vajra Essence*, forthcoming.
123. Düdjom Lingpa, *The Vajra Essence*, forthcoming.
124. Ibid., 257.
125. Ibid., 254.
126. Ibid., 254.
127. Ibid., 254.
128. Traktung Düdjom Lingpa, *A Clear Mirror: The Visionary Autobiography of a Tibetan Master*, trans. Chönyi Drolma (Hong Kong: Rangjung Yeshe Publications, 2011), 260.
129. Ibid., 181.

Bibliography

Source Texts

Düdjom Rinpoché Jikdrel Yeshé Dorjé. *Guidance Transmitted One-on-One to Those of Good Fortune: An Authentic Dharma Collection from the Profound Mind Treasure of Jikdrel Yeshé Dorjé Drodül Lingpa Tsel. 'Jigs bral ye shes rdo rje 'gro 'dul gling pa rtsal gyi zab mo dgongs pa'i gter gyi chos sde yang dag pa ste skal ldan gcig la chig brgyud du gdams pa.* From *Rang gter bla ma drag po gro lod kyi skor la spyi'i rtsa gzhung: yang gsang thugs kyi thig le las, lo rgyus lung gi byang bu.* In vol. 15 (*ba*) of *The Collected Writings and Revelations of H. H. Bdud-'joms rin-po-che 'jigs-bral-ye-ses-rdo-rje* (gsung 'bum/'jigs bral ye shes rdo rje), 128–29. Kalimpong: Dupjung Lama, 1979–1985.

———. *The Illumination of Primordial Wisdom: An Instruction Manual on the Originally Pure Stage of Completion of the Powerful and Ferocious Dorjé Drolö, Subduer of Demons. Bdud 'dul dbang drag rdo rje gro lod kyi rdzogs rim ka dag gi khrid yig ye shes snang ba.* In vol. 15 (*ba*) of *The Collected Writings and Revelations of H. H. Bdud-'joms rin-po-che 'jigs-bral-ye-ses-rdo-rje* (*gsung 'bum/'jigs bral ye shes rdo rje*), 423–33. Kalimpong: Dupjung Lama, 1979–1985.

Gyatrul Rinpoche, Ven. *Meditation, Transformation, and Dream Yoga.* 2nd ed. Translated by Sangye Khandro and B. Alan Wallace. Ithaca, NY: Snow Lion Publications, 2002.

Citations

Arkani-Hamed, Nima. "The Future of Fundamental Physics." Cornell Messenger Lectures, 2010, https://www.youtube.com/watch?v=SWWBuHszyD8.

Von Baeyer, Hans Christian. *QBism: The Future of Quantum Physics.* Cambridge, MA: Harvard University Press, 2016.

Bohr, Niels. *Atomic Theory and the Description of Nature.* Cambridge: Cambridge University Press, 1934.

Chagmé, Karma, and Gyatrul Rinpoche. *A Spacious Path to Freedom: Practical Instructions on the Union of Mahāmudrā and Atiyoga.* Translated by B. Alan Wallace. Ithaca, NY: Snow Lion Publications, 1998.

Cole, K. C. "In Patterns, Not Particles, Physicists Trust." *Los Angeles Times*, March 4, 1999.

Davies, Paul. "That Mysterious Flow." *Scientific American* 16, no. 1 (2006): 6–11.

Düdjom Lingpa. *Heart of the Great Perfection: Düdjom Lingpa's Visions of the Great Perfection*. Vol 1. Revised Edition. Translated by B. Alan Wallace and Eva Natanya. New York, NY: Wisdom Publications, forthcoming.

———. *The Vajra Essence: Düdjom Lingpa's Visions of the Great Perfection*. Vol 3. Revised Edition. Translated by B. Alan Wallace and Eva Natanya. New York, NY: Wisdom Publications, forthcoming.

———[Traktung Düdjom Lingpa]. *A Clear Mirror: The Visionary Autobiography of a Tibetan Master*. Translated by Chönyi Drolma. Hong Kong: Rangjung Yeshe Publications, 2011.

Düdjom Lingpa and Sera Khandro. *Buddhahood Without Meditation: Düdjom Lingpa's Visions of the Great Perfection*. Vol. 2. Revised Edition. Translated by B. Alan Wallace and Eva Natanya. New York, NY: Wisdom Publications, forthcoming.

Einstein, Albert, and Leopold Infeld. *The Evolution of Physics*. Edited by C. P. Snow. Cambridge: Cambridge University Press, 1938.

Feynman, Richard, Robert Leighton, and Matthew Sands. *The Feynman Lectures on Physics*. London, 1966; California Institute of Technology Online edition, 2013. Vol. 1, chap. 4, https://www.feynmanlectures.caltech.edu/I_04.html.

Fuchs, Christopher A., N. David Mermin, and Rüdiger Schack. "An Introduction to QBism with an Application to the Locality of Quantum Mechanics." *American Journal of Physics* 82, no. 8 (2014): 749–54.

Gefter, Amanda. "A Private View of Quantum Reality." *Quanta Magazine*, June 4, 2015, https://www.quantamagazine.org/quantum-bayesianism-explained-by-its -founder-20150604/.

———. "The Evolutionary Argument Against Reality." *Quanta Magazine*, April 21, 2016, https://www.quantamagazine.org/the-evolutionary-argument-against -reality-20160421/.

James, William. *Principles of Psychology*. 2 vols. New York: Henry Holt and Company, 1890.

———. *Talks to Teachers on Psychology: And to Students on Some of Life's Ideals*. New York: Henry Holt and Company, 1899.

Linde, Andrei. "Inflation, Quantum Cosmology and the Anthropic Principle." In *Science and Ultimate Reality: Quantum Theory, Cosmology, and Complexity*, ed. John D. Barrow, Paul C. W. Davies, and Charles L. Harper, 426–58. Cambridge: Cambridge University Press, 2004.

———. "Choose Your Own Universe." In *Spiritual Information: 100 Perspectives on Science and Religion*. Edited by Charles Harper Jr. Philadelphia: Templeton Foundation Press, 2005.

Lochhead, Jamie, dir. and prod. *Nova*. Season 46, episode 2, "Einstein's Quantum Riddle." Aired January 9, 2019 on PBS. https://www.pbs.org/video/ einsteins-quantum-riddle-ykvwhm/.

Padmasambhava, and Gyatrul Rinpoche. *Natural Liberation: Padmasambhava's Teachings on the Six Bardos*. Translated by B. Alan Wallace. Somerville, MA: Wisdom Publications, 2012.

Wallace, B. Alan. *Balancing the Mind: A Tibetan Buddhist Approach to Refining Attention*. Ithaca, NY: Snow Lion Publications, 2005.

———. *Minding Closely: The Four Applications of Mindfulness*. Ithaca, NY: Snow Lion Publications, 2011.

———. *Open Mind: View and Meditation in the Lineage of Lerab Lingpa*. Edited by Eva Natanya. Somerville, MA: Wisdom Publications, 2018.

———. *The Art of Transforming the Mind: A Meditator's Guide to the Tibetan Practice of Lojong*. Boulder, CO: Shambhala Publications, 2022.

Wallace, B. Alan, and Eva Natanya. *Śamatha and Vipaśyanā: An Anthology of Pith Instructions*. New York, NY: Wisdom Publications, 2025.

About the Author

B. ALAN WALLACE is president of the Santa Barbara Institute for Consciousness Studies as well as the Center for Contemplative Research. He trained for many years as a monk in Buddhist monasteries in India and Switzerland. He has taught Buddhist theory and practice in Europe and America since 1976 and has served as interpreter for numerous Tibetan scholars and contemplatives, including His Holiness the Dalai Lama.

After graduating summa cum laude from Amherst College, where he studied physics and the philosophy of science, he earned his MA and PhD in religious studies at Stanford University. He has edited, translated, authored, and contributed to more than forty books on Tibetan Buddhism, medicine, language, and culture, and the interface between science and religion.

After teaching for four years in the Department of Religious Studies at the University of California, Santa Barbara, he founded the Santa Barbara Institute for Consciousness Studies and three branches of the Center for Contemplative Research, which focus on the interface between contemplative and scientific ways of exploring the mind and its potentials—the latter of which has created a space for dedicated practitioners to be in long-term meditation retreat in order to reach the path in this lifetime.

Also Available by B. Alan Wallace
from Wisdom Publications

Stilling the Mind
Shamatha Teachings from Dudjom Lingpa's Vajra Essence

"A much needed, very welcome book."—Jetsun Khandro Rinpoche

The Attention Revolution
Unlocking the Power of the Focused Mind
Foreword by Daniel Goleman

"Indispensable for anyone wanting to understand the mind. A superb, clear set of exercises that will benefit everyone."—Paul Ekman, Professor Emeritus at University of California, San Francisco

Tibetan Buddhism from the Ground Up
A Practical Approach for Modern Life

"One of the most readable, accessible, and comprehensive introductions to Tibetan Buddhism."—*Mandala*

Natural Liberation
Padmasambhava's Teachings on the Six Bardos
Commentary by Gyatrul Rinpoche

"Illuminates the most profound questions about who we are and provides a roadmap for the journey through life, death, and rebirth in great depth and simplicity."—Tulku Thondup

About Wisdom Publications

Wisdom Publications is the leading publisher of classic and contemporary Buddhist books and practical works on mindfulness. To learn more about us or to explore our other books, please visit our website at wisdom.org or contact us at the address below.

Wisdom Publications
132 Perry Street
New York, NY 10014 USA

We are a 501(c)(3) organization, and donations in support of our mission are tax deductible.

Wisdom Publications is affiliated with the Foundation for the Preservation of the Mahayana Tradition (FPMT).

Thank you for buying this book!

Let Lama Alan Wallace continue to guide you in your Dzogchen practice with his classic Wisdom Academy online course Introduction to Dzogchen. Includes HD video teachings, guided practices, readings, and more. Save 15% with code ITDBOOK24. Begin your journey at wisdom.org.